EARLY
STUART

ssays in Honor of David Harris Willson

STUDIES

DITED BY HOWARD S. REINMUTH, JR.

NIVERSITY OF MINNESOTA PRESS · MINNEAPOLIS

Foreword

This collection of essays has been written by colleagues and former students of Professor David Harris Willson as a tribute to his many years of outstanding teaching and devotion to scholarship concerning the Early Stuart period.

Until quite recently the period 1603–1640 was neglected to a large extent, almost equally so on both sides of the Atlantic. For one thing it lay between two more alluring eras: the Elizabethan, colorful, dynamic, abounding in fascinating personalities including the dominant figure of Queen Elizabeth herself; and the Civil War, one of the remarkable times of ferment, political, religious, social, and intellectual, in all of English history.

It has been the lifelong work of Professor Willson and others to develop a new picture of the Jacobean age and of James I — an age which had an interest and importance of its own, and was neither merely an appendage to the reign of Elizabeth nor a prelude to the Civil War; a king whose complex and tortured personality made an even greater impact on his own reign than had that of Elizabeth, who so often subordinated her personal life and preferences to her sense of duty as a sovereign.

Nearly fifteen years have passed since the publication of Professor Willson's biography of James I, a work which like all important historical books is significant not only in itself but also as a stimulus for further research and scholarship. This volume of essays is intended to explore some of the topics suggested in part by Professor Willson's own work.

In the political sphere two figures other than the king dominated the era of James I, Robert Cecil, Earl of Salisbury, and George Villiers, Duke of Buckingham. Professor Coakley takes issue with the older view of Cecil as a mere appendage to his father, Lord Burghley, as a man who repeated obsolete policies in a new milieu. He shows him to have been a politician of great skill who managed the incredibly complex and diverse interests of Jacobean Englishmen, great and small, but who was finally unable to resolve the fundamental weakness of royal finances. Much of this interpretive essay deals with the intricacies of political patronage, a subject previously much better documented in the Elizabethan than in the Early Stuart period.

In dealing with James's great favorite, Professor Barcroft shows that the usual view of the Duke of Buckingham as one of the most successfully venial men of any age has been overdrawn. Though appointment to office was indeed controlled by Buckingham, it was not simply a question of bribes, of the purchase and sale of places. Much more complex ideas of office, closely connected with contemporary notions of property, were involved.

Further light on the Jacobean political scene is shed by Professor Jones's essay, which takes a major figure of the Elizabethan age, Thomas Egerton, Lord Ellesmere, and shows the difficulties of a man who, unlike Cecil, was unable to cope with the new political scene yet continued to hold high office and was powerful enough to influence Jacobean politics and law, albeit often negatively. By clinging to life and office he also helped frustrate the careers of promising younger men like Sir Edward Coke and Francis Bacon.

Although recent scholarship has contributed greatly to our knowledge of Elizabethan parliaments, the study of parliaments between 1603 and 1640 has lagged far behind. Professor Gruenfelder has taken the subject of the elections to the Short Parliament of 1640 to show that the Early Stuart period marked a

transitional stage in the history of elections between the Elizabethan period and the age of Walpole. The conflicts of the
Caroline age made national issues — political, constitutional, religious — prominent in many election contests. Competition for
seats, partly on an ideological basis, upset the carefully managed
Elizabethan system which ensured the crown substantial numbers of supporters in the Commons.

The study of the Jacobean Church has been neglected by
comparison with the Elizabethan Church or with the religious
complexities of the Civil War period. Professor Kautz has studied
a key issue of patronage in the Church, the appointment of
bishops, and summarized its impact on political life where there
was a revival of clerical councillors as well as on diocesan administration and the religious life of the laity. James I's highly personal manner of appointing bishops and his absorption in the
growing theological controversy of Calvinists and Arminians
help to explain why the Anglican Church drifted further and
further from Elizabethan comprehension toward the fierce con-
fessional struggles of the 1640's.

Concerning another aspect of religious life, Professor Hurstfield takes the Gunpowder Plot as a point of departure to examine the mentality of the Roman Catholic minority in England,
which gradually accepted its isolation and met the situation into
which it had been driven by the government and the actions of
a small number of its own members who attempted to regain
religious power by violence. Professor Hurstfield also makes a
major contribution to the study of the history of European religious toleration.

Most of the contributors have considered England as a whole,
but two have taken different perspectives. The editor has studied
the changing character of border society, to point out that for
many Englishmen the county was still the most important sphere
of their concerns, that there was still much diversity in the English scene. He also shows how one member of the Catholic minority succeeded without plots and violence in achieving a meas-

ure of political power and economic success while he carefully nurtured his dissenting faith in his extensive family.

Some Englishmen eschewed national politics for local, but others left England altogether and sought opportunities in the New World. Professor Johnson writes of a shrewd combination of Virginia Company directors and Londoners concerned with a social problem of vagrancy and a fiscal one of taxes who resolved their difficulties by exporting them to the New World; there at least a few unwilling expatriates found opportunities they would never have enjoyed in Great Britain.

This volume, then, combines a series of broad, interpretive essays with individual case studies to further knowledge of the Early Stuart period, especially in its political and religious aspects, but also in some of its social, economic, and legal characteristics.

Table of Contents

EARLY STUART STUDIES

David Harris Willson

In the fall of 1923 when new funds became available for the expansion of the department of history at the University of Minnesota, Guy Stanton Ford wrote to his old friend, Wallace Notestein, who had earlier been a member of the department for about a decade, asking him to recommend a young man to teach Tudor and Stuart English history. Notestein proposed David Harris Willson, and, as events were to prove, he had in fact sent his most promising student to Minnesota. Young Willson was only twenty-four years old when he arrived in Minneapolis; for the next forty-five years he served the University of Minnesota with distinction as instructor, assistant professor, associate professor, and, after 1946, as professor of history.

This young man, the son of Thomas Harris and Amelia Shryrock Willson, was born in Philadelphia on May 18, 1901. His family came from Anglo-American stock. The first Willson settled in Dedham, Massachusetts, in 1638; John Harris, who contributed another of the young man's names, was the founder of Harrisburg, Pennsylvania. His mother also came from a well-established family, which has produced another distinguished historian, Richard H. Shryrock. The Willsons sent their son to the Haddonfield Friends School, Haddonfield, New Jersey, then to the Friends Select School in Philadelphia, and finally on to Haverford College, where he graduated with honors in 1921.

3

From there he went on to Cornell University to work under Professor Notestein for a Ph.D., which he completed in 1925.

David Willson's interest in English history undoubtedly stems from his encounter at Haverford with Professor William E. Lunt, whose textbook history of England was standard all over the United States for at least thirty years. Young Willson's honors work was in English history, and his grades earned him a Phi Beta Kappa key as well as strong recommendations from Professor Lunt and Professor Rufus Jones for an assistantship at Cornell. He arrived there at the time when Wallace Notestein, Carl Becker, and Preserved Smith made the department at Cornell one of the best in the United States. It is small wonder that David Willson flourished in such an atmosphere. He won the Laura Messenger Prize in History in 1923, and enough money to travel to England for research on his dissertation. He left Cornell in 1924 to come to Minnesota; his dissertation was finished the next year.

His career at Minnesota began about the time when the department of history was emerging as one of the best in the state universities of the Middle West. Guy Stanton Ford, A. B. White, William Stearns Davis, A. C. Krey, L. B. Shippee, George Stephenson, S. B. Harding, Norman Gras, and Solon J. Buck were the senior men. L. D. Steefel had joined the department only a year before; A. L. Burt, Herbert Heaton, Ernest Osgood, Faith Thompson, Theodore Blegen, and Harold Deutsch were soon to come. This was Minnesota's first "important" department of history, as well as one famous both for its internal solidarity and for the production of scholarly books and articles. The young instructor did his part to bring luster to the department. In 1931 he published his first book, *The Parliamentary Diary of Robert Bowyer, 1606–1607* (University of Minnesota Press). In 1932–1933 he was awarded a Social Science Research Fellowship for study in England; 1940 saw the appearance of his *Privy Councillors in the House of Commons, 1604–1629* (University of Minnesota Press), based upon his doctoral dissertation and much additional research in England and the United States. These two books, published between the first two world wars, and numerous articles and reviews in learned journals in both England and the United States solidly established Professor Willson's reputation as a distinguished scholar.

These years were also the ones in which Professor Willson developed his style as a teacher. To those who did not know him, this young professor appeared a shy, somewhat diffident person, but in the classroom this facade dropped aside and there emerged an able, energetic, even brilliant lecturer, who had learned to pace his words so that the occasional burst of humor necessary to keep the attention of a class never seemed forced or extraneous to the material at hand. I shall never forget the series of lectures that Professor Willson gave to the naval history and strategy course prepared for the NROTC at Minnesota during 1943–1944; it was obviously the product of a master teacher, unexcelled in clarity, forcefulness of language, and precision of historical significance. It was evident that the young man who had come to Minnesota almost two decades earlier had learned his profession as a teacher as well as he had established himself as a scholarly historian.

In the first two decades Professor Willson also perfected his techniques as a graduate instructor. His seminars were models of academic excellence from which his students emerged exceptionally well trained. The second two decades of his career at Minnesota coincided with my own years there, and practically every one of my graduate students was fortunate enough to take his seminar. They were uniformly grateful for the meticulous care that he took in their training, especially in the correction of their seminar papers. A stylist himself, Professor Willson sought to teach both his craft as an historian and his skill as a writer. But my students were only a fraction of the non–English history M.A. and Ph.D. candidates who entered his seminar. The Minnesota requirements for these degrees were such that candidates in both United States history and European history found it advantageous to work with him. The result was less fortunate for Professor Willson than for his students. He found himself sitting on more oral examinations and reading more theses, dissertations, and seminar papers than anyone else in the department. Even a good friend on the Group Committee of the Graduate School could not save him from overwork.

As one might expect, Professor Willson also attracted attention beyond the boundaries of the University. In 1931 he taught summer school at the University of Chicago; in 1936, at Duke University. In 1941 he was named Secretary of the Modern European History Section of the American Historical Association for a five-year term. He served on the Robert Livingston Schuyler Prize Committee and the Advisory Board of the Yale Parliamentary Diaries Project. In 1959–1962 he was on the program committee of the Mid-west Conference on British Studies, and in 1965–1967 he was its president. During 1966–1967 he was visiting professor at the University of Texas. In addition to these outside activities, he served on numerous University and departmental committees, where his wisdom and understanding contributed to the formation of policy.

These years after 1940, however, were years largely consecrated to teaching and research. In 1941–1943 and again in 1948–1949, Guggenheim fellowships provided the time for the beginnings of the research on *King James VI and I* (Cape; Holt, 1956), a project that occupied much of Professor Willson's time for the next decade and a half. This brilliant, witty, incisive study won the Robert Livingston Schuyler prize in 1956, and earned for its author further recognition as a scholar and a writer. Johns Hopkins University and also the University of London invited him to give public lectures in 1957. Reviewers in the popular as well as the academic periodicals showered praise upon *James VI and I*. His colleagues at the University of Minnesota shared in the warmth of the reception of this book which they had seen in the process of development.

With the biography finished, Professor Willson listened to the

David Harris Willson

blandishments of his publisher and settled down to write a history of England for university undergraduates. The publishers had assured him that he could write the book with one hand tied behind his back, but they did not know how conscientious he was. It is one thing to present a series of lectures on specialized topics and trust the text to provide the factual basis for the course, and quite another to produce that text. Again I plead special knowledge for I recall the days when my colleague told me his problems. During those years when he was working on James I and the problems of the first years of the Stuart monarchy, a large company of scholars also was at work on the history of England from the time of the Anglo-Saxons to the present. The textbook writer who fails to include recent research does himself and his readers a great disservice. It was no easy thing to bring himself up to date on the research of a twenty-year period for so large a field. Even though the fact that there had been a war slowed down research, there was a great surge of new materials and new insights after 1945. Professor Willson, as an undergraduate, studied under the man who had written the most distinguished text in English history up to that time; his own *History of England* (Holt, 1967), the result of a decade of arduous labor, is unquestionably the best that has been written up to the present time and promises to be the standard text for a long period to come.

These years after the Second World War also saw an increasingly large number of young men and women come to Minnesota to study Tudor and Stuart English history and to write their theses and dissertations under Professor Willson. This present volume is evidence of the affection that they developed for their professor and the instruction that they received from him. Their theses and dissertations form a sizeable and respectable part of the work done by graduate students in history at the University of Minnesota under the post-1945 faculty.

Any recognition of David Harris Willson as a teacher and scholar would fall short of its intention, however, if it failed to note that at Minnesota he also had a private life as a husband, father, and friend. The young Willson who arrived in Minneapolis in 1924 was a bit shy and reserved. His colleagues suspected that he would always be a bachelor, wedded to his scholarly activities, but during his third year at Minnesota a young lady, Lillian Kemp Malone, arrived at the University as a graduate student in French. She received her M.A. in 1927, and the next year taught in a private school for girls. In September 1928, she and David Willson were married. He not only acquired a charming wife, but also as brothers-in-law two historians, Dumas Malone and Miles S. Malone, and a scholar in Old and Middle English, Kemp Malone. One son, John Harris Willson, was born to the marriage; he holds an A.B. from Yale University and did graduate work at the University of Minnesota. Recently he has made his father a grandfather.

All of us who know Professor Willson can testify to his loyalty as a friend, and to the pleasure of his companionship. The sly twinkle in his eyes, the clever sally of his wit, the careful judgment of his words, and the warmth of his personality toward those he knows and trusts have made him much beloved by colleagues and friends in Minnesota, in many parts of the United States, and in England. All of us have benefited from his wisdom and have been warmed by his friendship.

JOHN B. WOLF

THE ESSAYS

W. J. JONES

Ellesmere and Politics, 1603–1617

Sir Thomas Egerton, Baron Ellesmere and subsequently Viscount Brackley, was a great administrator, lawyer, and judge. He is mentioned in general political studies, but most references are painfully standard: his predicament on the day of the Essex revolt is repeated with tedious regularity, and under James he has been conventionally trotted out as anti-Spanish, an opponent of the Howards, a supporter of the prerogative, and a testy combatant of Coke. Chamberlain's verdict still holds sway: ". . . he left but an indifferent name, being accounted too sour, severe, and unplacable, a great enemy to Parliaments and the common law, only to maintain his own greatness and the exorbitant jurisdiction of his court of Chancery." A few years after his death, it was quipped that he had "died of conceit, fearing to be displaced." Yet no one denied that he was formidable, a monumental figure in the structure of law and institutions. Indeed, appreciation of this might emerge as flattery: a petitioner once coupled Ellesmere and Chief Justice Popham as "the two great lights of this commonwealth." As with so many historical persons, he has too often been placed in context by half-truths handed down from tome to tome. He once said that "a countryman would esteem and have more use for a whetstone than a diamond";[1] and perhaps this can be read as

1   J. Hawarde, *Les Reportes del Cases in Camera Stellata*, ed. W. P. Baildon (London: privately printed, 1894), 43.

a commentary upon his own role. The uneven, and at times rare, occurrence of his name in the obvious sources is no accident. Withdrawn and pragmatic by nature — until recent times he perished in comparison with Coke for lack of publication — he had his incapacities, and this is a study of a man in his declining years. Well past sixty at the Stuart accession, he was sometimes hapless, sometimes ill, sometimes lacking, sometimes weary, and sometimes caught up in Elizabethan preconsiderations which few others shared or understood. He is often important because of an inability to apply his talents, and his career under James is as much the story of aging excellence turned dull as it is of a brilliance which was realized.[2]

Ellesmere had enjoyed a distinguished career under Elizabeth, whom he served as Solicitor General, Attorney General, Chamberlain of Chester, Master of the Rolls, and Lord Keeper of the Great Seal. Promoted Lord Chancellor by James, he carried on until his death in 1617, and his ability to survive would surprise, sometimes unpleasantly, his contemporaries. Ill health often enforced his absence from the bench, the court, and Parliament. He was genuinely afflicted with what contemporaries called "the gout," but his habit of talking about his ailments, infirmities, and symptoms must have bored many people. Irritated by the inevitable medical bulletin and by assertions that his memory was weak and decaying, some came to believe that he was merely trying to cover up an avaricious nature. It is easy to see how these interpretations came about, and related characteristics of health and personality certainly illuminate both his reputation and his erratic impact in affairs of state.

Suspected at times of being selfish and overconcerned with

2   *The Letters of John Chamberlain*, ed. Norman E. McClure (2 vols.; Philadelphia: Memoirs of the American Philosophical Society, XII, 1939) (hereafter cited as Chamberlain, *Letters*), II, 65. *Diary of Walter Yonge* (London: Camden Society, 1848), 33. Henry E. Huntington Library [hereafter HEH], *Bridgewater* and *Ellesmere* MSS [hereafter *El.*], 2029. I am indebted to both the trustees and the staff of the Huntington Library, San Marino, California, for their assistance and courtesy.

imaginary woes, Ellesmere also acquired the reputation of being haughty — in his early days as an MP he was reproved for talking down to the House of Commons — and was thought by some to be a judge who lacked charity. In 1604, for example, when Serjeant Heale was prosecuted in Star Chamber, one of the background issues was the Serjeant's former attempt to secure the Mastership of the Rolls under Elizabeth. Ellesmere had opposed this ambition vehemently, but it was difficult since he himself had a material interest in retaining the office. On this occasion, the Lord Chancellor, who resented past insinuations and hated Heale, admittedly an unsavory character, unleashed his venom from the bench: "find him guilty in all of corruption and ambition, craft and covetous practices; fine [him] £2000, and suspend [him]." It would seem that although Heale was fined, the other members of the Star Chamber bench declined to follow the Lord Chancellor's view of the matter. There were other occasions when he appeared "hard" to contemporaries. Lord Zouche, who resented Egerton's attitude toward the Council in the Marches of Wales, professed to fear his "malice." On the other hand, he did make efforts to be gracious, although there is sometimes a suspicion of the grand gesture. He once told some of his tenants that he would rather lose twelve pence that was due to him than offer them a halfpenny wrong. With respect to a Chancery case, William Foorth petitioned the King to request Ellesmere to stay the grant of an injunction. James was agreeable, but only if it was consistent "with the rules of equity and justice," and he left it up to the Lord Chancellor. The injunction was granted, and Foorth again petitioned the King, stating "that the question now was whether the commandment of the King or the order of the Chancellor should take effect . . ." It was an arrant perversion of the facts. Foorth was sentenced in Star Chamber to lose his ears in the pillory, to suffer perpetual imprisonment, to have a paper put on his head, to ride with his face to the horse's tail, and to be fined £1000. The bench, exhibiting a fine fury, warned all men to "take heed how they complain in words against any magistrate, for they are gods . . .," wording which should caution us not to take some statements about monarchs out of context. However Ellesmere, who had withdrawn before sentence, solicited a pardon from the King, "which was a very honorable action in him, and added greatly to his many other honorable and worthy virtues."[3]

Ellesmere loved to visit the countryside, and made it clear that he preferred to live in such surroundings: here could be found good air, diet, and exercise, "the way to heaven." He was able to cast off his cares and even become jovial. Yet he could never become a senior country gentleman. He could rest in counties, but his authority stemmed from public office and his career in the law, interests which could not provide the stately quietude which he sought. Chancery, Star Chamber, and Parliament were closely linked to a physical presence in Westminster, and his duties called for attendance at York House in the Strand, which had come to be the official residence of Lord Chancellors. He loathed the place, partly because of its structure and partly because of its proximity to the Thames. He called it "unsavory" and complained about its "air and accidents," but it is probable that he would have disliked any other residence in the metropolis. Having lived in Islington during the 1580's, he had assumed a place in Chester and purchased Harfield, but he could never escape until he was willing or allowed to retire. After the death of Salisbury he did try to resign but the request was denied.[4]

Much can be understood in an old man who was depressed and sick. He freely admitted that his feet were fettered by "podogra," his heart by melancholy, and his movements by the fear of contracting disease. He hoped for little more than an intermission from sickness, and he lacked faith in his doctors. He likened his weary body to an ailing copyhold falling into the

3   W. J. Jones, *The Elizabethan Court of Chancery* (Oxford: Clarendon Press, 1967), 92. Hawarde, *Reportes del Cases*, 171–177. HMC, *Cal. Salisbury* MSS, XVI, 23–24. HEH, *El.*, 233, 2715.

4   HMC, *Cal. Salisbury* MSS, IX, 25, 412; X, 70, 74, 81. HEH, *El.*, 21, 75. HMC, *3rd Rep. App.*, 214; *11th Rep. App.*, VII, 286. CSPD, 1611–1618, 168.

lord's hand for lack of repair, and in the language of the theater cast the gout and the stone as principal actors in the unpleasant tragedy staged within himself. It was all rather dismal and martyred although optimistic flashes did appear: when his daughter-in-law recovered from measles, he wrote that "it pleaseth God mercifully to shake his rod, and to give us some warning strokes rather than chastisements."[5] Depressing, but not unnatural, unless we feel, as did some contemporaries, that woe was curiously mixed with an ambition that was very much alive. The problem is at its clearest in a letter, laced with biblical allusions, which he wrote to Salisbury in 1606.

Now Christmas is done, it is time for those that durst not presume to the feast to seek some part of the fragments. I found nothing in myself worth prizing or valuing to be a ground of suit, saving love and fidelity only, which being the duty of all, ought not to be esteemed as singular in any. This made me, being bashful by nature and lame in limbs, to lie still, as the poor lame man by the pool of Bethesda, in hopes that after the angel's moving of the water some would help to put me in at one time or other. The water is often moved and almost exhausted, many are cured and some are overflowed, and some perhaps surfeited, and yet I lie still lame and helpless but not hopeless. I see that presidents of provinces, and some honest petty chancellors and many others have been bountifully rewarded . . . I detract nothing from their worthiness, but commend their good fortunes. When I look back to my predecessors, I dare compare with none in desert, but with the last [Sir John Puckering, Lord Keeper, 1592–1596] I would I might also compare with him in the fruits of my service.

The writer apologized if he should be thought foolish. "Gifts given to old men serve but as Mary Magdalene's ointment, to help bury them; yet that comforts age, and in the end serveth for good and necessary use." He described his suit to the King: "if you mislike it, let this child die in the cradle, for I will never importune his Majesty in anything that may seem unto you inconvenient for me to ask, or for his gracious and princely wisdom

---

5   HMC, *Cal. Salisbury* MSS, X, 70, 81; XII, 583; XVII, 382. *The Egerton Papers*, ed. J. P. Collier (London: Camden Society, 1840), 394.

to grant."[6] He felt that he had been ignored, but he was still willing to abide by Salisbury's advice although there was an implied criticism of England's most influential minister. The letter illustrates Ellesmere's ability to fuse the themes of sickness and reward. It is not surprising that some discounted his protestations, and thought of him as greedy, unsatisfied, and even crafty, but by the standards of the world in which he lived, he had much justification for his sense of grievance.

From 1596 until her death, the old Queen had allowed him to hold simultaneously the positions of Lord Keeper, Master of the Rolls, and Chamberlain of Chester. Rivals and suitors for office were inclined to stress his good fortune, but he himself denied enjoying multiplicity of office, and implied that the material proceeds were exaggerated. As it was, his cluster of positions made it unlikely that he could benefit further from the struggle for Burghley's succession. He could hardly hope for additional office. Obviously he liked Essex, and just as obviously he recognized the strength and superior political ability of Robert Cecil. He adopted a position of neutrality, but he was in effect assisting the tilt of the balance toward Cecil, for he could have done a great deal to make Essex appear a more respectable contender, and after all the Devereux group had initially tried to read his appointment as a triumph. Neutrality was of no use to Essex as it became clear that he was in the weaker position. It is more than possible that Elizabeth hoped to witness the development of a third force which would play an active role and so inject some stability into the state of faction around her. Perhaps she had this idea in mind when she entrusted the Earl, after his tempestuous return from Ireland, to the Lord Keeper's care. Either way it was too late. Essex had revealed the paucity of his political acumen. In 1599, the Lord Keeper had a few good things to say in Council concentrated upon criticism of the Earl.[7]

6   *Egerton Papers*, 408–409. See also, HMC, *Cal. Salisbury* MSS, XVIII, 203–204.

7   Jones, *Chancery*, 61–99. BM, *Add.* MSS, 3828, fols. 47 ᵛ–63.

The bond with Cecil tightened, Essex had collapsed before his pathetic attempt at revolt, and the Lord Keeper could not participate in the fruits of victory. Of course, some people in his circle may have benefited. His son, John, was appointed Baron of the Exchequer in Chester in May 1600, but in view of the father's position as Chamberlain this does not require special explanation. George Carew and William Lambarde, friends and Chancery officials, received further recognition. However, Carew had served previous lord chancellors, Lambarde had been a follower of Burghley, and both were already renowned as lawyers and administrators, men appreciated by the Queen for their own sakes. Few people were exclusively indebted to the Lord Keeper. Even his household steward, Morgan Coleman, was a legacy from his predecessor, Puckering. Others, doubtless bright, were devoid of political stature. His secretaries included that scalawag John Donne, who was discarded amidst scandal, and Gregory Downhall, who was such a nuisance in the 1601 Parliament. John Davies was moving closer to him but he lacked repute and anyhow regarded Coke as his principal patron. The Lord Keeper was a self-made man, a bastard of decent gentry stock, who had made his own way and did not have the connections of a Cecil, a Fortescue, a Sackville, or even a Bacon.[8]

His first marriage had allied him with the Ravenscrofts, a respectable Flintshire family with a place at Lincoln's Inn. A second marriage, more ambitious, united him with the sister of Sir George More of Loseley. This lady, twice widowed, had once been the spouse of Sir John Wolley, the Latin Secretary. He mourned her death in 1600, but grasped the opportunity of making a greater connection. His third and last marriage, to the daughter of Sir John Spencer of Althorpe, and widow of the fifth Earl of Derby, allied him to the Stanleys. Previously, by virtue of friendship, legal advice, and his position as guardian to the late Earl's daughter, he had been close to the family. It

8   *Egerton Papers*, 306. HEH, *El.*, 6004. J. E. Neale, *Elizabeth I and Her Parliaments, 1584–1601* (London: Jonathan Cape, 1957), 377, 380, 387.

was an alliance of two impressive estates. The Lord Keeper, through industry and good fortune with respect to the deaths and dispositions of legitimate Egertons, was already a considerable landholder. But the marriage was a personal disaster, a hopeless union of incompatible temperaments; far from strengthening his position with the Stanleys and the Spencers, it almost certainly weakened it.[9]

Ellesmere was rarely, if ever, an open leader of factional interests, and his family position was not one which could have easily sustained such an ambition. He did, of course, have a strong base in the Inns of Court, especially Lincoln's Inn, and at Oxford University, his alma mater, where he became chancellor in 1610. Yet this sort of background, although always useful, might have less significance under James, just as it became clear that some of the big family groups no longer had the same impact. The Howards made a long and strenuous effort, and men like Southampton or Pembroke were always capable of standing on their own, but the limelight of the reign was to be seized by two men — Carr and Villiers — who lacked all the old advantages of family and education, and who were outstanding examples of the superiority of royal favor to the "old school tie." Villiers, having analyzed the fall of Carr, worked eventually to broaden his base through a network of marriage alliances, but this maneuver was irrelevant to his rise.

Outside his offices and professional reputation, Ellesmere did not have a strong political hand, but he could stand with Cecil among the leading men who had moved into clear authority by 1601 and who had smoothed the way for an orderly succession by James VI of Scotland. After Elizabeth's death, his son, John, who had gone north to meet the new sovereign, fell ill, but information was transmitted by Lord Henry Howard, the future Earl of Northampton, and by Sir Thomas Challoner, Cecil's agent. Assuming that Challoner had the ear of the King, he poured out a rebuttal of charges of "haughtiness, insolence, and pride" made

9   Jones, *Chancery*, 93–95.

against him. It was not an auspicious beginning. He had to relinquish the Mastership of the Rolls, which carried much patronage, and the office of Chamberlain of Chester, which had been a support for his authority and interests in the counties clustered on the northern border of Wales. He expected to lose these offices, indeed the temporary nature of his tenure had been apparent, but he was aggrieved that they might have been an obstacle to further reward under Elizabeth, and he was bitter that their surrender should now be taken so much for granted. It may have made it worse that he was succeeded as Master of the Rolls by a foreigner, Edward Bruce, whose naturalization could not be effected until Parliament met in the following year. As one who hated being tied to the court, he can hardly have appreciated James's remark that he would be too busy attending on the royal person to continue as Chamberlain of Chester. He may have pondered the assumption of the new Chamberlain, the Earl of Derby, that Cecil had been instrumental in this transfer of office. He began to petition the King for reward, stressing that his increment as Lord Keeper did not match his expenses in that respect. He was elevated to the title of Lord Chancellor and created a baron. It was nice to have a peerage which could be bestowed upon his son — Ellesmere made this notion very plain at the end of his life — but otherwise there was little ground for satisfaction. Many received commensurate recognition, and title did not substitute for loss of income and patronage. Yet this was the situation. The efforts of Essex, the struggle for Burghley's succession, the triumph of Cecil, the arrangements for a peaceful accession, and the distribution of jobs and honors in the new king's reign, can be seen as an entity. Ellesmere emerged no less fiercely loyal than before, but with a feeling that he had lost rather than gained. He could note how Cecil, confirmed as Secretary, was allowed to keep the Mastership of the Wards and was rapidly promoted up the scale of peerage. Other favored persons had been of negligible importance or even out of favor during the last years of Elizabeth. Of course, the difficulty was that it was almost impossible to "promote" a Lord Chancellor, and although he might have been transferred to some honored position — possibly as President of the Council in the Marches of Wales — James was not foolish enough to think that he could find a better Lord Chancellor, aged though Ellesmere was. Doubtless the viscountcy should have come earlier than 1616, but this apart the King did not have much to offer. As it was, the call for "remembrance" became incessant.[10]

By the time he composed his "pool of Bethesda" letter, Ellesmere's Jacobean character was formed. Christmas had passed in more than one sense: the initial spate of gifts and rewards was drying up. Opinions, friendly or adverse, were hardening. These personal matters have to be stressed. Since he tended to operate in politics as an individual and not as a member of a group, the degree of respect accorded to his advice and actions would be influenced by the assessment of the man.

The Lord Chancellor occupied the center of the stage at the end-of-term assembly in the Star Chamber when he delivered the "King's charge." This was intended to provide justices of the peace with inspiration and information while at the same time embodying a broad hint, perhaps a command, that it was time to leave the metropolis and go home. The performance symbolized both the Lord Chancellor's importance and the weak link in the chain of a governmental system based upon local control and cooperation. Ellesmere took these occasions seriously, although he had once, in Elizabeth's time, professed skepticism, feeling that "these admonitions and proclamations are no better

10   HEH, *El.* Calendar, 130, 162–165, 167, 1208. HEH, *El.*, 1271–1273. *CSPD,* 1603–1610, 27. *Egerton Papers,* 359–366. HMC, *Cal. Salisbury* mss, XX, 20. Among others who held multiple office under Elizabeth — a circumstance partly owing to the rivalries of Cecil and Essex — note may be taken of Sir John Fortescue, Chancellor of the Exchequer, Master of the Great Wardrobe, and Chancellor of the Duchy of Lancaster. When James came to the throne, Fortescue lost his position in the Exchequer — it was given to a Scotsman — but he retained the other two offices, and his position as Chancellor of the Duchy was confirmed with a life patent. D. Brunton & D. H. Pennington, *Members of the Long Parliament* (London: Allen & Unwin, 1954), 190–191.

esteemed than as matters of fashion, and so all grows out of fashion." He may have been a little on the defensive — he had failed to obtain instructions — but he had touched on the truth. Official policy was too often flouted, and ceremonial exhortations by a Lord Chancellor were outdated. His addresses were marked by ponderous reproof, and it could be noted that he "sermonized." Early in the new reign he expressed James's intention of enforcing proclamations, and urged that the "vulgar" should make use of the courts and refrain from rushing with their complaints to the King. These were conventional, general principles without much depth, and he was soon to make clear his disappointment with the local justices. In an outstanding speech delivered on February 13, 1605, he observed that they were supposed to "maintain peace, but they rather make war." Throughout the kingdom, he said, they forgot their oath to God and their duty to King and country. Their numbers were increasing but too many did nothing, living in London most of the time, and only valuing the office for the social prestige it brought. In the following year, he was again heavily critical. One of the traditional fears, evident under Elizabeth and exacerbated by the Gunpowder Plot, was that justices of the peace were lax toward papists. In 1606 there was a campaign to exclude men who had recusants in their immediate families and households from the commission of the peace. The Roman Catholic problem was peripheral. The real issue was that of controlling the justices in all their duties, and if this was ever to be achieved the government must exercise a proper control over appointments. Ellesmere and his generation were beginning to anticipate the later difficulties of Charles I. The choice of justices lay theoretically with the Crown and Lord Chancellor, but the position had tended to become a formal recognition of social status. The failings had been pointed out by Lord Keeper Puckering in 1595, and "corrupt" justices had been discussed in the 1601 Parliament. There was nothing new in the situation and Ellesmere, who appeared something of a cipher in the face of pressure from below, had been neither more nor less lax than his immediate predecessors. The government at the center was losing control – if it had ever really had it – and this among other things increased the scope for local faction. Naturally, he tried to go beyond expressions of verbal disapproval. In the summer of 1605, it was directed that new names were not to be included in commissions of the peace unless this was approved by the justices of assize, who were to receive recommendations from two existing justices of the peace in the county. It was also noted that he would not put father and son together in the same commission without a certificate from the justices of assize. He was seeking to improve the government's grasp while diminishing individual lobbying, but the value of certificates from justices of assize – and other letters of recommendation – were open to question. The situation was not mastered.[11]

The sinews of political reliability were becoming twisted. When it came to anxiety over the justices of the peace, religion should not have been a major concern, although it was, not surprisingly, one which attracted immediate attention. Early Stuart government danced to its death by producing short-term policies to meet immediate circumstances. With respect to spiritual matters, Ellesmere, despite a lack of conformity in early manhood, represented an establishment point of view. He was sarcastic toward those whom he called "puritan" and critical of those whom he called "papists." However he always believed that many Roman Catholics were simple and led by error. They were to be pitied rather than condemned, and should certainly be distinguished from those willfully seditious and traitorous persons who deserved severe punishment. This distinction doubtless lay

11   HMC, *Cal. Salisbury* MSS, XII, 48. Hawarde, *Reportes del Cases*, 161–162, 186–187, 263–264, 299–300. HMC, *Cowper* MSS, I, 62. J. Hurstfield, "Political Corruption in Modern England: The Historian's Problem," *History*, 52:16 (1967). *Letters of Philip Gawdy*, ed. I. H. Jeaves (London: Roxburghe Club, 1906), 157. *Calendar of Wynn Papers* (Aberystwyth: National Library of Wales, 1926), no. 537. T. G. Barnes, *Somerset, 1625–1640: A County's Government during the "Personal Rule"* (Cambridge, Mass.: Harvard University Press, 1961), 42. J. H. Gleason, *The Justices of the Peace in England, 1558 to 1640* (Oxford: Clarendon Press, 1969), 58–60.

behind his recommendation of 1604, as reported by the Spanish ambassador, that the King "would do well to hold them in check and enforce the laws against them." There was nothing unusual in this opinion, but Ellesmere must have been aware, as were other officials, that the treatment of English Roman Catholics could not be divorced from consideration of relations with the major Catholic powers.[12]

Ellesmere could hardly have avoided involvement in discussion of foreign affairs. In the last years of Elizabeth he had assisted with various negotiations, and in the reign of James some would gain the impression that he took a hostile line toward Spain. He had his own channels of information, such as that doubtless provided by Sir George Carew who went as ambassador to Paris. He may have received news from Sir Henry Wotton, and in 1608 one of his servants appears to have acted as an informant of Wotton, who was then in Venice. From other sources, sometimes indirectly through those who corresponded with his son, John, he might receive reports from abroad. This did not add up to anything of consequence and it was not extraordinary for a leading man and councillor. Common sense indicated a settlement with Spain in 1603, but even at that time it is difficult to describe him as either an avid supporter or an opponent of peace proposals. He was concerned to uphold the policies initiated by the King, and these pointed toward peace. After the treaty, he could support the notion that continuance of peace demanded a behavior fitting of friends and brothers, whereas the only alternative was to wage war as kings. The choice, clear and simple, had been made, and ambassadors who veered from the chosen policy should be recalled. These views were somewhat alien from Wotton's celebrated quip about ambassadors being men sent abroad to lie for their country — an early indiscretion which was later to occasion Wotton embarrassment and a royal repri-

---

12   Hawarde, *Reportes del Cases*, 164, 188. HEH, *El.*, 466. A. J. Loomie, "Toleration and Diplomacy: The Religious Issue in Anglo-Spanish Relations, 1603–1605," *Transactions of the American Philosophical Society* (new ser., pt. 6: Philadelphia: The Society, 1963), 56.

mand. Ellesmere expected conformity and obedience from those who were agents and not directly responsible for the promulgation of policy.[13]

How then did he acquire the label of being anti-Spanish? In part, explanation must be sought in the period of Sarmiento's embassy, when Ellesmere was clearly hostile to the Howards and therefore, by implication if not by direct action, opposed to much official action. Yet, even for the first decade of the reign, it is not difficult to discern how the notion of his enmity to Spain could be created out of a fascinating fusion of issues, external and internal, legal and political.

Peace had been concluded in 1604, but the Spanish were continually resentful of depredations at sea. Indeed, not long before Ellesmere's death, it was complained that Spain had lost more shipping than when she had been at war. England, it was charged, had done little to restrain the activities of her seamen, and had even encouraged pirates from other countries to seek a haven in her ports. The distinction between pirates and privateers was always open to discussion, and appalling complications could be raised around the status and activities of ships from countries such as Scotland. These things would always happen, but the Spanish were particularly aggrieved by their failure to secure restitution before the English courts. In 1607, and in subsequent years, possessory decrees obtained in the Admiralty were blocked by the ability of defendants to obtain commissions of appeal. In a complaint to Salisbury, the Spanish ambassador affirmed his willingness to wait upon proceedings before the English courts, but he protested that Ellesmere had delayed execution of an Admiralty sentence for three weeks under pretense of an appeal on the question of possession. A further complaint contained the argument that there could not be an appeal from a possessory decree awarded in the Admiralty.

13 HEH, *El.*, 419, 448. *The Life and Letters of Sir Henry Wotton*, ed. L. P. Smith (Oxford: Clarendon Press, 1907), I, 5, 428 n. 2. Loomie, "Toleration and Diplomacy," 17.

Equally objectionable was the way in which some litigants obtained prohibitions from the court of Common Pleas, and in at least one case it was felt that the Lord Chancellor was involved. The Spanish ambassador, irritated by interminable delays, scented a "denial of justice" inflicted by political men. Ellesmere, for his part, later retorted that the ambassador was misinformed and mistaken in his law. It hardly seems likely that he would consciously use his position to defend hostilities against Spanish shipping, but it is likely that there had been some change in procedure. In 1603, shortly after James's accession, the French ambassador had complained about appeals in cases of depredation, asserting that both Elizabethan practice and current pronouncements established that attempts at appeal were to be denied until the sum adjudged had been paid. In a list of matters needing remedy, submitted to the 1610 Parliament, James I suggested that defects in the law concerning piracy were giving England a bad name abroad. Furthermore, there was an element of reprisal in the situation, since Spanish complaints did little more than mirror those of the English. The House of Commons was much exercised by this matter and heard many complaints in 1607. The Spanish legal system was condemned, and the example was cited of one English merchant who had gained thirteen sentences of restitution without avail. Although some merchants are known to have received satisfaction, the English would continue with their complaints, notably in 1611–1612.[14]

Prohibition was an old prerogative writ. In the later years of Elizabeth and the early years of James I, there was a fair degree of dissension over the application of it against courts such as the Admiralty, the Requests, the High Commission, the Provincial Councils, and so on. This is not the place to attempt an explana-

14   HEH, *El.*, 1628–1633, 1636–1640, 1644–1645. *CJ*, I, 341–342, 344, 355, 372–373, 380–381, 383–384. *CSPD*, 1603–1610, 361. HMC, *Cal. Salisbury* MSS, XV, 374; XIX, 12, 510. *Proceedings in Parliament, 1610*, ed. E. R. Foster (New Haven: Yale University Press, 1966), II, 281. S. R. Gardiner, *History of England from the Accession of James I to the Outbreak of the Civil War, 1603–1642* (10 vols.; London: Longmans, Green, 1883–1884), II, 135, 149–150.

tion, but some points have to be made since this was a period when judges were also political animals — which is not to suggest that nonlegal considerations controlled their judicial activity. Two particular areas of uncertainty may be instanced. One has already been seen: the Admiralty; the other centered upon the issue of this writ against proceedings before the High Commission. Archbishop Bancroft and Chief Justice Coke had a splendid battle, and the King — whatever his own conclusions — tried to look like an impartial arbitrator. Something of a compromise may have been reached in March 1610, but in a few months, when Bancroft had been succeeded by Abbot, the debate was as lively as ever.[15]

Some — the Spanish ambassador and many churchmen — evidently considered that a legal process was being twisted by nonlegal considerations. Others, and Bancroft may have appreciated the point, felt that the difference represented a genuine confusion over the procedural rules surrounding the issue of prohibitions. If political interpretations were dominant, Ellesmere might appear to stand on both sides. With respect to Spanish attempts in the Admiralty, he could be accused of supporting the issue of prohibitions and the employment of other devices. With respect to the High Commission, he was reputed to stand with the establishment, although it must be confessed that his views were not always clear-cut and it does not follow that a similar conclusion can be reached for all other ecclesiastical tribunals. It is not, however, impossible that he was consistent in legal terms, and discerned important distinctions between the various kinds of proceedings and between the jurisdictional capacity of the courts. Indeed, this should be an obvious conclusion, and only the necessity of knowing more about the legal details compels one to be tentative. Contemporaries had a real difficulty in understanding the jurisdiction of the High Commission. Its position was sometimes as hard to deny as to support. Yet the technical grounds for

15 J. P. Kenyon, *The Stuart Constitution* (Cambridge: University Press, 1966), 91.

issuing prohibitions were difficult to challenge so long as it was deemed merely necessary to claim that the matter before the High Commission concerned temporalities and so long as the relevant rules of priority of suit were unclear.[16]

Throughout 1609, there were a number of conferences and consultations in which the King, Ellesmere, the Archbishop, the judges, and the Council were involved, but the results were mostly abortive. At the end of the year, the King's Bench justices and the barons of the Exchequer, summoned to give an opinion by Ellesmere, responded in a fashion apparently favorable to Common Pleas practices. Coke, at any rate, later stressed this opinion and asserted that in consequence the point ceased to be an issue. Nonetheless, it was not the end of the matter. Early in 1610, for example, James decided to get an opinion from the judges of the King's Bench alone. Through the Bishop of Bath and Wells, he requested Ellesmere to undertake the matter privately and without giving the judges time for deliberation. If they were difficult, Ellesmere might either insinuate that this was a personal wish of the King "for his own particular satisfaction" or he might put the question as though it were his own. The substance of the inquiry was a proposition that the judges of the Common Pleas did not have lawful authority to grant prohibitions save when their court was first possessed of the suit and in certain other restricted circumstances. The reply of the King's Bench judges acknowledged the truth of this supposition. Only, of course, the question and response did not dissolve the legal issues. In handling applications, the court of Common Pleas was not greatly concerned to define itself but rather to define, for example, the position of the High Commission. Common Pleas clearly assumed that it had broader powers in circumstances when it did not have priority of suit than the King's Bench judges could easily allow, but there was considerable disagreement among the judges — Coke himself was frequently

16   S. B. Babbage, *Puritanism and Richard Bancroft* (London: published for the Church Historical Society by S.P.C.K., 1962), 259, 269.

opposed by Walmsley on the Common Pleas bench — and it is clear that opinions would vary according to the particular group of judges which was solicited. Furthermore, it was not sufficient to discuss whether Common Pleas could issue prohibitions although there was not an action before that court. Even if this were allowed, there was doubt over prohibitions issued on surmise and in circumstances when the Common Pleas neither could nor cared to claim jurisdiction. Indeed, many of its disputed prohibitions were, as under Elizabeth, concerned rather to regulate than to deny the ecclesiastical courts. On a number of occasions the writ was issued because, it was insisted, the consistory court should first consider the case. The debate was bound to be futile unless temporalities and the bounds of High Commission jurisdiction were given proper attention. In 1611, when Ellesmere was again extremely active, an attempt was made to right the balance by issuing new letters patent which endeavored to provide the High Commission with a more substantial definition of its powers. In this situation, finding out about the courts and then about the different categories of legal dispute is far more important to the historian than attempting to lump all the prohibition disputes into an unlikely whole, even those disputes which only concern ecclesiastical courts. Nonetheless, it may be remarked that issue of the writ required an initiative taken by litigants, but they must have been encouraged by any suggestion that the bench was likely to be sympathetic. The prohibition was normal and traditional; only its increased use combined with the notion that its issue should be redefined or limited could raise a real crisis, and indeed it continued to be used after the events which are here noticed. To speculate an alternative would have been truly revolutionary.[17]

When legal problems of this kind came up, Ellesmere was

17   E. Coke, *The Fourth Part of the Institutes of the Laws of England* (London, ed. of 1669), 99–100. HEH, *El.*, 2008. Kenyon, *Stuart Constitution*, 178. R. G. Usher, *The Rise and Fall of the High Commission*, ed. P. Tyler (Oxford, 1968), 191–193, 217–218.

sometimes involved directly. Equally often he could act as an intermediary or provide a neutral opinion. This is a political sketch, but sharp lines of distinction among law, administration, and politics are alien to this period. In his decisions, arguments, notes, and legal writings he was bound to raise points which were relevant to political issues surrounding the Crown, Parliament, property, taxation, and so on. His speech in Calvin's case is an obvious example. In many ways impressive, it has flashes of the Lord Chancellor at his dogmatic and pompous worst. A number of straw men were dispatched, and Plato, Aristotle, and More's *Utopia* given short shrift. Many statements, if taken out of the context both of the speech and of the language of the times, help to explain Ellesmere's reputation as a King's man and vehement supporter of the prerogative. Yet, though the immediate case was sometimes submerged, the issue could hardly be analyzed without discussing the nature and varieties of allegiance. The tragedy both of the decision and of Ellesmere's discourse — he claimed that he had not originally intended to speak — is that it finalized the failure to reach a closer relationship between the crowns and countries of Scotland and England. Had this hope still borne life there might have been less emphasis upon the legal points involved. As it was, the dominant background which produced such a flavor was political, since the House of Commons had refused to distinguish between the *ante-nati* and the *post-nati*, and had indicated that if union was to take place it should represent an extension of English law and institutions to Scotland. The political dice had been thrown; the judges could do little more than assess the position of the *post-nati* as a matter of law.[18]

18   *The Speech of the Lord Chancellor of England, in the Exchequer Chamber, Touching the Post-Nati* (London, 1609). David Harris Willson, *The Privy Councillors in the House of Commons, 1604–1629* (Minneapolis: University of Minnesota Press, 1940), 52–53. David Harris Willson, "King James I and Anglo-Scottish Unity," *Conflict in Stuart England,* ed. W. A. Aiken & B. D. Henning (London: Jonathan Cape, 1960), 43–55. G. Donaldson, "Foundations of Anglo-Scottish Unity," *Elizabethan Government and Society,* ed. S. T. Bindoff, J. Hurstfield, & C. H. Williams (London: Athlone Press, 1961), 282–312.

On this and other occasions, Ellesmere raised or ranged over most of the contentious themes so familiar in textbooks. The King was the law, the King was the law speaking, and the prerogative was rooted in an ancient and high law. The common law and statute law "by way of explanation or declaration of the ancient law of the diadem and Crown did plainly show the King's ancient prerogative and jurisdiction." This had been of the utmost importance in the past when the Pope had usurped "the King's supreme and absolute authority in ecclesiastical as well as civil causes." Of course the prerogative has to be seen on many levels, but as it was noted in a mundane Star Chamber case of November 1605, Coke, then Attorney General, and Ellesmere argued strongly in favor of the King's prerogative royal and the necessity of purveyors, "being both as ancient as the fundamental laws of the kingdom . . ." Ellesmere would probably have considered any suggestion that he was minimizing the common or statute law less as a disagreement than as the product of confused thinking or a failure to attend to what was being said. Historically on the losing side, one can nonetheless understand his reputation, insofar as it was intended to be a criticism, as a doughty supporter of the prerogative — so easily mistranslated into an opponent of the common law. Sometimes the situation was that he himself was not always paying sufficient attention. In May 1613 he unleashed an invective against Whitelocke who, as counsel, was trying to keep a case in Chancery and prevent it from going before the Earl Marshal. The Lord Chancellor was annoyed at being confronted by an issue of the prerogative and by a stream of common law and statute precedents of which he confessed himself to be ignorant. The story was eventually carried to the King, Whitelocke vainly protesting that far from denying the King's power to issue commissions for the holding of an Earl Marshal's court he had only argued that such a commission had not in fact been issued. The attack on Whitelocke, as later with Coke, was political although the issues could only be discussed in legal terms. Northampton and Suffolk, who made use of Ellesmere's outburst, were interested in Whitelocke's other activities, and so, though he was first charged because of his speech in Chancery, this dubious item was soon forgotten. It was hard to imagine a clash with divine or natural law but, as More had discovered and Ellesmere doubtless came to perceive, it was dangerous to dig into the particulars and somehow a clash could be created by warring interpretations and political necessities. Common and statute law should suffice to justify the Crown's position, but it never harmed to call upon divine or natural law as an ultimate authority. Yet others could turn to these sources, as Ellesmere indicated to the Lords in 1614 when he suspected that the Commons might do so and the Lords be unprepared. Certainly the Crown did not have a monopoly of reaching beyond common and statute law.[19]

Ellesmere's views on the prerogative were conventional. Like his former henchman, Lambarde, he believed that only the sovereign was capable of exercising that general discretion which was necessary to all society. It was rarely a question whether the King should or should not exercise this power. The prevalent view of monarchy made any distinct alternative unthinkable, and Ellesmere — like Coke, Eliot, Noy, Wentworth, or Lord Say and Sele — was a conventional monarchist. The immediate question was whether the King was using his power of general discretion in what was really a personal and private fashion, possibly in support of friends and favorites. Likewise, Professor Willson has pointed out that at the Hampton Court Conference and on subsequent occasions there was nothing wrong in the King's trying to act as arbitrator, and he certainly meant well. Trouble came

19   Hawarde, *Reportes del Cases*, 188, 249. Gardiner, *History*, II, 188–189. L. A. Knafla, "The Law Studies of an Elizabethan Student," *Huntington Library Quarterly*, 32:237 (1969). Ellesmere composed a brief and conventional essay upon the prerogative. It can be found in a number of manuscript sources. I have used the copy in Northamptonshire Record Office: Finch-Hatton MS, 578.

when he appeared too easily as the controversialist seeking victory. James made many mistakes, and he did some things of which Elizabeth would hardly have dreamed, but the issue had not become too serious when Ellesmere died in 1617.[20]

However, one of the related problems was already becoming clear. Some people, while remaining conventional, were beginning to ponder the distinction, by no means entirely novel, which might be made between the King's person and the Crown. This was an issue played back and forth by Coke and Bancroft in the immediate period before the 1610 session of Parliament. The Church was involved, the notion of discretion would be, and in the end the structure of law and government would submit to this distinction. As an elder statesman of the law, Ellesmere had no wish to engage in argument but he was not averse to endowing others with the benefit of his authority on this and other topics. In the House of Lords, and doubtless in the Council, he managed to make his conclusions sound weighty. In Calvin's case he had warned against the dangerous potential which lurked behind distinctions being drawn between King and Crown, between King and kingdom. When the possibility arose in 1610 that some such distinction might be raised in the debate over the Great Contract, he made the position clear: ". . . all men hold their land of the King, either immediately or mediately, and the person of the King and his Crown cannot be divided." Here he was concerned with yet another facet. Doubtless he accepted that many categories of property belonged to the subject who, in the form of direct taxation, approved by Parliament, made a voluntary grant to the King. When he found that the subject was not willing to give voluntarily, he concluded that he would do so if handled properly. Procedure to Ellesmere was as important in the forum of politics as it was in proceedings

20   M. A. Judson, *The Crisis of the Constitution* (New Brunswick: Rutgers University Press, 1949), 29–30. W. Lambarde, *Archeion*, ed. C. H. McIlwain & P. L. Ward (Cambridge, Mass.: Harvard University Press, 1957), 66–67. David Harris Willson, *King James VI and I* (London: Jonathan Cape, 1956), 208.

before the courts, and he was particularly conscious of this when it came to controlling meetings of Parliament.[21]

During Ellesmere's Stuart lifetime there were, the need for replacements apart, only two elections. Since 1604 was so close to Elizabethan times, 1614 can be regarded as the first election which properly reflected the Jacobean structure of patronage. On both occasions his role was minor. He had some power at Brackley, expressed through his son, John, who had married Lady Frances Stanley, and possibly at Oxford where he had succeeded Essex as High Steward. At St. Albans, where he was also High Steward, he appears to have had some influence in 1614. In the same year at Cambridge, where he held a similar position, he was less successful. The corporation tardily agreed to acknowledge his interests, and he in turn was apparently prepared to accept one of the men already selected for election — Sir Robert Hitcham, the Queen's Attorney General.[22]

Ellesmere had a distinguished parliamentary career, being elected three times as an MP and serving in four Parliaments as "Speaker" of the House of Lords. He never sat in either chamber save as an acknowledged public official. On the three occasions in the 1580's when he was elected to the Commons he was already Solicitor General. In 1584 and 1586 he represented the county of Cheshire where his power in officialdom, coupled with personal fragments of influence, was becoming apparent. In 1589, he was a late choice at Reading, but having already received a writ of assistance to the upper house he apparently never attended the Commons, although that body made efforts to secure his presence. In 1593, as Attorney General, he did not seek election. This limited experience in the Commons, even if he was inclined to be the ponderous official, was valuable and in later days he would look back upon these years. In 1610 he recalled

21   Judson, *Crisis of the Constitution*, 39, 149, 152. *Proceedings in Parliament, 1610*, I, 64.

22   J. E. Neale, *The Elizabethan House of Commons* (London: Jonathan Cape, 1949), 168. T. L. Moir, *The Addled Parliament of 1614* (Oxford: Clarendon Press, 1958), 43, 50. VCH, *Cambridgeshire*, III, 70.

33

that it was not thought lawful for "any Member to draw a bill" and that the Queen's counsel could be relied upon to see that nothing was done in the House of Commons which might prejudice the sovereign. This last reflection was particularly nostalgic. Appointed Lord Keeper in 1596, he served in the last two Elizabethan Parliaments as moderator of the upper chamber, and as such played some part in the creation of a great parliamentary crisis. Addressing the Parliament of 1597–1598, he indicated that the legality of many patents and monopolies would be examined. He was transmitting a message from the Queen, but he should have been aware of the significance of this promise, and if anyone below the sovereign was responsible for its fulfilment, it was he. Furthermore, he was not a blind supporter of royal grants and in his own sphere of interest, the Chancery, was actively engaged in challenging certain patents. Yet, as with others, he does not appear to have understood the potential impact of his words, and the somewhat specific assurance would be recalled in 1601 and spark off some heated moments in that dramatic Parliament.[23]

The Lord Chancellor, as it was said in 1604, served as "the common mouth of that Great Presence," in other words, the sovereign. In this respect Ellesmere would always be important, but despite affairs of close interest to him, such as the Buckinghamshire election case of 1604 — he and Popham were intimately responsible for the wording of the election proclamation — the evidence is better and certainly more colorful for 1610 and 1614 than it is for earlier years. He was naturally involved in the preparations for a Parliament, notably the details of proposed legislation desired by the government. It may have been for this purpose that he compiled a set of notes — "Memorialles for Judicature" — which have occasional affinity with the fourteen articles presented to the 1610 Parliament by James I. The wording of his

23   HMC, *11th Rep. App.*, VII, 182. S. D'Ewes, *The Journals of All the Parliaments during the Reign of Queen Elizabeth* (London, 1682), 424, 441–442. *Proceedings in Parliament, 1610*, I, 154, 243. Neale, *Parliaments, 1584–1601*, 355, 379.

fourth general proposal is more or less identical with the first part of the King's twelfth article, the remainder of which covers the substance of Ellesmere's fifth proposal. However, and this was particularly true in 1610, it did not follow that he would be in agreement with all the government's policies and suggestions. One suspects that, as he grew older, he found increasing difficulty in the responsibility of being a mouthpiece for both King and House while having his own, and possibly divergent, views as a councillor. In this respect, the task of the man on the woolsack could be more complicated than that of the Speaker of the House of Commons. Furthermore, and unlike Elizabethan holders of his position, he was a peer and thus could play a more active role. In 1621, the then Lord Chancellor, Francis Bacon, recalled how Ellesmere sometimes gave up the Speaker's chair "and at his discretion went some time down to his place" in order to speak. An outstanding legal authority, it is somewhat ironic that Ellesmere should have presided over the House of Lords during a nadir of its fortunes. In 1621, the first Parliament after his death, the Lords were to assert themselves not least by a reassumption of judicial authority which was so dramatic as to involve the downfall of his successor. Bacon was assailed as Lord Chancellor and government official, but whatever the accusations of the Commons the Lords cannot have acted as they did without being aware that an assault was being made on their own chairman. Possibly there was some reaction to the futility of 1610 and the absurdity of 1614.[24]

It is often hard, and it must have been hard for contemporaries, to judge whether Ellesmere was revealing considered disapproval over the near stagnation of the House of Lords or whether he was merely behaving as a difficult old man. In March 1610, the House of Commons requested an audience with the King so that they might extend thanks for being given permis-

24   CJ, I, 149. Egerton Papers, 384–388. HEH, El., 2623. Proceedings in Parliament, 1610, II, 279–282. Notes of the Debates in the House of Lords Officially Taken by Robert Bowyer and Henry Elsing . . . 1621, 1625, 1628, ed. F. H. Relf (London: Camden Society, 1929), 29.

sion to discuss tenures. On Saturday, March 17, Ellesmere moved that the upper chamber should do likewise, but he asked to be spared the task because of his age and infirmities. He had made the motion, and he was also surely the spokesman and formal representative of the House. If he was indeed too infirm for this, then perhaps he should have retired. Salisbury, who was also reluctant to undertake the task, implied that the Lord Chancellor had that virtue of being "short" and "pithy" which was appropriate. The matter remained in the air and the House adjourned until Monday. On that day Ellesmere again asked to be relieved, but on being pressed requested instructions. He had, or so he asserted, given no thought to the matter over the weekend since he had hoped that another spokesman would undertake the task. In the face of this assertion — which hardly reflected the tenor of comments made on Saturday — Salisbury repeated his previous remarks about brevity, and insisted that Ellesmere was not the kind of person who really needed instructions: "seeing my Lord is no stranger in the matter, seeing my Lord is a master in the art of reporting, seeing my Lord doth oftener give advice than want . . ." When, on Tuesday, March 20, Ellesmere made his speech to the King he did not fail to seek pardon for his errors, "being now so far in the winter of my age and having one foot in the grave." Somehow he had managed to strike a chilling note, and concentrate attention upon himself. He had been ill in February, and still had a cold at the beginning of March. Yet one suspects that he was employing guerrilla tactics, and previously he had made it clear that he did not wish to be involved in the report on Cowell's book. It was only proper to insist that the House must give thanks to the King, and he doubtless wished to see some sign of the Lords' asserting themselves. The matter, the whole business of tenures, he had insisted, "concerneth us as much if not more than they [the Commons]." It is probable that he did not approve of the license which had been given, and had therefore wished to avoid the duty of addressing the King. If so,

Salisbury would have been aware of Ellesmere's thoughts and concerned to prevent him from escaping.[25]

If Salisbury could prick the hide of the Lord Chancellor's mixture of self-deprecation and pomposity, Ellesmere himself was quite capable of deflating formal nothings when they were mouthed by others. On one occasion in 1610, during a taut exchange with a Commons spokesman, he put to scorn the latter's profession of belief that the Lord Chancellor and the Lord Treasurer would never stoop to take an advantage. "Necessity," he warned, "will alter conscience." Perhaps he was thinking of some of his own performances. He had a grasp of politics but could not easily transform himself into a political activist. He always seemed to be waiting for some strong leader with whom he could agree. For a time Salisbury had filled that role, but by 1610 Ellesmere clearly had grave doubts over official tactics. In the end, Salisbury would have to bear much of the blame for the failure of 1610, and although he remained in office his last years have been fairly described as pitiable.[26]

After the first Parliament of James's reign had been sent home, Ellesmere produced a critical assessment of the events which he had witnessed. Even before this he had revealed doubts over government methods and the degree of reliance which could be placed upon the House of Commons. On November 14, 1610, he suggested that the Commons, by their lack of achievement, had failed to live up to the freedom of debate accorded to them. In February he had made his own position clear when speaking in the committee of the whole. He could not understand why the King had permitted such a broad discussion *before* supply had been granted. Likewise he could not comprehend the passivity of the Lords. ". . . For in all the Parliaments that I ever read of

25   *Proceedings in Parliament, 1610*, I, 38–43, 184, 193–195. H. E. Bell, *An Introduction to the History and Records of the Court of Wards and Liveries* (Cambridge: University Press, 1953), 140. CSPD, 1603–1610, 587.

26   *Proceedings in Parliament, 1610*, I, 118. Willson, *James VI and I*, 268. For an assessment of the Great Contract debates and of the role of Salisbury, see Bell, *Court of Wards*, 139–145.

in this kingdom, first the King by his Chancellor delivered the cause of assembling the session and then, after his ends were satisfied, would he give way unto the petition of the Commons of his lower House, who best understood the several grievances of the country. For as the King is the head of the commonwealth, so both our Houses make but one body. For a Kingdom without peers were but in a tottering state, so peers without the Commons were but in a weak case." It would seem that in 1610, probably throughout the sittings of Parliament, he was in disagreement with Salisbury over a number of crucial matters. Almost certainly he approved of Salisbury's broad plans and schemes of reform, of which the proposed contract was only part, but one is forced to guess that he had been defeated in Council with respect to the approach which was adopted.[27]

Ellesmere appears to have had two cardinal thoughts. The first, as he stressed in his answer to the Speaker's request for privileges in 1614, was that Parliament had a duty to grant supply. Only then could other matters be considered. He seemed to believe that Parliament would grant supply if it was not diverted, and he was also arguing that the sovereign must be trusted. James understood the latter point, but more as an expectation than as goal for himself to achieve: he told the Commons in 1610 that in the matter of impositions they would have to rely upon his word. As for diversion, this seemed to be provided not merely by MP's but also by the government. Mistaken strategy was creating much of the difficulty. Once the King appeared to bargain it was difficult to fall back upon the older notion that the sovereign would automatically listen to grievances after supply.

Ellesmere's second conclusion was that disaster must come if the House of Lords, whatever might be said of social prestige and conferences, took second place while the House of Commons ranged freely in debate. Certainly the power was there, if only to be witnessed in the upper chamber's exercise of veto which wrecked some of the work of this Parliament. With respect to

27   *Proceedings in Parliament, 1610*, I, 13, 170, 276–283.

the periodic institution of Parliament he evidently had some notion of "balance," but was even more concerned to think of the two Houses as "but one body." His position was based upon the obvious fact that the Commons did not constitute Parliament and in the end it was the total performance of Parliament which he criticized.[28]

It must be presumed that Ellesmere participated in discussions which developed the technique of using conferences between the two houses as a means of controlling the Commons. In 1606, for example, he appears to have encouraged free discussions in such conferences, but even at that time he could express his disappointment in the result or adopt a hectoring tone toward the Commons spokesman. The implication behind conferences was that the bounds of discussion could be extended in a fashion which was not normally allowed to the House of Commons. A sense of propriety was nonetheless observed: at conferences the representatives of the Commons stood bareheaded while the Lords sat covered. The House of Lords was much closer to the government, but this could become a weakness when, as in 1610, speeches were dominated by Ellesmere, Salisbury, and a handful of others. Even in 1610, as on November 13, Ellesmere could move a conference with the Commons. But with respect to some topics he was becoming hostile. He expressed a distaste for conferences on "religious" bills, and he made this position plain when one was suggested on the bill against swearing. The proper experts were the bishops in the upper house. He probably thought that conferences were valuable when delicate topics could be discussed in circumstances which did not involve the King and yet which were controlled. In 1610, when the Commons were reluctant to surrender the initiative to committees negotiating with the Lords, this system was being undermined. The very nature of the debate on taxation placed the onus on the Commons while providing the Lords with only limited oppor-

28   Moir, *Addled Parliament*, 84. Willson, *James VI and I*, 265. *Proceedings in Parliament, 1610*, I, 276–283.

tunities. This was inevitable, but as already noted he tried to galvanize the Lords by reminding them of their own interests, and warned that in any contract "not only tenures to the King but to your lordships are to be taken away . . ." Nevertheless, he might not have been so worried had the Commons sought the fullest participation. Clearly this was not the case, and on several occasions the Lords found themselves in the humiliating position of pressing for a conference and a conclusion to the matter whereas the Commons appeared unenthusiastic. Yet on other matters, such as religion, the lower house was more interested in the idea. The tables had been turned, the House of Lords was being negated, and conferences were of little use if the Commons would not subordinate themselves. No wonder he became disgruntled, and he doubtless agreed with Bacon that the King had bargained like a merchant and that the Commons had haggled like contractors. Only he may have felt that the latter followed from the former. In his "Observations" written after this Parliament, he asserted that whereas the King, prelates, and lords had declined, the "popular state" had gained strikingly in power and audacity: "and if way be still given unto it (as of late hath been) it is to be doubted what the end will be." [29]

Ellesmere appreciated Salisbury's efforts to obtain a novel settlement, but he did not like some of the methods being used and the events of 1610 probably mark a divergence between the two men. In 1614, addressing a new Lord Treasurer, Ellesmere would urge that he follow the example of earlier and not recent predecessors. The failure of Salisbury's endeavors had brought out as never before the financial straits of the Crown. In 1611 Ellesmere chaired the commission appointed to handle the first award of baronetcies. The situation, of course, was merely one of difficulty and there were many legitimate and even uncontentious

---

29   Willson, *Privy Councillors*, 234. *The Parliamentary Diary of Robert Bowyer, 1606–1607*, ed. David Harris Willson (Minneapolis: University of Minnesota Press, 1931), 42, 208 n. 1. *Proceedings in Parliament, 1610*, I, 65, 129, 169, 276. Kenyon, *Stuart Constitution*, 28. Bell, *Court of Wards*, 141–142. Moir, *Addled Parliament*, 72.

sources of revenue. Traditional devices were resorted to, and after a request to Ellesmere and the Master of the Rolls, a list was drawn up of persons connected with the court of Chancery who were able to make loans to the King. Looking to the future, this was a dangerous straw in the wind since the search for a loan followed close after a parliamentary failure. However, unlike 1626 or 1627, the government still had some credit, and the possibility of a genuine loan was not therefore exploded. After Salisbury's death the Treasury was put in charge of a commission headed first by Henry Howard, Earl of Northampton, and subsequently between June 1613 and the appointment of Thomas Howard, Earl of Suffolk, as Treasurer in July 1614, by Ellesmere himself.[30]

The worst experience of Ellesmere's parliamentary career was still to come. In 1614, and what was to prove his last Parliament, he may have hoped for a fresh degree of understanding with the Commons. The Speaker was his associate of many years, Ranulph Crewe, that same man who would be rapidly confirmed and dismissed as Chief Justice of England by Charles I. Yet the disaster was even worse than that which had occurred before, and Ellesmere as Lord Chancellor and leading councillor cannot be separated from the fiasco. Of course he showed dissent at some official procedures, and over the years he had revealed an increasing distrust of the policies and assumptions behind them. Yet lacking evidence, and granted his age and habits of sickness, one wonders how far he was willing to push his opinions. He was inclined to sound disapproval as a sick old man, and others may have taken him at face value. Whether it was due to age, illness, or character, he did not charge about like Coke. He might have served better if he had tried to make a similar impact.

Relations between James and his Parliaments, as Willson has stressed, should not be treated merely as a story of retreat. The over-all stance adopted by the King, although marked by experi-

30   H. R. Trevor-Roper, "The General Crisis of the Seventeenth Century," *Religion, the Reformation, and Social Change* (London: Macmillan, 1967), 84 n. 2. *CSPD*, 1611–1618, 244. G. P. V. Akrigg, *Jacobean Pageant* (Cambridge, Mass.: Harvard University Press, 1962), 234. HEH, *El.*, 1212, 2942.

ment, was not radically in variance with that of Elizabeth, but it was increasingly unsatisfactory. As the years passed, the King's approach began to look negative, and then defensive. His tactics were uneven. In 1610 he allowed the House of Commons an exceptional freedom of debate on vital economic and legal affairs. Naturally, he did not think that the Commons should normally exercise this freedom, certainly not on its own initiative. "To James," writes Willson, "the veto was a prerogative to be employed at will, the privileges of the Commons mere examples of royal indulgence, and the demand for change mere clamor. Thus he presented a blind conservatism to the aspirations of the Commons; all novelties are dangerous he told them; and his answer was purely negative at all points." There was a strong theoretical basis to such an opinion, and the sovereign could bask in a clear edge of legal advantage, but the political world is not a legal world. The two notions, often inseparable, can be brought into violent opposition. Whatever the system, law tends to rest upon what has been and what is. Politics is concerned with immediate movement and that which is becoming. The illegal and the improper can be reformed; only the legal has to be destroyed. This is a central clue to the fortunes of the first two Stuart kings.[31]

Ellesmere was conservative with respect to form. In 1614 he reacted sharply against some protests made in the House of Commons over the supposed illegality of the King's financial measures. Speaking of presumption and ignorance, the Lord Chancellor suggested that if this went on the Commons would become councillors and that the foundations of monarchy, as it was understood, would be destroyed. This sort of statement was not particularly reactionary in its own day; rather, by raising a possibility which was shocking and hypothetical almost beyond belief, it was intended to find a bridge of broad appeal. Ellesmere was certainly desirous of achieving conciliation and avoiding trouble. In the end, together with Winwood, he made a celebrated effort to cool tempers by trying to fashion a compact for the moment.

31 Willson, *Privy Councillors*, 4, 13.

The idea was to try to persuade the King to prorogue instead of dissolving, and to get the House of Commons to offer supply in return. The device centered upon his idea about priorities. It failed, and doubtless the attempt was naive. But Ellesmere had revealed his ability to combine conservatism with conciliation. He believed that supply should precede grievances, but that discussion of grievances should be as free as possible. He recognized that the Commons could not be fobbed off. Nor was this last-minute attempt a late gesture. He had earlier sought consultation with other councillors on the wording of the bill for conservation of woods, fearing that disputes over phraseology might disrupt the King's affairs in this "hopeful Parliament," and he had delayed sealing a patent which might cause contention. Ellesmere took great pains to avoid trouble. Only when this failed did he really appear to be conservative, and then his traditionalism might also be read as a criticism of those who supported the government's views.[32]

Ellesmere's reactions in 1614 may reflect the advice initially preferred to the King by Sir Henry Neville who had urged that, with careful management, supply might be effected within a few weeks. He had stressed that every care should be taken to avoid irritation, and had emphasized the necessity of living up to promises made in 1610 and continuing to show an appreciation of the grievances expressed in that year. He had indicated the advantage of dealing directly and squarely with the House of Commons. This position was based upon the assumption that the leaders of 1610 would be re-elected and that they could be satisfied. However, Neville clearly went much further than Ellesmere could have approved of concerning proposed concessions and in suggesting how James should handle the Commons.[33]

The underlying issue was the prerogative, the whole corpus

32 Judson, *Crisis of the Constitution*, 160. Willson, *Privy Councillors*, 141. *CSPD*, 1611–1618, 224. C. Roberts, *The Growth of Responsible Government in Stuart England* (Cambridge: University Press, 1966), 21 n. 2.

33 Moir, *Addled Parliament*, 15, 53–54, 70–71. Gardiner, *History*, II, 202–204, 228–229.

of the King's legal rights, although those who attacked impositions denied that they were attacking the prerogative. Men who
rushed defensively into the breach were being almost equally de-
structive. The very notion of arguing in the House of Commons,
as did Wotton, that James had a right to levy impositions was
repugnant to Ellesmere. The subject should not be discussed
unless royal consent were given, and accordance of this consent
was a question of timing in relation to supply. As things turned
out, it is clear that he did not think the subject should be discussed even in conference, although he was willing to conceive
the possibility of a rigidly controlled exchange of views about
particular details which would be agreed upon beforehand. Ellesmere did not have a closed mind, and almost certainly was not
committed to stand pat on the analysis of the judges in Bates's
case, which anyhow only covered some types of imposition. In any
case, the notion of substantive precedent was relatively unformed,
and despite Salisbury's activities as Lord Treasurer it is perhaps
significant that in 1614 some were urging action in the House of
Commons for fear that "precedent" might develop and thus make
impositions legal. In fact, although Ellesmere was very much concerned to defend the King's position, he was not greatly moved
about the rights and wrongs of impositions per se. He was anxious
to prevent a resort to unsatisfactory procedures which could only
have undesirable consequences.[34]

Throughout the brief 1614 Parliament, the House of Lords
was dominated by a discussion of what kind of communication
could or should be established with the lower house. The Commons made an approach, but there was disagreement in the
Lords. A meeting, as distinct from a conference, meant that the
views of the Commons would be heard, but debate would not
take place. Ellesmere argued that they should find out what
points the Commons wished to raise about impositions before
even a meeting was agreed upon, but Lord St. John and others
thought it best to agree to meet first. Archbishop Abbot sup-

34 Moir, *Addled Parliament*, 95, 114, 117–118.

ported the idea of a meeting, and Southampton pressed home the case by saying that if they did not then like what the Commons said they could refuse to confer. Ellesmere switched the trend of the discussion by taking up a suggestion that they should consult the judges on the legality of impositions before making any answer to the Commons. This was agreed, but the judges, through Coke as their mouthpiece, replied that an opinion could only be delivered after the matter had been argued. They were there to advise, to give their expert opinion, and not to dispute. They were willing to recognize that the subject might have the right to claim freedom from impositions, but the nature of the prerogative must be recognized. If, as the King claimed, impositions were part of the prerogative, then they were legal. The prerogative was part of the law, and therefore justified by the law. Coke would not delve further into the subject.

After this, debate again concentrated on the possibility of a meeting, and Ellesmere strove to make his fellows face reality: "the lower house desire a conference, and your lordships are disputing whether you should give them a meeting." The only possibility was a conference, and he for one was flat against it. Declaring that he would not attend, and stressing his age and incapacities, he also put a finger on one of the realities. The legal talent of the House of Commons was too impressive, and the judges had not helped the Lords. The Commons, on the other hand, "go both high and low and look of all things that concern their purpose, and we can say nothing, having not seen records. They perhaps will tell us of the law of nature and of nations, being learned and able gentlemen who have studied this case long. If any man in this House think himself able to dispute with them, let him do it; for my part I must desire to be excused . . ." This time there was no Salisbury to cut off his retreat. The House of Commons was eventually informed that the Lords would not agree to a conference at the present time. Unfortunately, some details of the debate leaked through to the Commons, who were

45

incensed by some supposed remarks made in the upper chamber. It served to add further poison to the atmosphere.[35]

Ellesmere experienced the House of Lords at a period of low ebb. He might feel that his advice was insufficiently heeded, but when he was listened to it cannot be said that the result was fruitful. The House had agreed to his suggestion about drawing an opinion from the judges, but the latter had declined to comply. The House in the end had agreed not to confer with the Commons, and this was surely a major stepping stone towards the total failure of the 1614 Parliament. It is, however, important to note that his rejection of the idea of a conference was coupled with alternative suggestions as to how the dispute over impositions might be settled and these suggestions were not implemented. The clue is to be seen in his approach to the judges.

Parliament represented the King's High Court at Westminster. It was possible to envisage the House of Commons as a court of record on its own. The Apology of 1604 had assumed this, and in 1610 an MP had asked how it was that judges could consider a matter of the prerogative whereas the Commons could not although a court and a very high one. It was also possible, but far more satisfactory, to consider the House of Lords as a court and, though only a matter of terminology, it is worth recalling how those who took notes of debates could conclude a day with the entry that "this court" was adjourned. There was certainly a medieval heritage behind the idea, but leaving all theory aside there was also a reality in the presence of the judges as assistants to the House of Lords. In recent years, the House of Commons had paid increasing attention to the counsel present in their ranks, whereas the utility of the judges to the upper chamber had reached near nullity. This was underlined by Ellesmere when he argued against a conference in 1614, yet at the same time both he and Coke had indicated some interesting possibilities.[36]

35 HMC, *Cal. Salisbury* mss, IV, 250–267.
36 *Proceedings in Parliament, 1610*, I, xvi and *passim*.

Ellesmere's first attempt to turn to the judges was thwarted when Coke held his fellows aloof from wrangling. The Chief Justice probably felt that an early opinion would not help. If the judges were divided, the situation would merely be more complex; if they were united, they would probably offend without having any guarantee that their assessment would carry political weight. It is, of course, hypothetical. We do not know what the judges would have said if compelled to produce an opinion at that time, whereas we do know that the Parliament failed. Yet it is difficult to escape the conclusion that Coke was right and Ellesmere wrong. This does not mean that Coke's answer cannot be reconciled with Ellesmere's sense of possible distinctions. The implication remained that a legal right could, if the King were agreeable, be modified through parliamentary activity. We cannot suppose that Ellesmere was opposed to the notion that Parliament, of which the King was a part, could change the law through statute. This had been the assumption behind the debates of 1610: he had not been opposed to it as such but only to the procedures which were adopted. The difference in 1614 was probably that Coke felt that political skills, subsequently aided by judicial assessment or even arbitration, were needed to settle this affair, whereas Ellesmere placed greater reliance on the effect of an initial judicial pronouncement. Hindsight tells us that royal positions in the future would often be supported by the bench, and that this fact would not improve either the King's position or, whatever their honesty, the repute of the judges.

Ellesmere made a second, and different, attempt to throw the onus upon the judges. In his speech against a conference and excluding the possibility of his own participation were one to be agreed upon, he reminded his audience of two broad principles: "I think both the King's necessity on the one side and the people's good on the other must be regarded." Furthermore, "the King hath no prerogative but that that is warranted by law and the law hath given him . . ." This being so, those who were aggrieved by impositions should arrange for proceedings under writ of error to be brought before the House of Lords. He was, in fact, suggesting that the solution was to be found in a test case heard by the House of Lords in its judicial capacity. The idea had previously been put to the House by the Bishop of Lincoln. In such a trial, the House would do no more than affirm the opinion of the judges for, as Ellesmere had stated years before in Calvin's case, "in all such writs of error, the Lords are to proceed according to the law; and for their judgment therein they are informed and guided by the judges; and do not follow their own opinions or discretions otherwise."[37]

All the evidence suggests that Ellesmere's suggestion in 1614 was the product of decades of reflection over that great paradox which disturbed him as much as it did Coke. The difficulty lay in defining, even distinguishing, the role of the judges and the role of Parliament. The *Discourse upon the Statutes*, which clearly represents Ellesmere's thought although it cannot be ascribed with full confidence to his pen, was much concerned with the effect upon traditional judicial practice of the growth of parliamentary authority and legislation. He was in no way antagonistic to the idea that Parliament could change the law, but as in Calvin's case he stood up for the right of judges to declare the law without waiting for a meeting of Parliament. This was change in the sense of novelty rather than destruction: the judges could decide on a new and difficult case. In Calvin's case he discussed the judges on the bench and the judges in Parliament. His speech was delivered after the somewhat unsatisfactory 1606–1607 session of Parliament, and printed not long before the 1610 session. Then, as in 1614, he discerned the kernel of a possible solution: the bridge which might be found in the judicial activity of the House of Lords.[38]

37   HMC, *Cal. Salisbury* MSS, IV, 263. *Speech Touching the Post-Nati*, 23.
38   *A Discourse upon the Exposicion & Understandinge of Statutes: With Sir Thomas Egerton's Additions*, ed. S. E. Thorne (San Marino, Calif.: Huntington Library, 1942). *Speech Touching the Post-Nati*, 16–24.

After the Addled Parliament had gone home, the financial situation was even more brutally clear. The structure of royal revenue, the possibility of calling another Parliament, and the tactics to be adopted became involved in the developing web of faction. When the Council discussed these matters in 1615, Ellesmere must often have agreed with Coke, who was beginning to emerge with an energetic analysis. Coke is important because of his ability to face facts, and because of his growing conviction that the system of financial expedients — royal patronage, grants, monopolies, favors — was poisonous to the political and fiscal interests of the Crown. Naturally, Ellesmere also had ideas of his own. He continued to reject the idea that the King's right to impositions might be opened up to free discussion, but he was willing to conceive debate on details such as convenience, rate, and time. This was consistent, and it again reflects upon his previous parliamentary performance. Above all, he reverted to his major theme. "He never liked of novelties, especially in Parliament, as were the new terms of contribution and retribution, which he thought had done much hurt. He wished the old course of Parliaments to be holden between the King and his subjects: that is, that his Majesty should grant them good laws, and they give him convenient relief, as his occasions should require." Now, of course, "contribution" and "retribution" had been terms much in vogue in 1610. They had helped to provide the formula upon which the freedom of debate and anticipation of a Great Contract had been based. Ellesmere, in these later years, was revealing his stubborn conservatism, but he was also harping back over the immediate years and revealing once again his doubts over the procedures adopted. Still a stickler for form, he represented a viewpoint which was losing ground. In 1628, Eliot said that "the ancient manner of Parliaments was to begin with the affairs of the commonwealth and to conclude with subsidies." This assertion represents an extreme opposite to Ellesmere's position. In practice, the parliaments of James I and of his son, up to 1629,

49

represented a constant endeavor to find a formula which would bridge this gulf.[39]

When the 1614 Parliament was dissolved, it was interpreted as a success for Henry Howard, Earl of Northampton, who was to die a few days later. Ellesmere is often labeled an opponent of the Howards, a family described by Willson as a "worthless and treacherous lot, ready to sacrifice the interests of the nation for their own ends." Although they came to be associated with a particular foreign policy, they owed much of their initial advancement under James to Salisbury. Ellesmere never appears to have liked them, and apart from disagreements over policy it is easy to see how he could have been disgruntled. Under Elizabeth many of the Howards had been distinctly out of favor, but early in James's reign they were brought to the fore and rewarded. They approached the role of a reversionary interest, whereas Ellesmere felt that he had provided continuous faithful service, essential to the succession, without receiving sufficient acknowledgment. However, in these early years the Howards were not portrayed in quite the same clannish light as thereafter. It was only when Salisbury had passed away, and Lady Frances Howard had captured Somerset, that the influence of the Howards, and the revulsion with which they were regarded, was intensified. It was only then that the King sought a stronger and more positive alliance with Spain, and it is only of this period that there is solid reason for using the particular label "anti-Howard" for men who might be united on little else. Nonetheless, by the 1614 Parliament, it would appear that such a negative emotion could be a force in politics and associate, for the time, persons such as Ellesmere, Abbot, Naunton, Pembroke, Southampton, and Winwood. By 1615 these were joined by Coke, and common ground was more apparent on such issues as foreign policy or the necessity of calling Parliament. We may guess that the division was

39   HEH, *El.*, 441, 1216, 2628. Willson, *Privy Councillors*, 3, 38–39. *Proceedings in Parliament, 1610*, I, 13. H. Hulme, *The Life of Sir John Eliot* (London: Allen & Unwin, 1957), 260–261.

widened by Council debates. Although Ellesmere did not live to see the trends in Jacobean politics reach their climax, he was witnessing and sometimes assisting the opening of a festering wound.[40]

Elizabeth had often experienced difficulties with her councillors and public officials. Sometimes, as in the 1570's, the Privy Council had been split over relations with France or Spain, and English interests in the open seas. Occasionally, as in the months before the execution of Mary, Queen of Scots, there might even be an impression that the majority of councillors were combining against the sovereign. Elizabeth, however, worked with a small number of councillors, each of whom was presumed to have a particular skill or distinction. Over the years, Burghley might prove to be the dominating man, but there was rarely the danger — as could happen in the enlarged Council of James — of leading councillors coming to loggerheads and of lesser councillors and officials lining themselves up behind the leaders. Classification according to religious or foreign policy is feasible, but over-all we tend to think of them as individuals — Burghley, Hatton, Leicester, Walsingham, Whitgift, and so on — until the decade of Essex is reached. Both the skill of the sovereign and the small number of councillors assisted in keeping disagreement reasonably restricted to the Council table and Court. Above all, for much of her reign, the councillors observed an unwritten set of rules. From 1563, when Lord Keeper Bacon suffered a severe reprimand, to the late 1590's, the councillors were fairly well behaved in that they did not carry their disagreements into a public forum, notably that of Parliament. Perhaps the worst moment in this long expanse of years came in 1593, when it might be suspected that Essex and some of his associates — including Bacon and Morris, not councillors but aspirants for power and office — were giving indications that they could not be trusted in this respect. Certainly, at the end of this Parliament, Lord Keeper Puckering on behalf of the Queen pointed with misgiving to

40   Willson, *Privy Councillors*, 18.

the irreverence which had been shown toward privy council-lors.[41]

Over the years there were many themes in the developing situation: the heritage of the Wentworth brothers; the growth of a committee system which drained initiative away from coun-cillors in the House of Commons; an increase in the number of councillors which helped to promote faction; James's illness after 1616, so important to the career of Villiers; and the King's failure to arrange an adequate correlation between his erratic move-ments and the need to communicate with councillors. No single theme or date can be selected, and yet it does seem that shortly after the accession of James it was apparent that a new day had dawned.

Elizabeth could rely upon a passable degree of Council soli-darity when it came to managing Parliament. This was still true in 1597 and 1601. Had it not been so, the notion of privy coun-cillors giving the House of Commons a lead would have been negated. In the sessions of the Parliament which first met in 1604 there were but a few councillors in the lower house. This was a weakness, but it was not important so long as the government had confidence in the sobering influence of conferences with the House of Lords. The fallacy behind this technique became ex-posed in 1610, but the gap was not too wide. In 1614, however, the fissure was more evident as pressure united some councillors against the dominance of the Somerset-Howard coalition. The events of this Parliament, and its failure, clearly reveal the pres-ence of conflicting advice. During its brief life, Ellesmere could exhibit his doubts over policy, and the Earl of Northampton could ride in triumph through the streets when the dissolution, which the Lord Chancellor had tried to avoid, took place. After-ward it was necessary to consider the financial situation and future moves, but at the same time there was always the possi-

41   Neale, *Parliaments, 1584–1601*, 267–279, 309–310, 320. W. Notestein, *The Winning of the Initiative by the House of Commons* (British Academy, Raleigh Lecture; Cambridge: University Press, 1924), 22–23.

bility of major offices' becoming vacant, and this both heightened the anxiety of the anti-Howard forces and split them, the more so as they considered what the rise of Villiers portended. Ellesmere's health, his expected demise, and the debate over his successor became a part of the situation. Against this background must be seen the blunders of Coke which aided his removal from the King's Bench, shortly to be followed by his readmission to the Privy Council. Ellesmere died in 1617, but in the years ahead the split in the Council, irrespective of the collapse of the Howards in 1618–1619, was to explode. Dissensions of 1620 were to be carried into the open. In 1621 and 1624, James should have had enough councillors in the House of Commons to exert some influence. But these men in both houses, not to mention the mass of officeholders and government servants, were not only split but willing at times to exploit a public forum in their disagreement. Furthermore, leading peers in the 1620's were willing to associate with critics in the Commons. The *reductio ad absurdum* came in 1624 when, in addition to the Council, the royal family was also split, and James found himself opposed and manipulated by his favorite and by the Prince. In the vacuum Parliament could sense an invitation to arbitrate. The Elizabethan practice of collective responsibility in public had collapsed in ruins, and the presence of councillors in both the House of Lords and the House of Commons had become irrelevant. In 1626, in particular, the strained relations between leading men were apparent. Clarendon later asserted, with reference to the failure of Charles I, that monarchy could never be sustained in England save "by a prudent and steady Council attending upon the virtue and vivacity of the King." Before he died, Ellesmere had witnessed the crumbling of both requirements.[42]

One of the last major involvements of Ellesmere's life was Coke's removal from the King's Bench, a story which belongs to broader studies of patronage and political faction. It can only be

42   Edward, Earl of Clarendon, *The History of the Rebellion and Civil Wars in England*, ed. W. D. Macray (Oxford: Clarendon Press, 1888), I, 261.

understood against the careers of Somerset, Villiers, Bacon, the Howards, and many others. There had previously been technical disagreements between the two men, and although these need not be dramatized, the situation was delicate in June 1615 when Coke was very "derogatory" about Chancery. Later in that year, the two were at judicial loggerheads over habeas corpus proceedings and several points of jurisdiction. Vital legal interpretations were, as ever, involved, but entanglements between courts over jurisdiction were a normal and inevitable occurrence. The Lord Chancellor, even though we may suspect him of interpreting disagreement in a personal rather than institutional light, joined the attack on Coke in the following year because he lost his temper, and this was apparently a reaction less against Coke's arguments than against the timing of his actions.

The old man was very ill, and as early as February 10, 1616, Lake had informed Winwood that Ellesmere's recovery was doubtful. Two days later Bacon, apparently wishing to advance his own claims while undermining those of Coke, wrote to the King regretting that Ellesmere "goes his last day." That very day, Coke finally authorized prosecutions for *praemunire*, and on the morrow made his attempt to force a grand jury to find two indictments. It was commented that these things were done when the Lord Chancellor was supposed to be dead or past all hope of recovery. One has to assume that this was Coke's presumption even though the *praemunire* proceedings must have been considered beforehand. At any rate he did not seek postponement or delay. However, on the fifteenth, Bacon could report that the Lord Chancellor, although afflicted with a bad cough, was recovering. Six days later, Bacon informed James that Ellesmere was "stirred" by what had happened. "He showeth to despise it, but he is full of it, and almost like a young duellist that findeth himself behind-hand."[43]

43   HEH, *El.*, 1668, 5971-5972. J. P. Dawson, "Coke and Ellesmere Disinterred: The Attack on the Chancery in 1616," *Illinois Law Review*, 36:145 (1941). *The Letters and the Life of Francis Bacon*, ed. James Spedding (7 vols.; London: Longmans, Green, 1864-1874), V, 239-240, 241-244, 246-249. *CSPD*, 1611-1618, 349.

Ellesmere evidently felt that Coke had struck a "low blow," and the Chief Justice had blundered by so offending the Lord Chancellor. The King told Ellesmere that Coke's action had been "unseasonable" and was censured by all for "partiality and barbarity." Many months would pass, and a stream of other issues, political and legal, would be involved before Coke was dismissed. The significance of the dispute over Chancery jurisdiction is not that it played an important role in Coke's defeat, but that it served to rank Ellesmere against him and thus dramatize the split among those who were opposed to the Howards. It was through the ruins of this association that Villiers raced to eminence and triumph.[44]

The man most concerned to press an assault on Coke had experienced a career which hardly matched his aspirations. Bacon was a strong candidate to succeed Ellesmere, but he had often been frustrated in the past. In 1612, he had failed to secure significant advancement, certainly the Mastership of the Wards and possibly the position of Secretary. However, in October 1613 he was promoted to the attorney generalship. The reshuffle of that month, prompted by the death of Chief Justice Fleming, saw a protesting Coke moved to the King's Bench, Hobart replace Coke as Chief Justice of the Common Pleas, and Yelverton assume Bacon's old job of Solicitor General. These men would have to work together, but there was an unstable relationship among them. Bacon probably feared that Coke or some other such as Winwood, whose name was rumored in March 1616, might secure the prize. In March and again in May, Ellesmere was willing to surrender his position but the King did not take up his offer. As Coke seemed to have gone out of his way to exhibit an interest in Chancery, perhaps to advance his own position, perhaps to embarrass another appointment, so Bacon sought to weaken Coke. Apart from incidents affecting Chancery, Ellesmere had subsequent disagreements with Coke, evidently played a part in

44   T. Frankland, *Annals of King James and King Charles the First* (London, 1681), 20.

his suspension and dismissal which went beyond mere concurrence, and was pointedly critical in his speech to the new Chief Justice, Montagu. Nor, on at least one occasion, did he instil common courtesy into his servants' demeanor toward Coke. Unwilling to apply any restraint, he did however try to withdraw from the matter as early as October 1616. Obedience to the King, or so he said, frustrated this desire. In any case it was too late. Once legal points were being debated, common honesty compelled further disagreement, as in objections to Coke's *Reports*. As for Bacon, even if he felt more assured of promotion – although there were rumors that he might get the Lord Keepership but another be appointed over his head as Lord Chancellor – he still had an incentive to press the case against Coke and submit him to a public defeat. It would all help to smooth his passage on the Chancery bench. Ellesmere had been drawn into participating in the struggle for his own succession. It was only a straw in the gale of other honors, but the Lord Chancellor's resignation of the position of Lord Lieutenant of Buckinghamshire enabled the post to be picked up in September 1616 by Villiers, the new star, with whom Bacon increasingly associated.[45]

Villiers was less influential in February than he was in November 1616, and even then he would only be a favorite, a man who was highly regarded by the King but still without having his fingers on the practicalities of power and policy. Somerset had been disgraced, but the Howards would not be shifted from their hold until more than a year after Ellesmere's death. Nonetheless, it was clear that Villiers was on the rise, and that his aspirations must be concerned with the bestowal of patronage. Coke's temporary disgrace was vital, and in its creation Ellesmere was an honest pawn. Bitterly offended, he made little attempt to cool the situation. Coke blundered, as when he hinted at further revelations during the Somerset trial, and Bacon added twigs of legal dispute and impropriety to the flames. In another climate it need

45 *CSPD*, 1611–1618, 354, 356, 366. C. D. Bowen, *The Lion and the Throne* (London: H. Hamilton, 1957), 319–336. *Diary of Walter Yonge*, 32. HEH, *El.*, 1694.

not have been so dramatic, and it is well known that Coke after his dismissal soon appeared to be back in favor. The reality of the episode was that the politician with the most ideas on how to improve and reform the royal situation — ideas which Ellesmere could often support — was being forced for the moment off the center of the stage at the very time when the King's health was beginning to disintegrate. The victors were Bacon and Villiers. A return to favor for Coke, public embraces, and a marriage alliance, would not conceal the fact that it was they, and not the old opposition, who undid — or rather took over — the decrepit Howard empire.[46]

Attention in this respect must be paid to a facet of Ellesmere which reveals him as standing in sharp contrast to other Elizabethan and Early Stuart chancellors. He believed that the Lord Chancellor had a duty to his sovereign which justified a refusal to apply the Great Seal, and on occasion he had stood his ground despite a direct command. The Great Seal might be a rubber stamp in most cases, but it happened to be a necessary stamp, and if the man in charge refused to use it a most embarrassing impasse could be achieved. The obvious weakness was that such action might be interpreted as representing the personal or political interest of the Chancellor. In the reign of Elizabeth, for example, Ellesmere's refusal to seal a few grants which concerned Chancery contributed to the impression that he was prone to disguise avarice with technicality. It was unfair, and he himself obviously believed in the purity and responsibility of the Chancellor's individual decision, but this sort of thing did not sway others from the suspicion that he had the knack of ennobling a private motive.[47]

The early years of James I were uneventful, although we may suspect some queasy moments when a patent for Francis Michell,

46   With respect to Villiers, I must acknowledge a debt to discussions with Mr. L. Falk.

47   Jones, *Chancery*, 69–70. See Roberts, *Growth of Responsible Government*, 5–6.

of whom so much was to be heard in 1621, and a grant of the Lieutenancy of Gloucestershire ran into delays at the Seal. Later, Ellesmere's refusal to seal a grant made to Sir William Uvedale amounted to a defiance of Somerset. In 1615, supporting the objections of Yelverton, the Solicitor General, he refused to seal a pardon designed to protect Somerset from any charges which might be brought against him. After discussion in the Privy Council, James ordered compliance, but Ellesmere first demanded a pardon for himself, other pressures were brought upon the King, and Somerset was thwarted. It was a political as well as a legal victory for the Lord Chancellor. A few months later, Somerset and his lady were under arrest, and Ellesmere, despite Somerset's protest, presided over the sensational legal proceedings of May 1616. Ellesmere held up the patent for gold and silver thread for seventeen months, and in the last days of his life, he refused to seal any more patents, including that for the licensing of inns suggested by Mompesson. He was sick, but even then it could be noted that one patent was for Gerard's appointment as Lord President of Wales, a position which the Lord Chancellor was believed to want for his son.[48]

At one time, Ellesmere made the point that he was repelled by innovations which could be interpreted during his own life as disreputable to his name. No man can be led by another's conscience, he affirmed on another occasion. When James requested his favor for Robert Wolverstone, who had aided the court position in the 1614 House of Commons, Ellesmere was unhelpful and when he heard of moves to reverse a decree he reacted with a somewhat exaggerated expression of disgust for the man. Initially the King had probably intended little more than to bring the case to the Lord Chancellor's attention, as was often the aim of great men when they solicited a judge on behalf of a litigant. But the manner of the approach was indelicate, and James had once

48   HEH, *El.*, 444, 1435, 1437–1438, 2947–2948. HEH, *El.*, Calendar, 2943–2945. Akrigg, *Jacobean Pageant*, 189. *CSPV*, 1615–1617, 58. Gardiner, *History*, III, 77 n. 2; IV, 2–3, 11.

again made the mistake of sticking his finger too readily into the fire.[49]

Ellesmere did not refuse something very often, but even a few instances must have raised a political question. What would happen if his successor took a similar line, or even expanded it? A chancellor opposed to Villiers might do a great deal of harm to that young man's ambitions. Coke was probably only an outside possibility for the job, and historical hindsight suggests that Bacon was quite the favorite candidate. Yet we can understand how Bacon would have uncertainties on this point. As far as someone like Villiers was concerned, it was not necessary to view Coke as an opponent. But Coke would have been nobody's man. Even to think of him as Lord Chancellor is as unlikely as to conceive of Charles V, a century earlier, actually making Wolsey Pope. Considerations like these must have allied neatly with Bacon's anxiety, Coke's errors, and Ellesmere's affront. In the end, Bacon, the obvious candidate, the ally of Villiers, and a man distinguished in all save personality, was appointed. That he did not adopt the same attitude can surely be deemed a vital element in his failure and fall. In his initial speech as Lord Keeper, he discussed the responsibility for passing or denying grants and, under the guise of rationality, in effect rejected Ellesmere's position. It was with reference to this problem and the nature of the King's commands that he said, "I mean to walk in the light, so that men may know where to find me." A multitude of objectionable patents were doubtless passed under Ellesmere; only rarely did he block grants. Yet it is hardly conceivable that Ellesmere could have been open to the kind of attack which swamped his successor in 1621.[50]

All told, 1616 was an exciting year. Spurred on by activity, Ellesmere made a remarkable recovery and received yet another

49   HEH, *El.*, 444, 5964–5968. Hawarde, *Reportes del Cases*, 221.

50   Spedding, *Letters and Life*, VI, 187–189. Some years later there was a dispute between the Lord Deputy of Ireland and the Lord Chancellor of Ireland, partly because of the latter's refusal to seal grants. *APC*, March 1625–May 1626, 403–406.

impetus when it was known that his daughter-in-law was pregnant. When a boy was born, the King wisecracked that he would not be named James, "but Edward, after the Lord Chief Justice." This was in September, and Ellesmere noted that the King was pleased to be merry. At the end of December, the household accounts noted an outlay in respect of blankets, cradle sheets, and woollens for the young master. This was an Indian summer and Ellesmere soon succumbed. He gave up applying the Great Seal, which had to be removed from his care. He died at York House in March 1617. The will was short and lucid. He found "no true comfort nor contentment in this miserable life," and he asked to be buried in "oblivion." The remains were carried into Cheshire and laid to rest alongside those of his first wife and first son, a victim of Elizabeth's Irish war. The Countess made an unsuccessful attempt to break the will. John, soon elevated to be Earl of Bridgewater, obtained letters of administration for his father's effects and a special probate after it was found that the testator was "sound in mind and in whole and perfect memory."[51]

Ellesmere was an individual of moderate social status who acquired the dignity of high position through his own ability. On the bench and in politics he could be sagacious and compromising, but when his moral wrath was stirred and he felt absolutely in the right he could be exceptionally dogmatic and unyielding. Yet this was a man who could only be effective politically by virtue of the respect in which he was held. His association with Salisbury crumbled. His identification with nebulous groups of men opposed to the Howards rested upon the easily shattered foundations of a justifiable but negative hostility. An individualist, he was a loner amid Jacobean faction. Unwilling to be just a follower, his personal position and age could not support the role of leader. He relied upon the prestige of his position and the weight which would be accorded to his opinions, coming as they did from an elder statesman, able minister, and renowned judge.

51 *Egerton Papers*, 479–480. HEH, *El.*, Calendar, 326, 706–707, 725–726. PCC, 22 Weldon. Chamberlain, *Letters*, II, 65.

To some extent this was justified, but it would seem that Ellesmere was not regarded with quite the awe he desired. Too many of his listeners or correspondents reserved second thoughts about his attitudes.

Ellesmere was undoubtedly old and sick. He could hardly be blamed for either condition, and although old men, to the irritation of younger men, talk too much and rehearse their ailments, this was all very natural. His continued ability as Lord Chancellor more than compensated for these difficulties. Likewise, although he was rich, had reached the top of his profession, and was appreciated by James, he had justification for thinking that others who deserved less had received more. He was concerned to enhance his line and his descendants, but he was not greedy. Gifts, awards of title, or personal attentions from the monarch were still extremely important. He did not really need land, money, or even title, but these were standard means whereby a man was publicly honored by his sovereign and which, in Ellesmere's own words, comforted age. Continually he craved to be so honored before his countrymen. These elements were all very human, his long-suffering mien, his ability to introduce senility and sickness when others could think that he was playing politics, diminished the influence of his opinions. Yet he was unavoidable. He could not marshal battalions, but his office gave him a powerful position if he cared to use it. The man who controlled the Great Seal, who monitored the House of Lords, could not be ignored in the calculations of others, and his support or compliance was continually solicited. Those who were interested in leadership, attained or desired, had to deal with him. He was indeed a whetstone in the forum of politics. Coke only ignored him when it was reasonably assumed that he was at death's door, and that proved to be a gigantic blunder. Ellesmere himself appreciated that his political power lay in his office, and he probably understood that this was a limited strength if he was in disagreement with the King, the official line, or with the majority of councillors. Sometimes, despite wiles and excuses which may or may not have been genuine,

61

he was defeated, as when Salisbury forced him to address the King on behalf of the House of Lords in 1610. Sometimes he was victorious, as when despite the King he used his position to rally critical councillors in 1615 and deny Somerset a premature pardon. His few attempts to act openly and in combination, witness the abortive eleventh-hour campaign to prevent dissolution in 1614, were not very successful. In the political employment of his reputation and of his position as Lord Chancellor he experienced the range of triumph and defeat.

Ellesmere's abilities and feet of clay were both apparent in the Jacobean period. Unwittingly, he spoke his own epitaph in November 1608 when he advised counsel not to act for themselves in lawsuits. "Men of judgment and discretion have always refrained so to do, for a man cannot look into himself with indifferent eyes. Every man naturally is a lover of himself, and partial in the judgment of himself." He had behaved almost consciously as an Elizabethan. Even this label might not seem satisfactory when Parliament is considered, for the tactic of complicating supply by an early reference to grievance had been understood by Elizabethan MP's. Yet his fundamental, and apparently naive, doctrine that there was an order of doing things, first supply and then grievance, was essentially Elizabethan. It depended upon the establishment of some kind of formula, execution of which must depend upon the general trust in the sovereign's reliability and word of honor. Elizabeth never lost this, though she had her difficulties. Both aspects could be seen in the 1601 Parliament, but faith in her emerged as the dominant emotion. James never acquired this magic gift, and without it all Ellesmere's ideas about the proper way of doing things were futile and could represent only a sterile conservatism. Even outside this parliamentary issue the King often acted as did his predecessor, and yet he ran into novel criticism. Sometimes James had distorted the situation, and sometimes the criticisms were unreasonable. Yet, even if variants are ignored, there is no reason to suppose that imitation or repetition has any fundamental justification in a political world. As it was, Ellesmere often looked as though he was groping for some familiar kind of Elizabethan pattern. Dubious of official methods in handling Parliament, his own favored approach increasingly seemed threadbare, remote from events and the passage of years. In the first months of James's reign he had observed, with an eye to religion, that "albeit there be a change of the governor, yet there is no change neither of government nor in government." He was wrong.[52]

52   Hawarde, *Reportes del Cases*, 163, 308–309.

THOMAS M. COAKLEY

Robert Cecil in Power: Elizabethan Politics in Two Reigns

It was said of Robert Cecil,[1] as of the Thames boatman, "he is an excellent wherryman, who you know looketh towards the bridge when he pulleth towards Westminster . . ."[2] When Sir Francis Bacon wrote this uncomplimentary judgment, he made a shrewd observation about Robert Cecil, perhaps in a sense different from that intended. Cecil remains one of those complex persons whose careers invite periodic reappraisal; his subtleties make him appear elusive, if not fully two-faced, as Bacon implied. Cecil's reputation with historians has been an indication of scholarly concern with the success or failure of conciliar monarchy, with the processes of change and of continuity in political administration, and also with the effects of the Reformation and the origins of the Civil War. Lacking the color and appeal of contemporaries like Sir Walter Ralegh and the Earl of Essex and devoid of the obvious impact on Anglo-American public life and

1 An essay similar to this was read before the Midwest Conference on British Historical Studies at the University of Notre Dame, South Bend, Indiana, on November 11, 1967. Robert Cecil is so called throughout this article without regard for his changing titles in the course of his career. Other persons are usually referred to by their names or their titles according to common usage.

2 Francis Bacon to the Earl of Essex, [November 10, 1593], Spedding, *Letters and Life*, I, 262. J. Hurstfield, *The Queen's Wards* (London: Longmans, Green, 1958), 305.

64

thought of men like Sir Edward Coke and Sir Francis Bacon, Robert Cecil achieved an ascendancy over these contemporaries which appears puzzling.

Cecil was, indeed, the heir of his father's political talents and position. The glib maintained that "the Lord Treasurer's wit was as it seems of Borough English tenure, for it descended to his younger son, Sir Robert."[3] He served an apprenticeship under the patronage of his father, Lord Burghley, in Parliament and also at the Council table. His initiation into the duties of the secretaryship began as Sir Francis Walsingham's informal, and then his formal, successor. Cecil's political methods and objectives had deep roots in the experience of Elizabeth's reign. His commitment to Elizabethan policies and practices made him reluctant to reckon with new situations and personalities; yet his capacity for facing challenges to established Elizabethan ways is indication of his grudging willingness to change in order to meet new circumstances. Religious comprehensiveness, political accommodation, and national unity before the powerful Spanish foe had been Elizabethan watchwords. A quiet succession, peace with Spain, and internal division brought new and different challenges. If the changes in circumstance were unaccompanied by the dramatic events which characterized the Reformation a generation earlier or the Civil War a generation later, these changes were no less real. It was Robert Cecil's political position which did much to preserve certain aspects of Tudor conciliar polity until 1610, if not longer; and it was he who made the first attempt at harmony with the newly articulate personalities who clamored for change. In the course of his career he confronted three major threats to his political position: the rivalry with the Earl of Essex for the favor of Elizabeth, the succession of James VI of Scotland to the English throne as James I, and the quarrels between Crown and Commons in the early years of James I's reign, which culminated

3   *Diary of John Manningham, 1602–1603*, ed. John Bruce (London: Camden Society, 1868), 82. Algernon Cecil, *A Life of Robert Cecil, First Earl of Salisbury* (London: J. Murray, 1915), 129.

in the failure of the Great Contract. These threats to Cecil's position or crises in his career will be discussed later in this essay.

Cecil operated under several political limitations. First, the advisory capacity in which a privy councillor stood imposed a formal and practical restriction. Cecil counted for naught without the confidence first of Elizabeth and then of James. Clever talk about the *"regnum Cecilianum"* of Lord Burghley or about the absolute kingship of Robert Cecil never deceived father or son. They knew that there were "so many ways to the wood . . ." and employed great skill to acquire, retain, and use royal favor.[4] Elizabeth's confidence in Cecil arose naturally by the transfer to him of her confidence in his father. This trust received additional confirmation from the cool, efficient manner in which Cecil dealt with the crises induced by the exertions of the Earl of Essex, the first major threat to Cecil's career. By the time of Essex's fall inheritance, training, and service had established Cecil's considerable position in the state, although he has been seen as then only one of a triumvirate including the admiral, Charles Howard, Earl of Nottingham, and the treasurer, Thomas Sackville, Lord Buckhurst, later Earl of Dorset.[5]

Elizabeth's advanced age meant that Robert Cecil probably would have to acquire the confidence of a new royal master before long if he hoped to retain his ascendancy. The task did not appear easy, since the most likely successor, James VI of Scotland, was thought to be greatly hostile toward Cecil. By means of a public silence and a discreet correspondence, however, James and Cecil established a binding understanding and a sure course of conduct. Cecil circumspectly refused to bargain with the King for future rewards for himself or his friends for their services.[6]

4   William Herlle to Lord Burghley, August 11, 1585, Lord Burghley to William Herlle, August 14, 1585, PRO, *SP* 12/181/32, fol. 138ᵛ; 42, fol. 159. *CSPV*, 1603–1607, X, 514–516. Robert Cecil to Sir Henry Bruncker, 1604, HMC, *Cal. Salisbury* MSS, XVI, 420.

5   F. M. G. Evans, *Principal Secretary of State: A Survey of the Office from 1558 to 1680* (Manchester: University Press, 1923), 57, 58.

6   *Correspondence of King James VI of Scotland with Sir Robert Cecil and*

After James's accession to the English throne, Cecil received almost immediate recognition of the King's gratitude for a quiet succession and at the same time assurance of continued political position and royal favor. Cecil rose from a mere knighthood to an earldom in a little more than two years. He had survived by then the second major crisis of his career. He had not only retained his position but also improved it by serving as James's principal agent in the fulfilment of the King's fondest dream, the English succession. Until the memory of this deed had grown cold and failures in other matters had begun to chafe, Cecil had an incontestable place in the counsels of the King. James, reluctant to attend to the routine of state, must have been impressed and relieved by the way in which Cecil executed the duties of his offices and administered the officials who served under him. The "little beagle" letters of James to Cecil reveal deceptive familiarity on the part of the King, who spoke and wrote to many people in an unguarded fashion. Cecil, however, rarely presumed upon these demonstrations of friendship to allow himself similar expressions of familiarity.[7] Financial problems introduced abrasive exchanges in their correspondence and prompted protests of economy from the King and humble appeals for restraint from Cecil. The exchange of elaborate assurances may indicate a coolness which increased toward the end of 1610.

Another dimension had re-entered English politics with the accession of James I. The royal family required Cecil's attention, and he found no direct equivalent in the political testaments of Elizabeth or of Burghley. Some antipathy existed between Queen Anne and Cecil, which might have been serious if she had had great influence in public life. Cecil, however, served on her council, acted as her high bailiff and steward, and labored long over

Others in England, ed. John Bruce (London: Camden Society, 1861), xxix–xxxi, xxxvii, xxxviii, 1–8.

7   Willson, *James VI and I,* 186–190. Frederick G. Marcham, "James I of England and the 'Little Beagle' Letters," *Persecution and Liberty: Essays in Honor of George Lincoln Burr* (New York: Century, 1931), 315–319, 327–333.

the estates in her jointure.[8] He had a considerable part in the discussions of policy concerning the older royal children, Prince Henry and Princess Elizabeth. The Prince's education and plans for his marriage naturally involved considerations of foreign affairs and of religious policy. Henry's death in 1612, like the death of Cecil a few months earlier, blighted a number of expectations of political recovery by conciliar monarchy under a vigorous successor schooled by an able councillor. The marriage of Princess Elizabeth also meant intricate arrangements of foreign policy and religion. In Cecil's last months at work he counseled caution and delay out of considerations of policy, but the King pressed for a rapid decision upon a marriage treaty. The Princess was married to the protestant Elector Frederick of the Palatinate within a few months after Cecil's death.[9]

If Cecil had been obliged to please only the King, his political position and practice could have been relatively simple; but the situation was not that simple. Although he did not require the popularity of a leader in a modern political party, he had to consider individuals and groups in English public life whose interests might sometimes be contrary to his own. A number of persons of social position, intelligence, or energy could not be reduced to the ranks of Cecil's "Followers and Dependents."[10] Most of these persons did not aspire to positions of political equality with him, but they could not for one reason or another consider themselves in any formal sense less than peers of Robert Cecil. He bore no definite or constant relationship to these politically active persons

8   CSPD, 1603–1610, 45. Jane Drummond to Robert Cecil, November 1611, PRO, SP 14/67/79. Goodman, Court of James I, I, 37, 38. Willson, James VI and I, 156, 157.

9   Robert Cecil to Prince Henry, December 1608, HMC, Bath MSS, II, 55–56. Adam Newton to Robert Cecil, October 19, 1609, Manuscripts of the Marquis of Salisbury (Cecil Papers) [hereafter Hatfield House, MSS Salis.], 128, fol. 13. PRO, SP 14/2-71, and BM, Lansdowne MSS, 90–92, contain much correspondence about the Prince and his household. Viscount Fenton to Robert Cecil, September 1, 1611, "Tidings from England . . .," December ?, 1611, CSPD, 1611–1618, 72, 104.

10   The phrase is applied to Cecil's clients in Sir Henry Neville to Sir Ralph Winwood, May 12, 1608, Winwood, Memorials, II, 399.

but was forced to choose those individuals and groups with whom he could cooperate and to reject those with whom he found himself in rivalry.

Cecil carefully avoided appearing in any sense more exalted than first among equals in his relations with the other privy councillors, officers of state, and the nobility with whom he shared many of the rewards of office and some of its burdens. His relations with these personalities consequently had an ambiguous character which almost frustrates analysis. The factionalism of the Elizabethan Council seemed not to be a continuous thing: Young Turks of one period appeared as elder statesmen in another; some issues seemed to find virtually all the councillors on one side and the Queen on the other. In times of crisis a kind of unanimity obtained, only to fall apart in quarrels which were more personal than political. A static, stratified view of social and political life may have been under attack, but the monarchy and the state retained many traditional notions of solid stability and regulated order. Although the Cecils personally demonstrated the upward mobility of the age, they would have been ineffective if they had not shown an appreciation of the countervailing pressures toward immobility. Surely, as late as Charles I's reign, if not later, the privileges of rank and of personal favor had more consequence than deliberate policy or consciously organized political programs in the attainment of influence and office.[11] Short of revolution, which was still more than a generation away, there were privileged classes and interests which had to be consulted or favored. Robert Cecil's association with persons drawn from these classes and groups may have been less an act of deliberate policy than a conventional reflex. His attitudes toward political figures derived much from the notion of full, implicit loyalty to the Crown, which Burghley had preached, if he had not always practiced it before the accession of Elizabeth. Cecil developed alliances with politicians who were likely to share his loyalty and

11   See G. E. Aylmer, *The King's Servants: The Civil Service of Charles I, 1625–1642* (London: Routledge & Kegan Paul, 1961), 10–12.

avoided opponents who might taint that loyalty. He also sought to quiet discontent upon which disaffected leaders might build up resistance or rebellion.

An example of this traditionally minded political style may be seen in what once was called the readmission of the old nobility into positions of influence in the Council and the Court. The stereotype of hostility between old nobility and new nobility may be incapable of proof and overdrawn, and thus the notion of a readmission overstated. As more and more of traditional leadership embraced Elizabethan and Cecilian policy, it was possible to draw at least some of this leadership back into their conventional places in the state. Several of the Howards; Gilbert, seventh Talbot Earl of Shrewsbury; Henry, ninth Percy Earl of Northumberland, still may have had sympathies with other political or religious causes; but their interests had been enlisted in support of Elizabethan policies, particularly when they received the approbation of King James.[12]

More important still for Cecil than concern with hereditary leadership were the close working relationships which he maintained with other holders of great offices of state and of the Household. With these principal officers and also with the judges Cecil had mainly congenial relations in spite of occasional friction. He rarely made major decisions without the concurrence of one or more of them; his primacy, never a tyranny over the Crown, never became a tyranny over the Court or Council.[13]

With the Scottish courtiers and favorites of James I, Cecil formed outwardly friendly relations. Out of obligation, if not desire, Cecil worked for the interests of impoverished Scots, for whom he seems to have been a channel to the wealth of England,

12   Lord Henry Howard to Earl of Mar, November 22, [1601], *The Secret Correspondence of Sir Robert Cecil with James VI, King of Scots*, ed. Edmund Goldsmid (3 vols.; Edinburgh: privately printed, 1887), I, 14, 15. HMC, *Mar and Kellie* MSS, 53 (where the letter is dated November 22, 1607). APC, 1601–1604, 495–497. John Chamberlain to Dudley Carleton, December 9, 1608, Chamberlain, *Letters*, I, 273. HMC, *Tenth Report, Appendix VI*, 83.

13   Bruce, *Manningham*, 78. Evans, *Principal Secretary*, 53. Earl of Dorset to Robert Cecil, [1605], HMC, *Cal. Salisbury* MSS, XVII, 590.

although he tried to place limits on the scope and nature of their suits. Whatever the intent of either party to this working arrangement may have been, Cecil and the Scottish officers of state, courtiers, and favorites maintained a friendly correspondence. With the exception of George Home, Earl of Dunbar, the Scots took little part in internal English affairs during most of Cecil's ascendancy; and Cecil, in turn, exercised a slight role in Scottish affairs. The complimentary correspondence continued with the Scots until Cecil's death in spite of the fact that Robert Carr, Viscount Rochester, later Earl of Somerset, the King's Scots favorite, had begun to convert personal favor into political influence after Cecil's failure to effect the Great Contract in Parliament in 1610.[14]

More complex, however, were the relationships between Cecil and certain intelligent or energetic English rivals. These rivals frequently aspired to the same sort of eminence that Lord Burghley and his son had achieved. These ambitious emulators of Cecilian power and influence — Essex, Ralegh, and the Bacons — grew too proud to accept positions of secondary rank but often had limitations of ability, temperament, or opportunity which kept them from the highest offices. Almost without exception Cecil had strained relations with such men. These ambitious dissidents often provided leadership for the disaffected persons or groups of other backgrounds, noblemen or gentlemen who were not welcome at Court or who absented themselves from Court by reason of religion, poverty, or political and personal disfavor. The dissi-

14   Ibid., XV, 94, 95, 171, 259, 274; XVII, 89, 90, 101, 105, 219, 298–299; XVIII, 319, 441; XIV, xii. CSPD, 1603–1610, 585. CSPD, 1611–1618, 9, 19. CSVP, 1603–1607, X, 67, 515. APC, 1601–1604, 499. David Lloyd, State-Worthies, 2nd ed. (London, 1670), 733. Francis Osborne, "Traditional Memoirs," in Secret History of the Court of James the First, ed. Sir Walter Scott (2 vols.; Edinburgh: John Ballantyne, 1811), I, 232, 233. Bruce, Correspondence, 19. Papiers d'état, ed. Alexandre Teulet (3 vols.; published for Bannatyne Club; Paris: Typographie de Henri Plon, 1851–1860), III, 708, 709. Illustrations of British History . . ., ed. Edmund Lodge, 2nd ed. (3 vols.; London: John Chidley, 1838), III, 21 n., 31 n. Willson, James VI and I, 175, 176, are only part of the vast literature which has helped to create the impression of Cecil's relations with the Scots as suitors for favor, as politicians, and as friends, and of Cecil's role in Scottish affairs.

dents had not always been opponents of the Cecils; some were drawn from Robert Cecil's former friends, cousins, even brothers-in-law. Cecil's relationships with these rivals and opponents have given an unsavory reputation to his political practice which persists to the present time in much opinion concerning his career.

Perhaps the first group of opponents might be called the followers of Robert Devereux, second Earl of Essex, and the survivors of Essex's Rebellion. Much of the politics of the latter part of Elizabeth's reign was a question of how the impetuous Earl would be assimilated into the state; the eventual solution, of course, was that he would not be. There may have been some possibility that the Court and Council might have been organized again around two leaders, a "noble favorite" and a "more dependable civil servant," comparable with Leicester and Burghley in the early years of Elizabeth's reign. If that solution, as suggested by Sir John Neale, had merit, the likelihood of its implementation faded with Essex's impolitic reactions to his reverses.[15] When Essex ultimately sought to rival the "domestical greatness" of the Cecils, he turned for assistance to Robert Cecil's cousins, Francis and Anthony Bacon.[16] With Essex, however, the emphasis remained on military rather than domestic greatness. The Cecils, father and son, and the very character of Essex's attempts frustrated these ambitious plans; and the Cecilians acquired the favor of the Crown lost by Essex at his fall.

Cecil's part in Essex's fall has been the subject of frequent study, but no one seems fully to have broken through the silence of the surviving evidence on material points. Cecil avoided appearing the principal actor or initiator. He may have allowed Essex to strike off his own head by granting the Earl easy access to the means of committing treason; but he permitted Essex's more outspoken opponents, men like Sir Walter Ralegh, to render innocuous, almost friendly, his own expressions of opposi-

15   J. E. Neale, *Queen Elizabeth* (London: Jonathan Cape, 1934), 330.
16   Francis Bacon to Earl of Essex, October 4, 1596, Spedding, *Letters and Life*, II, 40–45. A. Cecil, *Robert Cecil*, 102, 103. Neale, *Elizabeth*, 331–337.

tion. Cecil's personal intervention at Essex's trial ostensibly was intended to clear his own reputation and honor rather than to obtain the conviction of the prisoner.[17] Once Essex had been removed from the scene, Cecil had to develop a new set of relationships with the survivors of the Earl's faction, a considerable number since only six persons suffered death at Essex's fall. The noble and gentle followers of the Earl received protection and surprisingly rapid reintroduction into the established political order.[18] One former supporter of Essex, however, seems to have received little encouragement, although he detached himself from the Earl's faction before the fall. Francis Bacon, son of Elizabeth's first Lord Keeper of the Great Seal, nephew of Lady Burghley and so cousin of Robert Cecil, found substantial advancement in the state impossible during his cousin's primacy. Although Bacon, of whom much was expected, appeared from the first an intelligent, energetic young man with the proper connections, his expectations received setbacks for two decades. If his association with Essex provoked resentment among the Cecilians, it was concealed; yet Bacon always regarded Cecil as the stumbling block of all his efforts. Cecil probably had no personal animus against his cousin, toward whom he, the successful politician, had little reason to bear a grudge. It is likely that the industrious Secretary considered Bacon an unreliable

17   Sir Walter Ralegh to Robert Cecil, [between February and August 1600], Edward Edwards, *The Life of Sir Walter Ralegh* (2 vols.; London: Macmillan, 1868), I, 258–260; II, 213–223. *A Complete Collection of State Trials . . .*, ed. T. B. Howell et al. (42 vols.; London: printed by T. C. Hansard for Longmans, 1816–1898), I, 1351, 1352. William Stebbing, *Sir Walter Ralegh: A Biography* (Oxford: Clarendon Press, 1899), 151–154. Osborne, "Traditional Memoirs," in Scott, *Secret History*, I, 103, 107. Laura H. Cadwallader, *The Career of the Earl of Essex from the Islands Voyage in 1597 to His Execution in 1601* (Philadelphia: University of Pennsylvania Press, 1923), 67, 89, 92, 93. E. P. Cheyney, *A History of England from the Defeat of the Armada to the Death of Elizabeth* (2 vols.; New York: Longmans, Green, 1926), II, 485, 504, 509–511, 513, 515–516, 522–524, 534–535, 538, 540–542, 544–548.
18   Earl of Northumberland to King James, [n.d.], Bruce, *Correspondence*, 68. Spedding, *Letters and Life*, III, 75 n. 1, 138. Goodman, *Court of James I*, I, 167. Nicolo Molin to Doge and Senate, January 6, 1606 N.S., *CSPV*, 1603–1607, X, 308. Neale, *Elizabeth*, 376.

dreamer, whose ambition and disposition toward fine living might prove insatiable. Throughout Cecil's life Bacon could not rise high enough by means of his own influence to acquire any independent political position; he could not persuade Cecil to become his patron; and he could find no other who would promote his interests after his early dependence on Essex. Without being ruined, Bacon was kept next door to real power.[19]

The fall of Essex began a period of political realignment which was complete only when James had been seated firmly on the English throne. At first, as has been mentioned, Cecil shared leadership in a triumvirate in which the Lord Admiral Nottingham and the Lord Treasurer Buckhurst were his chief colleagues. Two enemies of Essex were not unimportant. Sir Walter Ralegh enjoyed some revived favor with Elizabeth, which he owed to Cecil's support. Lord Cobham, Cecil's brother-in-law, also became something of a favorite with the Queen shortly before her death. Ralegh and Cobham supported Cecil against Essex but showed no taste for their own secondary rank between 1601 and 1603. They entered into compromising conversations with the Earl of Northumberland. Lord Henry Howard, later Earl of Northampton, referred to them as the "diabolical triplicity." These three figures earned a reputation for discontent which made them increasingly a subject for suspicion by the Cecilians. Lord Henry Howard used all his powers of poison-penmanship to discredit Ralegh with Cecil and with James. Once Howard proposed and rejected a plan to trap Cobham and Ralegh by involving them in a correspondence with Scotland, which could be revealed to the Queen; in the same letter Howard hoped to injure Cobham by involving him with the Spanish.[20]

19   Spedding, *Letters and Life*, I, 237, 257, 295, 296, 346, 347, 354–358; III, 57, 79–82, 148, 277, 278, 288–292, 296, 297, 362, 367; IV, 11–13, 240–243. Lloyd, *State-Worthies*, 832, 833. Gardiner, *History*, I, 194, 195. A. Cecil, *Robert Cecil*, 78, 79. Willson, *Privy Councillors*, 114, 115.

20   Lord Henry Howard to Edward Bruce, December 4, 1601, Goldsmid, *Secret Correspondence*, I, 37. J. B. Nichols, *The Progresses, Processions, and Magnificent Festivities of James the First* (3 vols. in 4; London: J. B. Nichols, printer to the Society of Antiquaries, 1828), I, 66 n. 1. Lord Henry Howard to Robert Cecil,

In spite of these maneuvers, an outward show of friendship among Cecil, Cobham, and Ralegh persisted until James's accession. Political ruin, however, came swiftly; before the end of 1603 Cobham, Ralegh, and others had been accused of treason, tried, and condemned so that thereafter they owed their lives solely to the King's mercy. The conspiracies, the so-called Bye and Main Plots, were too complex to be discussed here; the trials a travesty on justice; the executions a farce, as the principal condemned figures had their lives spared at the last moment. Throughout, Cecil maintained a coolness in contrast to the abusive attacks of Lord Henry Howard and to the vengeful prosecution of Sir Edward Coke; he managed to appear as still friendly with the accused excepting always their disloyalty. Only the French ambassador detected interest and passion in Cecil's behavior. Whatever else may be said of the Bye and Main episodes, they rid Cecil of several former allies and embarrassing friends who thereby lost all political hope.[21]

Northumberland, an isolated figure in spite of his position at Court and on the Council, survived the fall of his brother-in-law Essex and that of his friends Ralegh and Cobham. Gunpowder Plot was to be his undoing. An exaggerated acount of Northumberland's involvement with the plotters became the justification for his imprisonment, which continued until 1621.[22]

After 1605 no leading figure in England lost office or came

[from a draft or minutes, probably between March and June 1602], Edwards, *Ralegh*, II, 436–444; same letter somewhat differently arranged in Edward Thompson, *Sir Walter Ralegh: Last of the Elizabethans* (New Haven: Yale University Press, 1936), 176–178. Stebbing, *Ralegh*, 171, 172; see also Gardiner, *History*, I, 117 n. 3.

21   Edwards, *Ralegh*, I, 339–456 (especially M. de Beaumont to Henry IV, August 13, 1603 N.S., 376, 377); II, 436–486. Thompson, *Ralegh*, 203–215. Gardiner, *History*, I, 108–140. HMC, *Cal. Salisbury* MSS, XV, 212, 216, 240.

22   Lord Henry Howard to Edward Bruce, c. April 1602, May 1, 1602, Goldsmid, *Secret Correspondence*, II, 5–9, 33, 34. King James to Earl of Northumberland, March 24, 1603, Bruce, *Correspondence*, 75, 76. APC, 1601–1604, 495. Zorzi Giustinian to Doge and Senate, May 18, 1606 N.S., CSPV, 1603–1607, X, 350. Henry Percy, Earl of Northumberland, *Advice to His Son* [1609], ed. G. B. Harrison (London: E. Benn, 1930), 5, 7, 8, 11, 15, 19–21, 26, 27, 32–34. Gardiner, *History*, I, 283–285. *DNB sub* Percy, Henry, ninth Earl of Northumberland.

under suspicion during the rest of Cecil's period of ascendancy. It was as if Cecil had succeeded between about 1600 and 1605 in adapting himself to a new political climate by changing his alliances from one group of politicians to another which was more acceptable to the new ruler. Survival through this transition required skill; emergence from it in full favor and authority indicated a political intelligence of the highest order.

Cecil also maintained his position by taking pains over the duties of the numerous offices which he held; he was not only the trusted adviser of the Crown and the principal politician of the realm but also the leading administrator of the state. Although it would be anachronistic to attribute to Cecil a control and direction over administrative and quasi-judicial staffs comparable with that exercised by the modern secretary of a department, he had a degree of authority over the secretariat, the Exchequer, and the Court of Wards which forced the subordinate officers and all persons who had business with these officers to reckon with him and to seek his patronage. Cecil had a mastery of the means whereby matters of state were transacted and this mastery rendered him almost indispensable to the performance of many official duties. He hesitated about delegating the substantial powers of his office, keeping his dependents mainly occupied with routine, from which they found it difficult to rise after his death.

Like three or four royal secretaries before him, Robert Cecil made of the office a clearinghouse for advice, for foreign and domestic correspondence, for parliamentary management, for administrative supervision, and for the maintenance of internal peace. If the fixed, formal duties of the secretary were few and relatively routine, they could be elaborated into numerous, significant powers when the secretary was a man who had the royal confidence and a mastery of politics as well.[23] Because of Cecil's

23   Evans, *Principal Secretary*, 1–12, 33–34, 42, 50–53, 335. "Nicholas Faunt's Discourse Touching the Office of the Principal Secretary of Estate, etc., 1592," ed. Charles Hughes, *EHR*, 22:499, 500 (1905). Robert Cecil, "The State and Dignity of

preoccupation with the flexible, political activities of the secretaryship, the fixed, formal routine tended to devolve upon others. His subordinates, nonetheless, derived little independent political position from their proximity to the mighty as long as Cecil retained royal favor. Under Cecil the "inward men" of the Secretary, at first his personal servants, tended to become public servants; and their master, relieved of the routine duties of the secretaryship by clerks and private secretaries, then devoted more of his time to the duties of his other offices and to the policy-making duties of the secretarial office. After Cecil's death the political and advisory powers of the secretaryship fell back into the Household, indeed into the Bedchamber, and shortly the office was filled with dutiful bureaucrats rather than with independent politicians. The King presumably hoped to prevent the emergence of a powerful minister likely to take advantage of his laziness by using the flexible position of the secretaryship, but James's dispensing with a secretary of Cecil's caliber had results injurious to those connections between the Court and the Country which Cecil had maintained throughout his career.[24]

The Privy Council was one institution which the Secretary's influence penetrated and, indeed, dominated. The distinction between Cecil the secretary and Cecil the councillor was vague and doubtful, if not completely indefinable. Some correspondents wrote to Cecil the councillor as if he were the Council; others wrote to the Council as if that body were merely an institutional extension of the Secretary. There was a striking similarity between the flexible duties of strong secretaries like Cecil and the activities of the Privy Council. The activities of the Secretary in the Council increased the tendency toward common action by the

a Secretary of State's Place with the Care and Peril Thereof . . .," ed. Sir Walter Scott, *A Collection of Scarce and Valuable Tracts . . . of the Late Lord Somers*, 2nd ed. (13 vols.; London: printed for T. Cadell & W. Davies, 1809–1815), V, 552–554.

24 Evans, *Principal Secretary*, 61, 62, 64–65, 155, 157–159, 202, 203, 205. Goodman, *Court of James I*, I, 175, 176, 256, 257. Alan G. R. Smith, "The Secretariats of the Cecils, *circa* 1580–1612," *EHR*, 83:481–504 (1968).

Council and its leading member. By dominating the Privy Council, Cecil exerted an influence upon English administration far beyond the scope of his own offices.[25]

One of the numerous demands upon the time and skill of a great secretary was the encouragement or discouragement of subordinate officials and of persons who held no office but sought his favor. Cecil, the channel of communication between the Crown and the subject, was the natural person for suitors to approach for favors. A pension, a grant of land, a title, the reconciliation of a disobedient subject to the Crown, or a place in the state — all these were matters for which the good offices of the Secretary might be sought and might be used to the satisfaction of the seeker. The ordinary suitor, indeed the uncommon suitor too, had to have a powerful patron at Court to protect him from difficulties or indifference. Noblemen and gentlemen, high officials and humble clerks, soldiers and servants sought a dependence upon Cecil, took heart from every sign of his favor, feared every cross to their suits. Lord Danvers looked for high employment; Edward Coke for a knighthood or promotion to the chief justiceship of the Court of Common Pleas; a ship captain for the vice-admiralty in the Narrow Seas; Sir Richard Trevor for the King's promised benefit in spite of Cecil's displeasure. A writer on behalf of a Mr. Violet begged Cecil to "besprinkle with the dew of his comfort this withering Violet." Relatives, friends, clergymen, the unemployed, and debtors sought the Secretary's comfortable words and deeds.[26]

25   Evans, *Principal Secretary*, 222–237. E. R. Turner, *The Privy Council of England in the Seventeenth and Eighteenth Centuries, 1603–1784* (2 vols.; Baltimore: Johns Hopkins Press, 1927–1928), I, 110. *APC*, 1613–1614, 4–6, especially for the similarities between the oaths of a principal secretary and a privy councillor.
26   Elizabeth Stapleton to Countess of Shrewsbury, February 20, 1605?, Lodge, *Illustrations*, III, 156 n. Wallace Notestein, *Four Worthies* (London: Jonathan Cape, 1956), 69. Edward Coke to Robert Cecil, May 4, 1603, Sir Arthur Chichester to Robert Cecil, July 17, 1603, Dr. Robert Soame to Robert Cecil, November 14, 1604, Thomas Lord Grey to Robert Cecil, [1604], Dr. Robert Soame to Robert Cecil, June 5, 1605, Matthew Bredgate to Robert Cecil, June 20, 1605, Sir Edward Coke to Robert Cecil, February 2, 1606, Dr. Robert Soame to Robert Cecil, February 5, 1606, Lord Danvers to Robert Cecil, [1606], HMC, *Cal. Salisbury* MSS,

The most important offices in which Cecil's influence or power of secretarial patronage operated were the ambassadorial posts, the clerkships of the Council and of the Signet, the secretaryships for the Latin and French tongues, and the unofficial or personal secretaryships which he might fill. The holders of these places by the beginning of the reign of James I consisted primarily of Cecil's dependents, who, if they did not owe their first appointment to his patronage, had been promoted or sustained by him. The relations between Cecil and his clients and among the clients themselves are indicative of Cecil's political methods in two related ways: the retention of all independent political leadership in the hands of the great patron and the reluctance of the patron to prepare a successor to this independent leadership. Perhaps it is out of place to accuse Cecil of irresponsibility in these matters, since thorough administrative delegation and foresight still may have been in the future. Cecil's reluctance to hazard rivals among his dependents was, nonetheless, in sharp contrast to the way in which he had been prepared for state employments by his father and by others.

The evidence of Cecil's reluctance to share power and position with his dependents is necessarily indirect or unintentional. It is clear that he did not encourage his dependents; however, throughout their youth — and early middle age — they lived in expectation. Hopes grew particularly bright when Cecil received the white staff of the lord treasurer in 1608. Thomas Cromwell and Lord Burghley, indeed no other officeholder, had achieved such a formal pre-eminence in the state. Would Cecil remain principal secretary of state and master of the Court of Wards as he advanced to the great office of lord treasurer? The answer was yes; but the

XV, 72, 196, 197; XVI, 355, 436, 437; XVII, 242, 268, 269; XVIII, 42, 43, 390. Edmund Lassells to Robert Cecil, February ?, 1608, Grant to Edmund Lassells, February 11, 1608, Sir Richard Trevor to Robert Cecil, June 20, 1608, Sir Daniel Norton to Robert Cecil, August 23, 1609, William Butler to Robert Cecil, October 26, 1609, Sir Henry Gunderrot to Robert Cecil, December ?, 1609, Warrant to Sir Henry Gunderrot, December 11, 1609, *CSPD*, 1603–1610, 403, 441, 538, 553, 570. John Chamberlain to Ralph Winwood, October 12, 1605, Chamberlain, *Letters*, I, 209.

dependents continued to nurse false hopes of high preferment through his influence.[27] Parallel to Cecil's caution as a politician was his caution as a patron and public administrator. He advanced no one with the training and practical experience in affairs of state by which he had been prepared. He knew how to do what needed doing and did not feel the necessity of relief from the burden of affairs strongly enough to advance anyone who could offer him relief. He undertook no reorganization of the increasingly busy secretariat in spite of a contemporary proposal to divide the labor into home and foreign departments, but he enlarged and reorganized his private secretariat along similar lines. Although Cecil gave some consideration to reform of the office, he did not formally adopt that division of the secretarial function, which only was introduced fully in 1782. In part, an impediment to this solution of the Secretary's problems seems to have been Cecil's unwillingness to share with any of his dependents the policy-making powers which he exercised.[28] The office of principal secretary eluded his ablest dependents for years — Ralph Winwood until 1614, George Calvert until 1619, and Dudley Carleton, then Viscount Dorchester, until 1628. Many of the Cecilians fell by the way-

27   John More to Ralph Winwood, December 2, 1604, Dudley Carleton to Ralph Winwood, January 1605, Samuel Calvert to Ralph Winwood, March 28, 1605, April 6, 1605, Levinus Munck to Ralph Winwood, May 14, 1605, Sir Henry Neville to Sir Ralph Winwood, May 12, 1608, John More to Sir Ralph Winwood, June 25, 1608, Winwood, *Memorials*, II, 35–36, 45, 54, 57, 58–59, 398–399, 412. John Chamberlain to Ralph Winwood, February 16, 1605, Chamberlain, *Letters*, I, 205. Earl of Northampton to Sir Thomas Edmondes, March 2, 1606, Thomas Birch, *The Court and Times of James the First*, ed. R. F. Williams (2 vols.; London: Henry Colburn, 1849), I, 54. Sir Thomas Edmondes to Earl of Shrewsbury, September 30, 1606, Lodge, *Illustrations*, III, 188–190. Sir Thomas Edmondes to William Trumbull, May 11, 1608, Jean Beaulieu to William Trumbull, May 11, 1608, Sir Thomas Edmondes to William Trumbull, May 25, 1608, June 15, 1608, HMC, *Downshire* MSS, II, 56, 57, 61, 63. Sir William Waad to Robert Cecil, August 14, 1605, Sir Thomas Edmondes to Robert Cecil, March 7, 1606, HMC, *Cal. Salisbury* MSS, XVII, 368; XVIII, 73. Zorzi Giustinian to Doge and Senate, May 7, 1608 N.S., CSPV, 1607–1610, XI, 131.

28   Robert Cecil to Sir Henry Wotton, July 22, 1608, *Letters and Memorials of State*, ed. Arthur Collins (London, 1746), II, 326. Jean Beaulieu to William Trumbull, September 14, 1609 (two letters), October 26, 1609, Sir Thomas Ed-

side. It may be argued that Cecil had the misfortune to be surrounded by men of little political capacity or that the men about him remained unimpressive because they did not have the challenge of large responsibilities. Irrespective of the cause, the result became apparent at Cecil's death. None of the dependents possessed a capacity for enlarged, imaginative statesmanship.

Cecil's second major office, the mastership of the Court of Wards, had a considerable place in his political position in spite of the disparaging comments which he once made about that office. He was not candid when he wrote that he had "resigned a better Place," meaning the chancellorship of the Duchy of Lancaster, for the mastership out of nostalgic attachment because his father had held it. The previous masters, their incomes, the Crown revenues which they supervised, and the potentiality for patronage and prestige indicate an office of great political significance, a kind of training program for the lord treasurership.[29]

In contrast to Cecil's reluctance to release or reform the secretaryship, he demonstrated at the Court of Wards a willingness to make innovations, according to Professor Joel Hurstfield, with a view to efficient administration, increased revenue for the Crown, and, on the contrary, decreased income to the master, to the other officers, and to buyers and sellers of wardships. From a superficial view Cecil seems at first to have been engaged in activities at the Court of Wards similar to his father's and indeed to the practice of most Elizabethan politics. In short, he used the potentiality of the office for personal income and for patronage in

mondes to William Trumbull, November 2, 1609, Jean Beaulieu to William Trumbull, November 16 & 23, 1609, Sir Thomas Edmondes to William Trumbull, November 24, 1609, William Davick to William Trumbull, May 2, 1610, HMC, *Downshire* MSS, II, 126–127, 172, 178, 186, 190–191, 286. Maurice Lee, Jr., "The Jacobean Diplomatic Service," *AHR*, 72:1266–1269, 1280, 1281 (1967). F. M. Powicke & E. B. Fryde, *Handbook of British Chronology*, 2nd ed. (London: Offices of the Royal Historical Society, 1961), 111, 115, 116. Smith, "Secretariats of the Cecils," 500–502.

29   Robert Cecil to Sir Henry Neville, May 23, 1599, Winwood, *Memorials*, I, 41. Edward Curle to Robert Cecil, [1603], HMC, *Cal. Salisbury* MSS, XV, 371. John Chamberlain to Dudley Carleton, October 24, 1605, Chamberlain, *Letters*, I, 211. HMC, *Egmont* MSS, I, pt. I, 488.

order to create and maintain a political faction or interest. Gradually, however, Cecil demonstrated a willingness to forego the income of the office. Eventually he was willing to accept the extinction of the Court and of its servants in order to set royal finance on a firm footing and also to silence criticism of the abusive use of fiscal vestiges of feudal rights.[30]

These projects did not reach their highest pitch until Cecil had attained his greatest position in the state, the lord treasurership. The treasurership extended that patronage which Cecil could distribute, enhanced his prestige, and increased his income directly. The offices of the Exchequer, of the receivers and escheators of the counties, and of the customs were places in which the patronal influence of the Lord Treasurer might be exerted. In addition, the contracts with farmers, or lessees, of various customs and taxes fell under the Lord Treasurer's supervision.[31] If attainment of the treasurership carried Cecil to the full measure of his political position, it also gave him personal responsibility for royal finances. This responsibility was to have serious consequences for Cecil's position, since he was called to his greatest office in time of severe financial crisis. The financial difficulties provoked a political controversy, the third major crisis of Cecil's career, which will be considered later.

In addition to holding numerous temporary or local offices, Cecil received the honor of knighthood (1591) and the titles of Baron Cecil of Essendon (1603), Viscount Cranborne (1604), and Earl of Salisbury (1605). His installation as a Knight of the Garter in 1606, beginning with a procession from his house in the Strand and concluding in a splendid ceremony in St. George's Chapel, Windsor, so impressed the Venetian ambassador that, according to his report, all observers compared it favorably with the King's coronation and furthermore they considered complete

30   Hurstfield, *Queen's Wards*, 297–325, esp. 300–316. Bell, *Court of Wards*, 48–50, 58–60, 116, 117, 136, 137.

31   *CSPD*, 1603–1610, 425, 427 (Virtually every volume of *SP* 14/32–70 attests to the political significance of Cecil's activities as lord treasurer.). Aylmer, *King's Servants*, 69. Bell, *Court of Wards*, 42.

the ascendancy of Cecil, based as it was on "prudence and ability." Although dignities of this kind were shortly to be debased
by the great numbers who were to receive them and by the bar-
gains through which they were to be acquired, this debasement
had not yet proceeded very far in Cecil's time and his honors duly
impressed his contemporaries and contributed to his political
position.[32]

There would be difficulty in finding any part of Cecil's income that was unconnected with his political position. His
income from land inherited or acquired, from the sale of lands,
from the farm of the customs, from privateering or commercial
speculations, from pensions, and from gratuities which poured
in from all quarters, depended upon his political offices or upon
those of his family. His income from these sources arose from his
political position as much as did the wages, fees, diets, and liveries which he received directly from his offices. Virtually all of
his income derived directly or indirectly from his official position
and reinforced his political strength. Before one becomes censorious about gratuities and other unofficial income, it is well to
notice the circumstances. The restraints upon official expenditure during the Spanish War and the Irish Rebellion in the latter
years of Elizabeth's reign and the continuing inflation before,
during, and after Cecil's ascendancy forced servants of the Crown
to look elsewhere in order to increase their incomes. Since the
recipients of gratuities received payments in kind and in services
as well as in money, the total value, merely in terms of the money
of account of the period, must remain difficult to establish. Cecil's
Spanish pension may seem a particularly reprehensible exploitation of his position. Cecil served as principal negotiator of the
peace with Spain in 1604; therefore, the Spanish gifts came well
within prevailing practice, which virtually encouraged envoys

32   G. E. C[okayne], *Complete Peerage*, XI, ed. by G. H. White (13 vols.;
London: St. Catherine's Press, 1910–1940), 402, 403. *CSPD*, 1603–1610, 145, 214, 312.
Nichols, *Progresses of James I*, II, 48; III, 1056, 1064 n. 1, 1070. Zorzi Giustinian to
Doge and Senate, May 31, 1606 N.S., *CSPV*, 1603–1607, X, 354. Sir Philip Gawdy to
Bassingbourne Gawdy, May 11, [1605], HMC, *Seventh Report, Appendix*, 526.

83

to find part of their support from princes or states with which they were negotiating. There is little reason to suspect that Cecil favored peace with Spain out of motives of personal profit. Peace had long been the preference of Cecil and of his father. At least by 1606, according to Father Albert J. Loomie, Cecil had begun to receive from Philip III of Spain a pension or other payments, of which one payment in 1608 was the equivalent of £12,500, in return for assistance and information. This arrangement may have contributed to the diplomatic flexibility with which the Secretary could serve the interests of king and country as Cecil saw those interests. Reports of Dutch and French payments to Cecil also circulated privately.[33]

Although Cecil's income may have been largely derived from office, his total income considerably exceeded his total official and unofficial receipts from the three major offices. On the basis of records which survive from the years 1608–1612 Professor Lawrence Stone sets Cecil's receipts at more than £49,800 annually. One must recognize that much of this income may have arisen from nonrecurring sources, so that the figure may leave a misleading impression. Cecil's complex dealings in land involved both income and expenditure for him. Between 1611 and 1613, before and after his death, his agents carried off a great sale of lands which did much to assure the future fortune of his house regardless of political favor or disfavor.[34]

Were Cecil's activities corrupt? The question has no simple answer. The man himself wrote that he had been appointed lord treasurer because "the condition of my fortune (if not my hon-

33   Lawrence Stone, "The Fruits of Office: The Case of Robert Cecil, First Earl of Salisbury," *Essays in the Economic and Social History of Tudor and Stuart England*, ed. F. J. Fisher (Cambridge: University Press, 1961), 89–116, esp. 91, 97, 98, 103, 115. Hatfield House, MSS *Salis.*, 129, fols. 129, 130. Nicolo Molin to Doge and Senate, September 1, 1604 N.S., *CSPV*, 1603–1607, X, 179. Don Diego Sarmiento de Acuña to Philip III, October 17, 1614 N.S., Turner, *Privy Council*, I, 85 n. 83, quoting PRO, *Spanish Transcripts*, 2/8. Gardiner, *History*, I, 214–217. Albert J. Loomie, S.J., "Sir Robert Cecil and the Spanish Embassy," *Bulletin of the Institute of Historical Research*, 42:30–57, esp. 54–57 (1969).
34   Stone, "The Fruits of Office," 103, 105–113.

esty) divert me from the errors of corruption . . ." Again the
censorious may find this remark not unlike the special pleading
which Burghley sometimes affected. Without endeavoring to
exonerate Cecil by invidious comparisons, it might be noted that
many contemporaries took an alarmed view of increasing corruption and some contemporaries testified to Cecil's incorruptibility.
Yet one may find numerous incidents, particularly in the papers
of his friend Michael Hickes, which demonstrate that Cecil was
not above the temptations of the age or at least that suitors offered
the temptations in confident anticipation of his favor. His early
practice in the Court of Wards seems to substantiate the judgment that Cecil took advantage from gratuities and from private
sale of wards. Hurstfield sees Cecil as willing, nonetheless, to
dismantle the Court of Wards, one of the principal edifices of
Elizabethan politics and a chief source of his income. Stone, more
severe in his judgment than Hurstfield, acknowledges that Cecil was not the "unscrupulous careerist described by his enemies. . . ."[35]

Why did Cecil need this great income? Quite obviously, he
needed it because he had great expenses, shown to be greater
than £49,014 a year from 1608 to 1612. These expenses, no less
than the means whereby Cecil acquired his income, appear unsavory to the squeamish. In the political and economic structure
in which he had to work many of these expenses were unavoidable. Cecil's position in the state and in the society demanded a
measure of display analogous to the display of the Court — elab-

35 Robert Cecil to Sir Henry Wotton, July 22, 1608, Collins, *Letters and
Memorials*, II, 326. Lord Burghley to William Herlle, August 14, 1585, PRO, *SP*
12/181/42, fols. 159, 160. Earl of Northumberland to Robert Cecil, August 13, 1605,
HMC, *Cal. Salisbury* MSS, XVII, 367. Robert Cecil to Michael Hickes, January 3,
1602, October 6, 1602, Sir Samuel Saltonstall to Sir Michael Hickes, July 1, 1608,
Pierce Pennante to Sir Michael Hickes, September 19, 1608, petition referring to
allegation of bribe offered by Robert Cecil, Francis Herrys to Sir Michael Hickes,
February 27, 1610, Captain Humphrey Covert to Sir Michael Hickes, [February
1612], BM, *Lansdowne* MSS, 88/25, fol. 56, 45, fol. 91; 90/97, fol. 194, 110, fol. 218;
91/49, fol. 110, 57, fol. 123; 92/85, fol. 147. (A few examples of the vast materials
on gratuities and more serious profits of office to be found in this correspondence.)
Hurstfield, *Queen's Wards*, 299–311. Stone, "The Fruits of Office," 113–116.

orate residences; household finery; numerous servants; expensive education, travel, and matrimonial arrangements for his children. These activities had a place in Cecil's political behavior which ought not to be ignored. The possibility of loss of office and influence and the fear of attainder concentrated a politician's efforts at creating and protecting an estate. Cecil bought, built, conveyed by secure forms, and bound to his family as thoroughly as he might when he had the rich opportunities of royal favor, especially in the years immediately before Elizabeth's death and then again immediately before his own death.[36]

If Cecil had survived the first two crises of his political career, the struggle with Essex and the accession of James I, with his power not only intact but growing, he was not to be so successful in meeting the third great crisis, the worsening relations between Crown and Commons in the midst of serious financial difficulties. The problems which confronted Cecil on the eve of the meeting of Parliament in 1610 were neither new nor simple. The degree of success with which the Tudor rulers had acquired power for the Crown and for its centralized administration had often depended upon their ability to solve the financial problems which beset them. The reluctance of Parliament to vote taxes, the dependence of the Crown upon similarly reluctant local officers for the collection of the parliamentary revenue, and the inelasticity of certain traditional revenues still imposed practical limitations upon the solution of the financial problems. In order to explain fully the Great Contract, which was the critical episode in Cecil's fiscal policy as well as a principal indication of his political practice, it would be necessary to examine royal finances meticulously. In this present setting no such thorough examination of the background is possible.

In brief, however, it may be said that the war with Spain and the rebellion in Ireland revealed all the weaknesses in the mod-

36   Lawrence Stone, *The Crisis of the Aristocracy, 1558–1641* (Oxford: Clarendon Press, 1965), Appendix XXIII following 782. Stone, "The Fruits of Office," 89, 90, 104–113. Smith, "Secretariats of the Cecils," 500.

estly successful fiscal policy of Elizabeth's early years. Although the war with Spain came to a close in 1604 and the rebellion in Ireland was suppressed, inflation continued and new occasions of expense replaced the old ones. James, his consort, his family, and his Scottish favorites and servants put new demands and strains on the Exchequer. The King was expected to "live of his own" and at the same time to live like a king. Cecil himself would not and could not deny the King and the Court the expenditure which set them apart from the rest of the kingdom. The difficulty arose in attempting to draw a line between politically necessary display and wasteful extravagance. Cecil was forced to think of means to raise the revenue without being able to entertain much hope of reducing the expenditure or, in fact, of keeping the expenditure from rising further. He had to content himself principally with efforts to expand the revenue in order to reduce the deficits and then, it was hoped, ultimately to reduce the debt.[37]

Proof of the seriousness of these difficulties may be found in the royal accounts for the years immediately following James's accession to the English throne. In spite of the transition from war to peace, total expenditure continued near the level reached in the latter wartime years of Elizabeth. The ordinary, or expected recurrent, expenditure expanded rapidly without commensurate increase in the ordinary, or expected recurrent, revenue, so that down to 1606 the annual deficits mounted and consequently the debt soared. The concerted efforts of successive lord treasurers, Buckhurst (by this time Earl of Dorset) and Cecil, reduced the indebtedness appreciably between 1606 and 1610. The acknowledged debt of the Crown shrank to less than £160,-000 by means of various methods devised by the lord treasurers, by defaulting on the last forced loan of Elizabeth, but chiefly by reason of the parliamentary grant of 1606.[38]

37   Frederick C. Dietz, *English Public Finance, 1558–1641* (New York: Century, 1932), 113. HMC, *Cal. Salisbury* MSS, XV, 2. Robert Ashton, "Deficit Finance in the Reign of James I," *EcHR*, 2nd ser. 10:15,16 (1957).

38   Speech of Lord Treasurer Dorset, February 19, 1606, Willson, *Parliamentary Diary of Robert Bowyer*, 373, 374. "The Lord Treasurer Dorset's Declara-

The methods devised by Cecil and Dorset included the reintroduction of customs farming; the preparation of two new books of customs rates; the levying of other impositions on foreign trade; the careful management of the Crown lands and then sale of some of the Crown lands; the further exploitation of the feudal and prerogative rights of the Crown, such as purveyance and wardship; and a composition in lieu of a feudal aid upon the knighting of the King's eldest son. Each of these devices presented political problems and revealed aspects of Cecil's political methods. For example: Customs farming, an abandoned Elizabethan experiment, was revived because of the hazards of direct administration of the customs service at the time. Although two of the farms, in which Cecil was personally interested, augmented the revenue by £60,000 yearly and assured a fixity and certainty of revenue to the Crown, they also were accompanied by considerable diversion of profits into the pockets of Cecil and others. Customs farming hardly constituted an unmixed reform. The new books of customs rates and additional impositions had short-run advantages, but they provoked hostility in the House of Commons when Parliament met in 1610. This hostility partly explains the failure of the Great Contract. Devices like the sale of large tracts within the Crown lands also meant a depletion of the resources of the Crown in return for short-term revenue. The prerogative revenue of purveyance and the feudal incident of wardship increasingly provoked charges of abuse which made the stringent exercise of these rights of the Crown politically inopportune. Composition for an aid upon the knighting of the King's eldest son aroused suspicion among precisely those groups whose goodwill would be necessary for any serious long-term solution of the fiscal difficulties.[39]

tion of the State of the King's Receipt at the Parliament *anno tertio*," [March 14?, 1606], PRO, *SP* 14/19/45. Ashton, "Deficit Finance," Dietz, *English Public Finance*, 125, 126, 130.

39 "Annual Augmentation of Revenue in the years hereunder specified . . .," January 12, 1610, BM, *Lansdowne* MSS, 165, fol. 114. Earl of Dunbar to Robert Cecil, [April 6, 1610], "Medium of the general customs & subsidies . . .,"

In spite of the prodigious amount of work which Cecil devoted to financial affairs before 1610, he could not completely pay off the debt or end the deficit in the ordinary accounts. The partial retirement of the debt in the ordinary accounts, which had taken place between 1606 and 1610, had been possible only because of extraordinary revenue. Cecil, furthermore, had managed to pay off most of the debt arising from past extraordinary expenditure. He could not, however, close fully the gap between rapidly increasing ordinary expenditure and sluggishly increasing ordinary revenue. He had approached a solution of the problem of the existing debt from extraordinary expenses (war, rebellion), but he had failed to solve the problem of accumulating ordinary deficits, which continued to generate new debt in the future. No device existed to meet this specific problem. The solution for extraordinary difficulties rested with Parliament. Supply, of course, was the name given to these traditional parliamentary grants. Although Parliament recognized an obligation to grant extraordinary supply in time of war or of grave emergency, no precedent existed for Parliament to make grants for ordinary expenditure. To meet the specific problem for which there was no existing device Cecil turned to an entirely new scheme, a composition or bargain to replace the various feudal and prerogative rights and revenues of the Crown with a fixed annual revenue. Support was the name used by Cecil and others for this fixed annual revenue for the Crown which, once approved, would be independent of parliamentary grant. In short, Cecil became will-

"Concerning the raising of the rates," Hatfield House, MSS Salis., 128, fol. 112, 129, fol. 130; 130, fol. 164. G. D. to A. W., July 28, 1610, enclosing Robert Cecil's speech on impositions, HMC, Downshire MSS, II, 330–339. Robert Cecil to Sir Charles Cornwallis, June 30, 1608, Winwood, Memorials, II, 415. Spedding, Letters and Life, IV, 58 n. CSPD, 1603–1610, passim. CSPD, Addenda, 1580–1625, 423, 440, 490, 497. A. P. Newton, "The Establishment of the Great Farm of the English Customs," Trans RHS, 4th ser. 1:129–155 (1918). Robert Ashton, "Revenue Farming under the Early Stuarts," EcHR, 2nd ser. 8:310–314 (1956). Sidney J. Madge, The Domesday of Crown Lands (London: Routledge, 1938), 40–43, 47–57. G. E. Aylmer, "The Last Years of Purveyance, 1610–1660," EcHR, 2nd ser. 10:81,82,84,91 (1957). Dietz, English Public Finance, 299, 325–338, 346 n. 24, 360, 362–372, 420–424.

ing to replace the irregular, arbitrary revenues, which had come to be thought abusive, with regular, fixed annual support.

The proposed composition for the feudal and prerogative revenues came under serious discussion precisely at the time when the House of Commons had become aware of its capacity to frustrate schemes which it considered more favorable to the Crown than to the subject. Because of the breakdown of conciliar leadership in the House of Commons, Cecil, as Earl of Salisbury, had to lead delicately from his position in the House of Lords if he hoped to obtain parliamentary acceptance of a composition for the feudal revenues sufficiently generous to satisfy the King and also to solve the financial problems. The parliamentary device by which he attempted to exert his leadership in the fourth session of James's first Parliament in 1610 was the conference of committees drawn from both houses. At these conferences he could speak freely, persuasively, and extemporaneously in a setting in which his remarks would be heard directly by influential members of the House of Commons and indirectly in the House by report. If conferences failed to reduce the growing independence of the Commons from conciliar management, they had a prominent part in the negotiations for the Great Contract.[40]

Cecil's opening device was to speak specifically of the financial needs of the Crown but to refer only vaguely to grievances and to the satisfaction of grievances. Throughout the session he attempted to minimize the fact that he was obliged to bargain away the feudal and prerogative revenues of the Crown in return for fixed annual support. Cecil's behavior was essential if he were to get sufficient supply and generous support at the same time. Too quick or too conciliatory a composition might mean an unduly low price; yet too high or too harsh a demand might make the King appear to be seeking advantage from his subjects' misery. Cecil found himself both partisan and conciliator at the same time. In fact, his expressions were so qualified that some commen-

40 Willson, *Privy Councillors*, 56, 58–60, 82, 83, 104–106, 109–111, 118–120, 123–125, 225–236.

tators seemed to doubt that Cecil favored the composition for the feudal revenues, much less that he managed its unsuccessful journey through Parliament.[41] Indeed, he "looketh towards the bridge when he pulleth towards Westminster . . ."

The Commons responded to Cecil's opening by turning to their best parliamentary device, the discussion of grievances. From February to July 1610 a duel went on with thrusts and parries exchanged by the principals, occasionally relieved by their seconds. Both sides wanted substantial advantages for the concessions which they made. The Commons began to speak early in the session of proceeding by a contract so that they would retain written, legal assurances that specific grievances would be suppressed in return for the annual financial support. The King acceded to the discussion of the composition for feudal tenures and expressed a willingness to part with purveyance and other rights considered burdensome by the subject. By the end of March the principal difficulties attending the proposed Great Contract had been discovered and discussed, but none of them had been resolved. Cecil continued to strive for £600,000 supply and £200,000 annual support before any composition for the feudal or prerogative revenues. The Commons balked at this proposition, which looked very much like a way of getting £300,000 annual support when they had offered only £100,000 for the suppression of wardship alone. The King's concession regarding impositions and Cecil's great speech on impositions in early July helped to keep the negotiations alive. After some private politicking among members of the Commons, reinforced by threats of immediate dissolution, a tentative agreement was reached. A scheme providing annual support at £200,000 including composition for wardship, purveyance, and other concessions

41   *Parliamentary Debates in 1610*, ed. S. R. Gardiner (London: Camden Society, 1862), 1–9, 13–16, 19–22. Spedding, *Letters and Life*, IV, 153–155. Robert Cecil's speech in the conference, February 15, 1610, PRO, *SP* 14/52/70. Jean Beaulieu to William Trumbull, February 23, 1610, March 1, 1610, March 8, 1610, Winwood, *Memorials*, III, 123–126, 129. *CSPD*, 1603–1610, 589, 590. Gardiner, *History*, II, 64–66.

carried the Commons by a majority of sixty "or thereabouts." The project was to be concluded formally following the summer adjournment. A memorial on the Great Contract was drawn up by the Commons and accepted by the Lords. Cecil deserved the greatest credit for securing the provisional agreement on the Contract.[42]

The adjournment gave opportunity for both parties to the Contract to reconsider what they might gain and what they might lose by the terms which they had accepted. Neither Crown nor Commons had achieved the full objectives for which the project had been undertaken. Shortly after the beginning of the fifth session of the first Parliament the King raised his terms again to £200,000 clear annual support before any composition for feudal tenures. On November 6, 1610, the Commons decided, as one man, not to proceed with the negotiations. The King accepted their refusal.[43]

Acute as Cecil's disappointment must have been, he still tried quietly to salvage something from the wreck. He accepted failure mildly although it had become plain that the King's vexation with the Commons had begun to fall also upon him since Cecil had so consistently advised the efforts to come to agreement with

42 Gardiner, *Parliamentary Debates, passim,* esp. 25–30, 45–48, 121–124. Sir Thomas Edmondes to William Trumbull, March 22 & 29, 1610, April 5, 1610, Jean Beaulieu to William Trumbull, April 19, 1610, Sir Thomas Edmondes to William Trumbull, May 2, 1610, HMC, *Downshire* MSS, II, 267, 269, 271, 279, 285. Jean Beaulieu to William Trumbull, March 29, 1610, April 26, 1610, May 2 & 9, 1610, John Pory to Sir Ralph Winwood, July 17, 1610, Winwood, *Memorials,* III, 144, 145, 153, 159, 160, 193, 194. Sir Thomas Lake to Robert Cecil, April 30, 1610, Hatfield House, MSS *Salis.,* 128, fol. 118. Dudley Carleton to Sir Thomas Edmondes, July 13, 1610, Clement Edmondes to Sir Thomas Edmondes, July 16, 1610, Dudley Carleton to Sir Thomas Edmondes, July 17, 1610, July 25, 1610, Birch, *Court and Times of James I,* I, 122, 123, 126, 128, 129, 131. Sir Roger Aston to Lord _____, July 24, 1610, CSPD, 1603–1610, 625. Gardiner, *History,* II, 68–84.

43 Gardiner, *Parliamentary Debates,* 124, 126–131, 164–179. Sir John Holles to Robert Cecil, September 22, 1610, the answer of the Commons to the King, November 9, 1610, the Speaker's address to the Commons, November 17, 1610, CSPD, 1603–1610, 633, 641, 643. Spedding, *Letters and Life,* IV, 208, 210, 221–224. M. de la Boderie to M. de Puisieux, November 17, 1610 N.S., November 25, 1610 N.S., PRO, *Paris Transcripts* 41. Gardiner, *History,* II, 84–87, 105–108. Dietz, *English Public Finance,* 139 n. 20.

the Lower House. There was nothing to do in view of the positions of the King and the Commons except to adjourn, prorogue, and ultimately dissolve Parliament.[44]

Cecil not only had failed to save any part of the Great Contract; he had lost that special confidence of the King which he had enjoyed since the beginning of the secret correspondence. He was not overthrown or dismissed; he continued to hold the position which he derived from his offices. He still received the respect of other politicians and kept much of the support of his dependents. Still, one can see the growing influence of Robert Carr in politics. The young Scot without experience or special political intelligence could not assume control of the administration; consequently Cecil, falling back on expedients and forced to try new "projects" of doubtful utility, plodded on for more than a year until his final illness and death brought relief from his great burden.[45]

Cecil's policies and practice did not mean blind devotion to the past; he recognized the need for change. Yet it was his misfortune to be unable or unwilling to make changes in policy and practice sufficient to deal with the changed political circumstances which confronted him. By the superficial criteria of political success Cecil seems a failure. He was responsible for no great

44   Sir Thomas Lake to Robert Cecil and other councillors, November 21, 1610, Sir Thomas Lake to Robert Cecil, November 22, 1610, King James to Robert Cecil and other councillors, November 23, 1610, Sir Thomas Lake to Robert Cecil, November 23, 24, 25 (two letters), 26, 27, & 28, 1610, December 2, 1610, *CSPD*, 1603–1610, 644–647, 649. Gardiner, *Parliamentary Debates*, 132–146. Gardiner, *History*, II, 108–110. David Harris Willson, "Summoning and Dissolving Parliament, 1603–1625," *AHR*, 45:281–283 (1940).

45   Sir Thomas Lake to Robert Cecil, December 3 & 4, 1610, Robert Cecil to Sir Thomas Lake, [copy of a letter endorsed December 9, 1610], Sir Robert Carr to Robert Cecil, December 12 & 16, 1610, King James to Robert Cecil, December 6, 1610, Robert Cecil to King James, [copy of a letter written between December 3 and 6, 1610], [after December 6, 1610], King James to Robert Cecil, [two letters, n.d.], Hatfield House, mss *Salis.*, 128, fols. 168v, 169, 171–172, 174; 134, fols. 117–118, 142–143, 144, 149, 154. Sir Thomas Lake to Robert Cecil, December 6, 7, 1610, *CSPD*, 1603–1610, 650. Goodman, *Court of James I*, I, 39–45. Willson, "Summoning and Dissolving," 283, 284. Marcham, "James I of England and the 'Little Beagle' Letters," 331–333.

legislation, unless very indirectly he is given credit for the eventual composition for feudal tenures, of which the end was proposed again in the Civil War and confirmed at the Restoration. He made no refinement of the secretarial administration or of the Exchequer, but he carried out drastic reforms in the Court of Wards. His best devices to deal with the political, administrative, religious, and financial needs of the time generally fell short of success. Like some latter-day Sisyphus he seemed destined to roll the stone almost to the top of the hill only to see it tumble back down again.

May he, then, be condemned, according to the judgment of Francis Bacon, because his leadership was able only to keep "things from growing worse . . ."? Hardly. If he were a mere "pen-gent.,"[46] a nobleman of the robe recently risen from New People, he had a sense of the tradition in which he stood, one which sought to provide stability and continuity without resistance to change. He was no Richelieu or Mazarin endeavoring to make his king supreme; like Thomas Cromwell, Burghley, and Walsingham he was too much of an old parliamentary hand for that solution. His efforts may not have been a complete failure. If the circumstances with which Cecil had to contend are carefully considered, his political career was not without luster. He used his considerable abilities quietly without posturing and bore his physical and political weaknesses without self-pity. Although he lacked the capacity or desire to transform the politics of his age, he faithfully served its ideals. He accepted triumph without arrogance and failure with resignation.

46 "Reasons for the remove of Coke," Spedding, *Letters and Life*, IV, 381. HMC, *Cal. Salisbury* MSS, 589. Stone, *Crisis of Aristocracy*, 60.

JOEL HURSTFIELD

Gunpowder Plot and the Politics of Dissent

In an excellent chapter in his biography of James I, D. H. Willson explores with characteristic scholarly irony the King's contribution to the religious controversy of the age.[1] That controversy was touched off by the events at Westminster in the early days of November 1605 when a small group of Roman Catholic extremists staked their lives and the future of their faith in England upon the destruction of Parliament and government in one holocaust. The Powder Treason, as contemporaries called it, has itself been the subject of continuous debate, ranging in time from the very November in which these events occurred until today. This debate has focused mainly upon the authenticity of the plot; but in so doing it has obscured a larger and more fundamental issue in the history of English society, the issue of toleration. In this essay I shall attempt to examine the significance of the plot in the historic framework of religious dissent in England; but the question of the authenticity of the plot itself forms part of that analysis.

NOTE: Part of this paper was broadcast by the British Broadcasting Corporation and published in the *Listener*, 80:625–627 (November 14, 1968), under the title "The Causes and Consequences of Mr. Guy Fawkes." I acknowledge with gratitude the help given me by Mrs. Elizabeth Russell, my research assistant for the year 1967–1968.

1   Willson, *James VI and I*, 228–242.

"Sir Thomas Parry," wrote Robert Cecil, Earl of Salisbury, James I's Secretary of State, on November 6 to the English ambassador in Paris, "it hath pleased Almighty God, out of his singular goodness, to bring to light the most cruel and detestable practice. . . ."[2] *The most cruel and detestable practice* was nothing less than a plan to blow up Parliament at a time when the royal family and the nobility, the leading ministers, the clergy and judges and members of Parliament were assembled for its opening. And already on November 5 the government had in its hands an important conspirator, "one Johnson" as they had put it, "a Yorkshire man." There was, in fact, no such person. On November 7 they knew indeed that this man was Guy Fawkes. What had brought Guy Fawkes out of his Yorkshire obscurity to the very center of the political scene? It is impossible to tell the whole story here but the central events must be briefly recalled.[3]

On October 26 Lord Monteagle, a Catholic peer, while at supper with some guests, was handed a note which had been brought to his door. The note was unsigned but Monteagle quickly grasped its importance. Yet, instead of hastily putting it safely away, he handed it to a member of his household to read with him. The letter was a warning to Monteagle not to attend the opening of Parliament, and it went on: "for though there be no appearance of any stir, yet I say they shall receive a terrible blow this Parliament and yet shall not see who hurts them." Monteagle hurried with the letter to the Earl of Salisbury, who hardly needed to exercise any great analytical skill to detect that this language almost certainly meant a plan to blow up Parlia-

2   Cited in S. R. Gardiner, *What Gunpowder Plot Was* (London: Longmans, Green, 1897), 22. There is some doubt whether the letter was sent off on November 6. A similar letter, dated November 9, was sent by Salisbury to Sir Charles Cornwallis, English ambassador to Spain. *Memorials of Sir Ralph Winwood*, ed. Edmund Sawyer (3 vols.; London, 1725), II, 170–172. An unprinted copy of a similar letter, addressed to Sir Thomas Edmondes, English ambassador in Brussels, is at Hatfield House (see HMC, *Cal. Salisbury* MSS, XVII, 481–482), of which the original is at the British Museum (*Stowe* MSS, 168, fol. 213).

3   I follow here the narrative as set out in Willson, *James VI and I*, 223–226, and Gardiner, *What Gunpowder Plot Was*, 14–37.

ment by means of gunpowder. However, Salisbury went through the pantomime, several days later when he showed the letter to King James I, of leaving it to that kingly Solomon to unravel its meaning to the admiration of his ministers and courtiers.

It is clear that, once the letter had been read, first by a member of Monteagle's household and then by Salisbury, the whole plot and all the plotters were in jeopardy. Yet they held to their purpose, this strange band of men gathered together in an extraordinary conspiracy. They were led, not by Guy Fawkes, but by Robert Catesby, a man of great charm, strength, and personal magnetism. There is reason to think that he may have been a convert to Catholicism and, as is sometimes the case, he may have carried an inherited guilt over the treatment of the Catholic Church by his forbears. Certainly he was single-minded and idealistic, deeply resentful of the inequality and injustice inflicted upon members of his faith by the established order. Many men felt as bitterly as he did about the persecution of the Catholic Church in England but few were so brave — or so foolhardy. But some of these few were drawn to Catesby's leadership and remained loyal to him until the last. There were two brothers, Thomas and Robert Winter, and their brother-in-law, John Grant; there was Thomas Percy, a member of a distinguished Catholic family; there were the brothers John and Christopher Wright, and Sir Everard Digby, Ambrose Rokewood, Francis Tresham, these three men wealthier than the rest; there was Bates, Catesby's servant; and there was Guy Fawkes, the experienced soldier, in the plot almost from the start. At the fringe of the plot there were three Jesuit priests, who knew something about the plot as it developed but were not directly involved in either its preparation or execution.

The plot itself had two simple components: the first was to be the destruction of Parliament and government in London; the second was to be a summons to arms of the Catholic gentry. Hence for part one, there was the provision of gunpowder at Westminster; for part two, there was the hunting party at Dun-

97

church in Warwickshire, in the heart of a Catholic complex of estates, although it must be at once observed that the Catholic gentry had no notion of the role reserved for them. All this, and a good deal more, we now know, but little of this was known to the government. Hence, as often happens, even when they had knowledge of the plot they waited until the last possible moment for fuller information and evidence to come in before they took the decisive step.

It is probable that Tresham, who is widely — and, I think, correctly — believed to have been the writer of the Monteagle letter,[4] wrote it to warn the plotters rather than the government, in the hope of persuading the plotters to abandon the whole thing while there was time. In that case, Monteagle himself may have been part of the conspiracy within the conspiracy — that is, resolved to save the plotters from themselves. That would explain why he asked a member of his household to read it: to warn the plotters that their secret was no longer a secret. But this is still hypothesis.

What is clear, however, is that the plotters rejected so easy an escape. Even on November 2, when Catesby, Fawkes, and three of the others were told that Salisbury and the King were familiar with the plot, they held fast to their commitment. Tresham's plea to them went in vain.

On November 4 the government organized a search of the cellar below Parliament. On the first visit they found nothing but coal and wooden faggots, in the care of a certain John Johnson. On the second visit that night barrels of gunpowder were found underneath the coal and faggots, and Johnson was arrested. That was the end of the business. The plot was unmasked before a tinder could be struck. On the following day, November 5, Catesby and the others fled, hoping somehow that the second part of the plan, the Catholic rising, might yet be put into effect. But the Catholic gentry to a man rejected the call and would have nothing to do with the enterprise. On November 8 at Holbeche in Staf-

4   In HMC, *Cal. Salisbury* MSS, XVII, xvii and 550, there is a suggestion that the writer may have been Percy.

fordshire, Catesby and the Wright brothers were killed by the sheriff's troops, Percy mortally wounded, Thomas Winter and Rokewood wounded and taken prisoner. Those who survived were taken to London for trial. Inquiries were pressed forward, with torture and the threat of torture at hand. The trial followed in January, and at the end of that month and the beginning of February the conspirators were executed.

But the government from the start had been resolved that the affair would not end in anticlimax. The King addressed Parliament, an official account of the whole business was issued, the surviving conspirators were, after trial, barbarously executed in public, and an act was passed ordaining that November 5 should henceforth be celebrated for ever as a day of national deliverance.[5] This act was in force until the middle of the nineteenth century; and still now, a century after its demise, November 5 each year continues to bring profit to the pyrotechnics industry and delight to small boys of all ages. And here is another paradox. For every one person who recalls the name of the Earl of Salisbury, regarded in his own day as the most powerful statesman in Europe, a thousand now recall the name of Guy Fawkes, the minor Yorkshire gentleman and captain who was more brave than he was wise, more devout than he was intelligent. There is really no need for London street urchins — in search of contributions to the cost of their fireworks — to appeal to passers-by to "remember the Guy," for our folk-memory has preserved him. Guy Fawkes believed that his plans for November 5, 1605, would give him a secure place in history. He was right.

And yet, it might be said, surely this brief tragedy — which has also something of comedy in it — is hardly worthy of lengthy historical investigation. Nothing could be further from the truth, for we are only at the beginning of our understanding of what Guy Fawkes signifies in the history of England. The developments which prompted him to attempt what he did form part of the tragic story of European liberty: as such, it is a worthy theme

5   3 Jac. I c. 1.

for the historian. For this microcosmic situation, the events leading up to November 5, 1605, has in it the basic ingredients of the whole human order. Any consideration of the plot in its larger historical context prompts two questions: The first is, What brought Guy Fawkes to that tragic moment in Westminster when, as he stood at the door of his cellar, the Westminster magistrate put out his hand and arrested him? The second question, closely relevant to our own age, is, Can such a situation ever again recur in various parts of the civilized world? (I mean, not the plot but the situation in which gunpowder seems, to brave and honest men, to be the only answer.) This second question falls outside our context but the first — what brought Guy Fawkes to Westminster — is germane to any study of modern history.

The story of Gunpowder Plot is, then, the story of an explosion which never took place. But behind this story there lay long years of bitterness and despair. For Guy Fawkes belonged to an oppressed, disfranchised, and dispossessed minority, the English Roman Catholics who, for half a century, since 1559, had been increasingly isolated from their fellow countrymen. How this arose is, of course, well known. The mid-sixteenth century saw the outbreak of religious struggles of great intensity and intolerance in many places in Europe, which were to culminate in the Thirty Years' War from 1618 to 1648. In ideological warfare mercy is neither expected nor given. Moreover, religious struggle was identified with national survival: those who did not accept the established faith were, it was held, enemies of the existing order, perhaps even agents of an enemy power. We recall, too, that in 1570 the Pope formally deposed Elizabeth from the English throne and thereby set free her Catholic subjects from their due obedience; and in 1588 a Catholic crusade in the shape of the Spanish Armada was launched against England. We know also that several attempts were made to assassinate her, as they were made to assassinate her fellow Protestant, William of Orange; and that in 1584 the attempt against William proved successful.

In 1610 James I's contemporary, Henry IV of France, was also assassinated.

Aware of these things, we are able to explain the savage penalties which the English government inflicted on Catholics. I shall mention only a few examples. All Catholic services were prohibited; and failure to attend the Anglican Church on Sunday and Holy Days was punished with 1 shilling fine per week in 1559, raised in 1581 to £20 a month.[6] In some cases failure to pay the fine could lead to the seizure of two-thirds of a recusant's lands for the whole period of his recusancy, and to imprisonment. After 1585 any Catholic priest found in England was ipso facto subject to the penalties for high treason; and even harboring a priest carried the death penalty.[7] The oath of supremacy, required of all men in any branch of public service, barred Catholics from access to office. The same oath was intended to keep them out of office in the universities;[8] and the only schools to which they could send their children would instruct them in the Protestant faith. Nor was there any available outlet for honest dissent. The heavy hand of official censorship reached out relentlessly to every corner of the kingdom.

In the historical context we can understand how such savage measures came to be introduced. For this was an age when independent thought, outside the official channels of church and state, was suspect. Heresy — that is, dissent — corrupted the soul just as coining corrupted the currency. The penalty for coining was death; how much more necessary then was it in the contemporary outlook that he who attempted to corrupt the soul and deprive it of eternal life should be punished by death? Nor should we, who live in the twentieth century, be surprised at this draconic policy. One illustration must suffice: "I would rather give a healthy boy or a healthy girl a phial of prussic acid than this novel. Poison kills the body, but moral poison kills the soul."

6   1 Eliz. c. 2; 23 Eliz. c. 1.
7   27 Eliz. c. 2.
8   1 Eliz. c. 1.

The writer of this passage was not some benighted Tudor persecutor but the editor of the London *Sunday Express* in 1928 warning his readers about *The Well of Loneliness* by Radclyffe Hall.[9] The only sign of progress that one can detect is that the editor of the *Sunday Express* reserves the death penalty for the reader rather than the author. This was a matter of private morality. The power of political censorship (with the severest penalties for dissent) in many parts of the modern world needs no illustration.

The function of government is to govern and to preserve the security and independence of the state and the existing order. But it would be a grave lack in the historical imagination not to see that a fervent Catholic minority could not accept an order of society in which their faith was proscribed, their sons and daughters sent into exile for their education, their priests executed, their leaders imprisoned, their lands sequestered. On top of this, the new king, James I, having promised all things to all men found it impossible to fulfil any promise to any man. James was not himself vindictive against the Catholics but he was under heavy pressure in Parliament and elsewhere. In any case, the Exchequer was short of funds, and recusancy fines — the fines for not attending church — were a wonderful means for serving God and the Exchequer. But they were imposed sporadically, and Catholics continued to be fed on hopes that better times were coming. *Hope deferred maketh the heart sick.* So the English Catholics swung wildly between optimism and despair; and it was in the downward swing of despair that Guy Fawkes threw in his lot with the conspirators.

It is significant that the plotters were all country gentlemen, mostly of moderate means and limited prospects. Such estates as they or their families retained were under continuous threat of savage exactions and, as recusants, they lived under severe disabilities in education and in professional advancement. They

9   Cited in review in *The Spectator*, 221 (no. 7317):399, of *Radclyffe Hall: A Case of Obscenity?* by Vera Brittain.

were also officially barred from the whole government service. This is not to suggest for one moment that it was with the aim of improving their individual fortunes and prospects that they embarked on conspiracy. It was simply that they could not live at peace in a community which reduced a whole section of that community to the level of second-class citizens, criticized, distrusted, and, where occasion served, denounced by any influential demagogue who chose to set fire to false rumor and dark prejudice. Guy Fawkes — so he told his captors — had from the beginning prayed that "he might perform that which might be for the advancement of the Catholic faith and saving of his own soul."[10] Here indeed was an alienated minority in what was becoming a multi-religious society, a minority rejected by that very society to which they claimed to belong as equals.

But before examining the consequences of the plot, we must face a question which has dominated its historiography almost from the start. Everyone who has worked on the materials for the reign is aware that for centuries it has been suggested that the Plot was an invention of the government; and these allegations have been repeated, enlarged, refurbished, all the while building up to a mountainous indictment of the man who is said to have been its true author, the Earl of Salisbury. I cannot in my own lifetime recall a time when there was not someone, somewhere, announcing the discovery of new evidence to confirm these dark suspicions. Of this new evidence I only want to say one thing. Some of it is old; the rest is very old. Guy Fawkes was on trial for one day; the Earl of Salisbury has been on trial for three and a half centuries.

Let us admit at once that the man who should have benefited most from the plot was the Earl of Salisbury. This extraordinary man, one of the subtlest politicians in the whole history of England, had been advanced to office, late in Elizabeth's reign, in the shadow of his famous father, Lord Burghley, minister of the

10   HMC, *Cal. Salisbury* MSS, XVII, 479.

Queen for thirty-seven years. Salisbury himself was a hunchback, some five feet tall, with an inordinate ambition for power and wealth. He also had an unrivalled capacity for making enemies. He had a few close friends who worshiped him, but outside his narrow circle he must have been the most unpopular man in England, loathed by the people, never in the full trust of the King. Moreover, his greatest prospect, to become Lord High Treasurer of England, was in 1605 as yet unfulfilled.

If there was anything that would bind his monarch to him — and perhaps even win some measure of gratitude from the people at large — it was the dramatic rescue of the King, his ministers, and therefore the nation itself from some dastardly plot to plunge the country into blood and confusion. There was, moreover, a religious aura to be gained. Salisbury would emerge as the savior of Protestantism, protecting the guardians of the reformed faith against the dastardly machinations conceived in Rome and designed for England. Long regarded by Catholics as their principal scourge, what he needed was just such a plot to discredit the Jesuit activists, divide Catholic from Catholic, and reduce the moderates to subjection.

We are aware, too, that some of the confessions were obtained by torture or the threat of torture; and that parts of these confessions were never made public at all — as is sometimes the case today when treason trials are held *in camera*. Apart from this, at various times writers have come forward to point out that from their examination of the topography of Westminster they consider it impossible for anyone to have carried the gunpowder without being seen. Others have found mysterious callers at Salisbury's house who, they think, were his *agents provocateurs* among the plotters. Some have satisfied themselves — but no one else — that the confessions were forgeries. Much of this was thrashed out more than seventy years ago in a celebrated debate between Father Gerard and the historian S. R. Gardiner.[11] Not

11   J. Gerard, *What Was the Gunpowder Plot?* (London: Osgood, McIlvaine, 1897). Gardiner, *What Gunpowder Plot Was.*

a single piece of major evidence has since been brought forward to alter the case as made out by Gardiner and as accepted by the independent scholars who have worked in this field.

Much of the debate, then, has focused upon the career of the Earl of Salisbury. The view which contemporaries formed of him — and it is a view shared by many historians — is that he, like his father, Lord Burghley, was an inveterate enemy of the Catholics and bent on their destruction. No maneuver, his enemies believed, was too complex or too villainous to be unacceptable to him. Indeed, it was said that his peculiar genius lay in fabricating these devices with a spectacular degree of success. Michael Drayton's poem, "The Owl," written in 1603, may almost be taken as an anticipatory charge of Salisbury's guilty involvement in the plot of 1605.[12] In his poem Salisbury is the vulture, who employs a bat as his agent with a special capacity

> To urge a doubtful speech up to the worst
> To broach new treasons and disclose them first,
> Whereby himself he clears, and unawares,
> Intraps the fowl, unskilful of these snares . . .

If this is what Drayton could write in 1603, we should not be surprised to learn, according to one report, dated November 13, 1605, that the whole Gunpowder Plot has been described in Paris as "a fable."[13]

Yet this approach is simplistic. It is hard to discover, for example, whether the same opinion was widely held in French government circles or whether Dudley Carleton, who transmitted the news, had special reasons for sending such a report. We know that he had a link with the plotters — as the Earl of Northumberland's secretary he leased them the vault in Westminster where the gunpowder was stored. He was subsequently under suspicion of being involved in the plot; but there is no evidence to support

12   *The Works of Michael Drayton*, ed. J. W. Hebel (5 vols.; Oxford: Blackwell, 1932), II, 493. *Ibid.*, ed. Kathleen Tillotson & B. H. Newdigate (Oxford: Blackwell, 1941), V, 179.
13   *CSPD*, 1603–1610, 255.

this allegation.[14] Nor should we forget that most conspiracies from Gunpowder Plot to the murder of President Kennedy have been taken by someone to be the work of government agents. However, I have found no other record by either an English or a foreign diplomat at this time to indicate that similar suspicions of government involvement existed elsewhere. Molin, the Venetian Ambassador, reporting home on December 8 says that the government would be delighted to be able to prove that the Earl of Northumberland was the leader of the plotters. He reports that Salisbury would be glad to establish this because of the personal enmity between the two men; but as to the authenticity of the plot itself, the ambassador expresses no kind of doubt.[15] Father John Gerard, who wrote his narrative of the plot in 1606 — not under torture but in freedom and in a report to the papacy — makes no such charge against the government. He expresses doubts about the Monteagle letter and goes on: "But although many were of opinion that this [the letter] was not the first means of this discovery [of the plot], yet none that ever I could hear of was able to give a certain judgement which way indeed it was discovered."[16]

In these early days it was widely believed that the government was aware of the plot before the officials began their search of the vault on November 4 and perhaps aware of it before the Monteagle letter. There is nothing unreasonable in this supposition, for there is something dramatic and contrived about the delivery of the letter; and at least two people, Monteagle and Tresham, may have hoped that way to end the plot or, failing that, to clear themselves. This hypothesis is, however, quite different from the charge that the government (i.e., Salisbury) organized the plot, that it was a fabricated affair into which a few innocent Catholics were drawn. We do meet this allegation openly debated, but not

14   Chamberlain, *Letters*, I, 12.
15   *CSPV*, 1603–1607, X, 301–302.
16   John Gerard, *The Condition of Catholics under James I*, ed. John Morris (London: Longmans, Green, 1871), 101–102.

until a generation had passed, although there is evidence that it was being rumored before then.[17]

The argument is sometimes put forward that Shakespeare's *Winter's Tale* was a commentary on the Plot and, in its title, a reference to the confession of Thomas Winter, one of the conspirators; but there seems to be no evidence either internal or external, to support this interpretation. On the other hand, Ben Jonson's *Catiline His Conspiracy* does by implication deal with the allegations that the Plot was not genuine, and comes to the conclusion that it was. Jonson, however, enjoyed for a time the patronage of Salisbury and was involved, too, in informing on the plotters.[18] The surviving evidence, therefore, shows widespread rumors of Salisbury's prior knowledge of the Plot and somewhat later allegations of his instigation of it, which is a separate and more serious charge. In the mid-seventeenth century when Godfrey Goodman was writing his memoirs, he said of Salisbury: "The great statesman had intelligence of all this [Catholic plotting]; and because he would show his service to the state, he would first contrive and then discover a treason; and the more odious and hateful the treason were, his service would be the greater and more acceptable." He goes on: "some will not stick to report that the great statesman sending to apprehend these traitors gave special charge and direction for Percy and Catesby, 'let me never see them alive,' who, it may be, would have revealed some evil counsel given."[19] A tract of 1642 reports, though it discounts as false, "that there was no such treason intended but that it was an invention of him, whom in reverence I forbear to name."[20] By the time of the Restoration, amid the controversy over the emancipa-

17 See, for example, [William Lloyd], *The Late Apology in the Behalf of the Papists* (London, 1667), 32.

18 Cf. B. N. De Luna, *Jonson's Romish Plot* (Oxford: University Press, 1967).

19 G. Goodman, *The Court of King James I*, ed. J. S. Brewer (2 vols.; London: Richard Bentley, 1839), I, 102, 106–107.

20 *Plots, Conspiracies and Attempts* . . ., collected by G. B. C., 2nd ed. (London, 1642), 5.

tion of the Catholics, the charge of instigation is openly laid against Salisbury, though one of his defenders dismisses it as, "a very groundless and impudent fiction." "Others perhaps," he says, "have spoken this in raillery; yet you are the first, that we know of, that has asserted it in print." Then he goes on to present his argument against the whole thesis:[21]

Bellarmin[e] and his fellow Apologists in that age never pretended it. The parties themselves, neither at their trial, nor at their execution, gave any intimation of it. Can you tell us which of the conspirators were Cecil's instruments to draw in the rest? Or can you think he was so great an artist that he could persuade his setters to be hanged, that his art might not be suspected? For 'tis well known that he saved not any of those wretches from suffering. And they which did suffer charged none other but themselves in their confessions.

His opponent (thought to be Roger Palmer, Earl of Castlemaine), returning to the controversy, reaffirms that the Plot "was made, or at least fomented, by the policy of a great statesman." His reason was to destroy any prospects of improved conditions for Catholics under James; and it was no difficult task for a secretary of state to get hold of "turbulent and ambitious spirits" to join in the scheme. Indeed, as a reward Cecil was made an earl.[22] (This last observation may be taken as a measure of the evidence now coming forward, sixty years after the event. Gunpowder Plot was centered on the early days of November; Salisbury had been made an earl six months before on May 4.[23])

By now we are entering the apocrypha of the Plot. The men who were alive at the time had died, and it was becoming possible to attribute a string of fantasies to people who were no longer available to contradict them. Father John Gerard — not the contemporary priest, but the nineteenth-century controversialist — gathered together some of this material in his book *What Was*

21   *The Late Apology in the Behalf of the Papists*, 32.
22   [Roger Palmer], *A Reply to the Answer to the Catholique Apology* (London, 1668), 203, 208.
23   G. E. C., *Complete Peerage*, XI, 403.

the Gunpowder Plot?, published in 1897. Following are some examples of his evidence. We have a confession by the second Earl of Salisbury to William Lenthall that "it was his father's contrivance which Lenthall soon after told one Mr. Webb, a person of quality, and his kinsman, yet alive." Or again, we have the opinion attributed to Sir Henry Wotton that it was "usual with Cecil to create plots, that he might have the honor of the discovery, or to such effect." Here is another witness: Sir Kenelm Digby, son of one of the conspirators, "would often say it was a state design, to disengage the King of his promise to the Pope and the King of Spain, to indulge the Catholics if ever he came to be king here; and somewhat to his purpose was found in the Lord Wimbledon's papers after his death" — Lord Wimbledon was a nephew of Salisbury. Here is yet another: "Mr. Vowell, who was executed in the Rump time, did also affirm it." Finally, we may learn that "Catesby's man [George Bartlet] on his death-bed confessed his master went to Salisbury House several nights before the discovery, and was always brought privately in at a back door."[24]

It only needed a deathbed statement to complete the series; and it is manifest that, like the rest of the evidence, it can hardly attract serious examination. Perhaps the most useful comment upon this kind of material comes from a contemporary of these men, Thomas Fuller in his *Church History of Britain*, first published in 1655: "there is a generation of people who, to enhance the reputation of their knowledge, seem not only, like moths, to have lurked under the carpets of the council-table but, even like fleas, to have leaped unto the pillows of princes' bedchambers — thence deriving their private knowledge of all things which were, or were not, ever done or thought of."[25]

To sum up, there are odd and puzzling things about some of the plotters, Tresham in particular; but if one tries, as some

24   Gerard, *What Was the Gunpowder Plot?*, 160–161. These are drawn from Bodleian Library, CCC. 297/no. 50 Corpus Christi, *Fulman* MSS.
25   T. Fuller, *The Church History of Britain*, ed. J. S. Brewer (6 vols.; Oxford: University Press, 1845), V, 353–354.

writers have tried, to demonstrate that this shows the government to be the instigator of the plot, then this hypothesis is riddled with far more contradictions and improbabilities than the traditional, and I think reasonable, view that the plot was the work of brave but incompetent idealists who wasted their lives in a noble cause. In short, the question of the authenticity of Gunpowder Plot is no longer a rewarding subject for historical research. Nothing of major significance has emerged since Gardiner examined the Plot in 1897. Trying to prove that it was a fabrication has become a game, like dating Shakespeare's sonnets: a pleasant way to pass a wet afternoon but hardly a challenging occupation for adult men and women.

If then this one-time lively controversy has now run into sand, it releases the subject for much larger consideration. For one of the most interesting historical questions in this context is, What was the social framework of English dissent? — in which I include *all* dissent, Catholic, Protestant nonconformist, Jewish, agnostic, atheistic; and with this I join the related and still broader question of the historical causes of social alienation. Many historians are scarcely aware of this question; and those who are trying to work on it find their materials rich but their tools blunt. It will be decades before we come within sight of an answer, but the subject cries aloud to be studied.

The problem of Guy Fawkes, as we have seen, goes back at least to the Reformation. That fundamental movement — or series of movements — in human affairs no longer admits of a single or simple all-inclusive explanation. It is too complex in its social, cultural, religious, and political origins to submit much longer to the narrow bounds into which textbook writers have confined it. Nor can we find in it, as some have too often implied, a straight highway from medieval to modern times. Instead there is a vast labyrinth of roads, some of which turn back on themselves and others vanish inexplicably into desert. One winding path, badly marked and very obscure in places, leads toward a notion of toleration. In that respect, the Reformation is one major phase in this story.

Arising from new evidence and new approaches now at the disposal of historians, some of us are no longer able to see the Reformation as a gigantic struggle between two great religious movements, Catholic and Protestant. To us the Reformation is part of a large and longer struggle within religion as a whole and extending beyond Christianity itself.[26] In short, it is part of the long-lasting never-ending struggle between the laity and the priesthood, or, conceived even more broadly, between order and dissent. If this is so, then the Reformation period sees one of the great rebellions against the priestly order. The fundamental change in the doctrine of the Mass, which the Reformers carried through, deprived the priest of his special role of indispensable intercessor between God and man. To put the matter in its most extreme form, the Anglican Church was in essence secularized. For the first time in English history a king, Henry VIII, became its supreme head. The bishops were reduced almost to the role of clerical civil servants. But the victory over the priesthood was by no means complete; English puritans lamented that in the Protestant Church of England the power of the priest had returned in the shape of the bishops. Hence Peter Wentworth's celebrated rebuke to the Anglican archbishop Parker: ". . . That were but to make you popes. Make you popes who list, for we will make you none."[27] This explains, too, those famous satirical tracts which their authors wrote under the pseudonym *Martin Marprelate*.[28] But the puritans — or certain sections of them — in time developed their own priesthood. In spite of all the trappings of

26   The best recent discussion will be found in H. R. Trevor-Roper, *Religion, the Reformation and Social Change* (New York: Harper & Row, 1967), chs. 1–4.

27   Cited in J. E. Neale, *Elizabeth I and Her Parliaments, 1559–1581* (London: Jonathan Cape, 1953), 205.

28   See, for example, *An Introductory Sketch to the Martin Marprelate Controversy, 1588–1590*, ed. E. Arber (London: published by the editor, 1895); W. Pierce, *An Historical Introduction to the Marprelate Tracts* (London: A. Constable, 1908); *The Marprelate Tracts* (1589 ed.), ed. W. Pierce (London: Clarke, 1911).

spiritual equality, Calvin's Geneva gave enormous powers to the minister, and the Calvinists in Scotland under John Knox tried to establish the same system. James I — "I that was persecuted by Puritans there" — was perfectly familiar with this from his years in Scotland as king, this struggle for power by a new priesthood: "Jesuits," he cried, "are nothing but Puritan-papists."[29] Milton put it better when he said: "New presbyter is but old priest writ large."[30] When the priesthood is strong and the laity weak, orthodoxy and intolerance flourish; factions of the faith are exclusive; one religious community is spiritually segregated from another. This has nothing to do with the validity of faith but with its government.

This process, then, is clearly visible. But Roman Catholicism, even though it won back and held large parts of Europe, was experiencing the same tensions. Catholicism without a priesthood would, of course, not be Catholicism at all; and it is to the credit of the Jesuit order — but not to it alone — that it identified this danger to the faith and took vigorous measures to counter it. It is possible that without the Jesuits, and other ecclesiastical missionaries, Catholicism in England might not have survived the Tudor period, save in an attenuated and demoralized form. The Jesuits also realized that survival depended itself on the preservation of Catholic separateness, indeed isolation. Hence they forbade their followers ever to attend the Anglican Church even though the fines for nonattendance were heavy. So we see persecutors and persecuted pursuing the same policy; so in Elizabethan England we see the ghetto walls rising, not of bricks and mortar but the more impregnable ghettos of the mind.

Lord Burghley, though a deeply religious man, had seen in the Anglican Church the power of the priest reviving, and he had gone out of his way to warn Archbishop Whitgift that there were limits to his power; he gave broad hints elsewhere that he favored

29   *The Political Works of James I*, ed. C. H. McIlwain (Cambridge, Mass.: Harvard University Press, 1918), 126.
30   "On the New Forcers of Conscience under the Long Parliament."

restraints upon episcopal authority. His son, the future Earl of
Salisbury, different from his father in many ways, shared his views
on this. He sought to restrain the power of the Anglican bishops
and reduce their wealth, making a profit in the process; and he
also directed his attention to the Jesuits. At the end of the sixteenth century there was a curious and complex maneuver, sometimes described as the archpriest controversy, in which Salisbury
played a prominent part.[31] Salisbury, along with Bancroft and
others, had tried to drive a wedge between the Jesuit section of
the Catholic leadership in England — that section which looked
to the papacy and Spain to carry through the reconversion of England — and their rivals, especially some of the secular priests, who
hoped to negotiate terms from the English government which
might make their position more secure as a tolerated minority.
The terms offered to the moderates did not — in spite of some
transient hopes — grant toleration: if it had, then English history
might thereafter have taken a different shape. At most there was
an informal understanding with a small section of the secular
priests that persecution would diminish and they, in turn,
pledged themselves not to obey papal instructions to help depose
the Queen.

The sincerity of Salisbury and Bancroft in these negotiations
is very doubtful. In essence Salisbury's aim had been to break the
hold of the Jesuit priests, separate the leaders from the led, and
somehow bring the moderate Catholic priests and laity into some
measure of conformity with the established order. He had failed;
and his struggle against the priesthood went on. He told the Venetian ambassador in 1605,[32]

These are the laws, and they must be observed. Their object is undoubtedly to extinguish the Catholic religion in this kingdom, be-

31   T. G. Law, *A Historical Sketch of the Conflicts between Jesuits and
Seculars* (London: D. Nutt, 1889); P. Renold, *The Wisbech Stirs* (London: Catholic
Record Society LI, 1958). Cf. J. Hurstfield in *Elizabethan Government and Society*,
ed. Bindoff et al., 382–389.

32   Cited in Gardiner, *What Gunpowder Plot Was*, 166. An alternative
translation will be found in *CSPV*, X (1603–1607), 230–231.

cause we do not think it fit, in a well-governed monarchy, to increase the number of persons who profess to depend on the will of other Princes as the Catholics do, the priests not preaching anything more constantly than this, that the good Catholic ought to be firmly resolved in himself to be ready to rise for the preservation of his religion even against the life and state of his natural Prince. This is a very perilous doctrine, and we will certainly never admit it here, but will rather do our best to overthrow it, and we will punish most severely those who teach it and impress it on the minds of good subjects.

Salisbury failed; the power of the priests was not broken; but they recognized their true enemy. And it is not surprising that Salisbury holds a special place in the Jesuit historiography of Gunpowder Plot.

This is what one of his Catholic opponents wrote to him in 1606: "We know no other mean left us in the world, since it is manifest that you serve but as a match, to give fire unto His Majesty . . . for intending all mischiefs against the poor distressed Catholics."[33] To this Salisbury replied that he was no enemy of the Catholic faith itself. Nor did he wish to charge the Catholics as a whole with treason for, as he said, he knew of their loyalty to the Crown: "I do remember, upon the death of the late Queen of happy memory, with what obedience and applause both professions [Catholic and Protestant] did concur to His Majesty's succession, and now observe how little assistance was given to these late savage Papists." None the less, he went on; "my prayers shall never cease that we may see the happy days when only one Uniformity of true Religion is willingly embraced in this Monarchy." But he would avoid persecuting Catholics as such. "Yet I shall ever (according to the law of God) make so great difference in my conscience between seeing sins, and sins of ignorance, as I shall think it just by the laws of men."[34] He said more or less the same thing to the Venetian ambassador, in the passage earlier

33   R. Cecil, Earl of Salisbury, *An Answere to Certaine Scandalous Papers* (London, 1606), Sigma B 4.
34   *Ibid.*, Sigma F 1.

quoted. "Sir," he said, "be content as to blood so long as the Catholics remain quiet and obedient."[35]

The overwhelming majority of Catholics did remain "quiet and obedient." Only a tiny minority saw treason as the only way out of a desperate situation. But here was the crux of the matter. The Catholic protest movement could not write off its past history. Even if, wrote a Catholic two generations later, "the design [the Plot] had been suggested by papists alone, and unanimously approved by all, *yet we that live now are guilty of no sin*" — and he underlined the words as he wrote them.[36] By his act Guy Fawkes transmitted the taint of guilt to the unborn innocent generations who suffered for an irresponsible decision in which they had played no part; just as throughout the long centuries those of the Jewish faith expiated an ancestral act done at the beginning of the Christian era, in which they, too, had played no part. In both cases it was the organized faiths opposing them which fastened a charge of guilt upon the innocent and the unborn. *Tantum religio potuit suadere malorum*: the bitter words of Lucretius after so long return to taunt us.

Nothing should be taken to suggest, however, that, if the Plot had succeeded, if Parliament had been blown up, the King and his ministerers murdered or in flight, the surviving members of the royal family seized, that Catesby, Fawkes, Tresham, and the rest would have inaugurated an era of religious toleration under the benign patronage of the Papacy and Spain. Granted the contemporary belief that there was only one true religious faith and that all heresy was an offence to God and a threat to the soul of man, everything else followed: injustice, persecution, plotting, assassination. There is no reason to believe that the Catesbys in power would have been any more humane or tolerant than the Salisburys in power. Catesby and Salisbury alike were prisoners of the same harsh dogma of the uniqueness of religious truth, and the identification of ideological unity with political security. For

35   Gardiner, *What Gunpowder Plot Was*, 165.
36   [Palmer], *A Reply to the Answer*, 203.

this inexorable doctrine many thousands would have to give up their lives in the bloody decades now beginning in Europe compared with which Gunpowder Plot was no more than a trivial incident in the wings.

It is necessary, therefore, to ask, Could the government have tolerated with safety a minority in its midst when that minority belonged to a different faith? The government did not believe that it could, but this was probably a misjudgment of the situation as we now see it in the larger perspective of time. The evidence which was emerging by the early sevententh century was that the Catholics in England were not likely to bring in a foreign power to wage war on their behalf. There was a tiny intransigent wing which was prepared to attempt anything, but these were contained and restrained; and their efforts were wholly neutralized. The overwhelming majority of Catholics rejected these hotheads on every single occasion when any contact was made. Salisbury, in trying to split the Catholics, had glimpsed the possibility of an agreement with the moderates. But he had no intention of establishing religious toleration, nor did anyone else in the government envisage such a settlement. The question of blame or praise for holding these views does not arise. These men were caught up in the web of their time, as we are in ours, and they could not envisage a time when all men of all races and faiths would live in equality and peace with their neighbors. Because neither they nor their successors could foresee such an age the succeeding centuries would accumulate a vast, bitter record of suspicion, injustice, and bloodshed, all transmitted from one innocent generation to another until, at last, in the nineteenth century the whole apparatus of repression began to be dismantled.

I come now to my final question, What were the consequences of Guy Fawkes? His importance lies not in what he did, or tried to do, but in what he was taken to symbolize. Having destroyed the plotters, the government made the maximum political capital out of the Plot. Hence the address to Parliament, the publication of an official record, the inclusion henceforth of a special service in the Book of Common Prayer, and the establishment of November 5 as a day of national salvation. Nor should we think of Guy Fawkes Day in the seventeenth, eighteenth, or a good part of the nineteenth century as merely an excuse for gathering a few friends in the back garden to entertain the children. All too often in provincial England it was an occasion for whipping up hostility against the Catholics; and in the capital itself the same was often the case. In 1850 when the Catholic hierarchy was restored in England by the Papacy, one mob omitted the customary effigy of Guy Fawkes and replaced it with one of Cardinal Wiseman.[37]

So, in the seventeenth century and beyond, English Catholics carried the inherited taint of the plotters' guilt. "Sir," said one such critic of them, "I condemn you not all; but I condemn the religion of you all: for your religion bindeth you all to attempt the like . . . your religion bindeth you all to play the traitors."[38] And Catholicism was indeed easily identified with the foreigner by those who wished to denigrate it. In the sixteenth century it was said that the Catholics would bring in Spain; in the seventeenth, at first they were identified with Spain, and then with barbarous and treasonable war in Ireland, and then with submission to the France of Louis XIV. In the eighteenth century it was still France until almost the end; and in the middle of the nineteenth century the Catholics were, by their enemies, linked with the dark forces of repression anywhere. The existence of a minority looking to other traditions provided marvelous material for demagogues to whip up xenophobia, never far below the surface in a modern nation-state. Lord George Gordon, whose name will always be associated with the anti-Catholic riots of 1781, was not the last of his line.

The consequence of these centuries of repression was a grievous impoverishment of the whole nation. We recall that there was nowhere in England where a Catholic — or any other noncon-

37   *The Book of Days*, ed. R. Chambers (2 vols.; London: published by the editor, 1864), II, 550.
38   Cited in De Luna, *Jonson's Romish Plot*, 40.

formist — could gain a university degree. Until 1797 they could not vote in local elections; until 1829 they could not vote in parliamentary elections. It was not simply that Catholics were the losers: the whole nation lost, persecutors and persecuted alike. It is true that many nonconformists, Catholics and others, found outlets in those activities for which the 39 Articles or the Oath of Supremacy were not required: in medicine, in commerce and industry. Many sought in settlement overseas the right to practice their faith in dignity and peace. Of these Catholic settlements, Maryland is the most famous and it goes back almost to the time of Guy Fawkes. This process continued, culminating in the great Irish Catholic settlements of the nineteenth and twentieth centuries in Boston, New York, Chicago, and elsewhere, settlements which recall a long, bitter ancestry of repression and humiliation, and whose consequences may still be detected in Anglo-American relations of our own day.

History (alas!) does not fall neatly into the dates and epochs of textbooks and examinations. Long after battles have been fought and won, the scars refuse to heal, the memories decline to fade, and new generations are summoned to defend a cause which no one any longer wants to attack. To these surviving memories of injustice and persecution may be attributed a good deal of the meretricious and tendentious writing on Guy Fawkes which has plagued the study of the seventeenth century for so long.

Here then is a situation familiar enough throughout the whole history of organized religion in Europe: the doctrine of the uniqueness of religious revelation, that only one religion or one form of a religion has access to divine truth; and the consequent fragmentation of European society, the persecution, the martyrs, the oft-repeated cycle of war and oppression, the ineradicable memories of injustice. And here is the final paradox. Even as one admires the deep courage, the noble service and devotion of the priesthood to their faithful, one knows also that they were themselves a divisive force, separating by laws against intermarriage, by dietary laws, by ritual, one member of the European community from another. They were men of great ideals, and they did what they believed to be right. Those within their own community who dissented were ostracized, excommunicated, and, if they were priests, forbidden to minister to their own people. So we see, if we consider any minority or persecuted faith, that the isolation at first imposed from without was, in due course, perpetuated from within. It was the priesthood which performed this special role of continuing the isolation of their own faithful from other creeds. The fragmentation of Europe was not caused simply by the Protestant Reformation, as has so often been said, but by the leaders of all branches of the Christian faith; and the same pattern is to be seen beyond that faith in the long, checkered, and tragic history of the Jews. This is the high price that is paid for believing in the uniqueness of revealed truth, in the superiority of one faith or one community over the rest. Isolation thus becomes welcome to persecutor and persecuted alike. In any history of a ghetto there are two stages. The first is the erection of the wall from without, the second is the renewal of that wall from within. Many recent examples of this second stage can be seen all over the world.

The movement of Catholic protest in England thus passed through two stages, familiar enough in our own times but in a different context. The first stage saw the attempt to win recognition as a tolerated minority among majority groups. This phase ended in failure and Catesby emerged in 1605 as the leader of the party of action, the party which would take its rights by force. But it was a tiny party, and the events of November destroyed it. The movement now entered on its second phase when in despair it turned inward, emphasizing its distinctiveness as a community within the nation, passionately resolved to preserve its separate identity. In gunpowder few of the Catholics believed and in any case it was discredited. They turned instead to a different weapon, the press; and the vast polemical literature is a measure of their devotion and resourcefulness. Meanwhile many of them withdrew into themselves. But it would be quite false to imagine that all over the British Isles a patient minority endured their disabilities until a better time would dawn. In one area continuous repression was answered with endemic violence: the tragic history of Ireland since the sixteenth century, where racial and religious protest were combined, provides a perfect casebook of how not to treat a dissenting minority.

Deep below this controversy, inseparable as it is from the history of England, is the issue of liberty: the liberty of a minority within society but the liberty, too, of an individual within that minority, his liberty from the ideological domination of the priestly caste. The rationalist movements of the eighteenth and nineteenth centuries took up again the work of the sixteenth century in weakening the power of the priestly order in all faiths; and it achieved a remarkable degree of success. But success did not last. The second half of the nineteenth century saw the emergence of a whole series of secular theologies, comparable in inspiration, ideals — and intolerance — to the greatest religions in the world; and in the twentieth century pressures of ideological commitment have intensified. Just as the old priestly order was relaxing its grip, a new priestly order asserted its authority, backed now by all the apparatus of the printing press and the mass media. In many cases the state triumphed over the church and assumed its powers. Nor should one think of this solely in terms of government. The intolerance of minority leaders in many cases measures up to or exceeds that of the men who sit in the seats of authority. The events of the centuries since Guy Fawkes seen in this general context underline for us the tragic destiny of man: for how brief a time he enjoys his liberty and how precarious is his hold upon it.

Yet there are grounds for hope. In the 1530's, under Henry VIII, two measures were passed by Parliament. The first was designed to end the official use of the Welsh language in every part of Wales, the second, as it said, to abolish diversity of opinion in religion.[39] But diversity of opinion survives, so does the Welsh language; and as we read those two acts after so long we marvel at the pretentious littleness of some who lead us, and at the courage and power of those who dissent.

39   For example, "And also that from henceforth no person or persons that use the Welsh speech or language shall have or enjoy any manner office or fees within the realm of England, Wales or other the King's dominions upon pain of forfeiting the same offices or fees unless he or they use and exercise the speech or language of English." 27 Hen. VIII c. 26; 31 Hen. VIII c. 14.

JOHN H. BARCROFT

Carleton and Buckingham: The Quest for Office

As emphasis is placed upon institutional factors in explaining the English civil wars of the seventeenth century, the history of the royal administration plays an increasingly important role; for it is clear that the prestige of the monarchy depended in large measure upon the success with which it governed. Successful government, in turn, depended upon the caliber of the men who were placed in office. It therefore becomes necessary to establish the conditions under which men achieved office, since the methods of gaining office and promotion helped create the attitudes which the royal officials carried with them into their positions.[1]

The very long campaign which Sir Dudley Carleton (1573–1632) waged in order to obtain an office shows, in microcosm, the world of office seekers and officeholders during the ascendancy of the Duke of Buckingham. It illustrates the circumstances un-

[1] Relatively little work has been done on Early Stuart administrative history. The best general treatment is Aylmer, *The King's Servants*, which however does not deal save in passing with the period of the Duke of Buckingham, 1616–1628. The section of Stone's recent work *Crisis of the Aristocracy* entitled "Office and the Court" offers information of general relevance, but its emphasis is upon the peerage rather than upon the great bulk of the courtiers and officeholders. K. W. Swart, *Sale of Offices in the Seventeenth Century* (The Hague: M. Nijhoff, 1949), offers a brief comparative survey of venality in European and non-European nations.

der which they functioned, the stratagems which they employed, the reverses which they suffered. It illuminates the role of patronage in officeholding, the lack of specialization in the Early Stuart administration, and the limits which proprietary notions of office placed upon transfer of office. Particularly, Carleton's story is typical of the slowness and confusion which surrounded the quest for preferment at the courts of James and Charles.

From 1610 to 1616 Carleton was James I's ambassador to the Republic of Venice, from 1616 to 1625 his ambassador to Holland. With the exception of a brief visit in England in 1616 between the two embassies, Carleton spent fifteen years abroad; however, during the latter half of his diplomatic service abroad Sir Dudley repeatedly sought a position at home. He wanted an office at home for two reasons; first, to strengthen his financial position (there was no money to be made in ambassadorial posts); second, to have a greater part in the affairs of the government. The first reason led him in 1617 to attempt to secure the reversion to the provostship of Eton, a lucrative and prestigious scholarly office; the second to try in 1618 for one of the two secretaryships.[2] These offices were also lucrative; but, more to the point, they were key positions in determining policy, for the secretaries handled the King's governmental and some of his personal correspondence. In addition the two secretaries tended to exercise a supervisory function over the other government departments. Carleton failed to win either the provostship of Eton or a secretaryship, but his attempt at the latter demonstrates his method of operating.

Throughout his frustrating quest for preferment, Sir Dudley relied upon his nephews, John and Dudley, to act as his intermediaries. In the midst of his negotiations for the secretaryship in 1618, John Carleton wrote him that the Duke of Buckingham,

2　Carleton to Chamberlain, September 12, 1617, PRO, *SP* 84/79, fol. 45; John Carleton to Carleton, November 9, 1618, PRO, *SP* 14/103, fol. 80. Sir Dudley Carleton had two nephews, Dudley and John. In the following notes "Carleton" refers to Sir Dudley Carleton; other relatives will be cited with first and last names.

the King's favorite, spoke of Carleton "comfortably enough," but that his uncle's friends thought the best strategy would be for Sir Dudley to offer £3,000 for the office, since they were afraid that if they spoke in his behalf, Buckingham would be jealous, and think that Carleton was not enough dependent upon him. In any event, Sir Dudley ought to send John immediately a letter to be delivered to Buckingham, and let John know what to do about offering money, because one secretary, Robert Naunton, was seeking other preferment, and the other secretary, Thomas Lake was in disfavor. Thus, it seemed likely that one or both of the secretaryships might soon be vacant.[3]

Lake fell from office early in 1619, and Sir George Calvert was given the vacant secretaryship, apparently without a money payment.[4] Almost immediately Carleton began dealing with Calvert and with Naunton for their offices. In April 1619 Carleton was told that Calvert sent for one of his friends, and asked upon what terms Carleton would part with his house at Weston; when told, Calvert said "that he would not meddle with it at any hand." A week later the same friend approached Naunton, and reported discouragedly, ". . . I have known that man [Naunton] a great while, [and] I am of the opinion that upon these terms that your lordship offers, the other secretary (who has more cause to make use of the times) would be sensible of it."[5] Again, nothing came of the negotiations.

For a few years Carleton seems to have resigned himself to a waiting game, for there is no record of his being a suitor for office again until 1623. In the intervening years, several events occurred which were to establish the conditions under which he again sought office. In January of 1620, Sir Henry Wotton, newly re-

3   John Carleton to Carleton, November 9, 1618, PRO, *SP* 14/103, fol. 80. Lake had gotten into trouble with the favorite partly because Lake's wife circulated malicious rumors about some of Buckingham's allies and partly because of Lake's connection with the Howard family, whom Buckingham was purging from the royal administration in 1618 and 1619.

4   Chamberlain to Carleton, February 20, 1618, in Chamberlain, *Letters*, II, 216.

5   Locke to Carleton, April 24, 30, 1619, PRO, *SP* 14/108, fols. 71, 85.

turned from a term as James's ambassador to Venice, was given
the reversion (i.e., the promise of appointment to an office after
the incumbent relinquishes it) to the mastership of the rolls; the
grant is worth quoting, for it shows the customary form which
written reversions took: "At the intercession of the Marquis of
Buckingham I [James] do promise the next reversion of the mastership of the rolls after Sir Julius Caesar, who now holds that
place, unto Henry Wotton, knight, in remembrance of his honest
services past, and for encouragement of the future."[6] In 1622
when Lionel Cranfield was lord treasurer, Buckingham attempted to move Sir Julius Caesar into Cranfield's former office
of master of the wards, thereby giving Wotton the choice of oc-
cupying Caesar's old office through his reversion to it, or of taking
instead a reversion after Caesar to the mastership of the wards.
However, Cranfield and Caesar were apparently both reluctant
to shift about, and the plan came to nothing.[7]

Also in 1622, Buckingham decided to replace Secretary Naunton with Edward Conway. Naunton had been in difficulties with
James and Buckingham since 1620, first for indiscretion in handling correspondence relating to the Palatine crisis, then for in-
discreet conversation with the French ambassador.[8] Naunton was
not in Buckingham's deep disfavor, he was merely declining in
usefulness in the office. Buckingham dealt gently with him. In
September 1622 Naunton[9] wrote the favorite to plead that he be
kept in his office until his wife gave birth to her child, since a year
previously she had miscarried as a result of a rumor that Naunton
was to lose his office.

She is a woman, and a woman naturally subject to stronger apprehension than I could wish, weak some ways, as all mankind is, fearful and

6   January 16, 1620, *ibid.*, 112, fol. 18. Buckingham was not created a duke
until 1623.
7   Buckingham to Wotton, January 2, 1622, in *Fortescue Papers*, ed. S. R.
Gardiner (London: Camden Society, 1871), 172–173.
8   Gardiner, *History*, III, 391.
9   Naunton to Buckingham, September 23, 1622, BM, *Harleian* MSS, 1581,
fol. 115.

mistrustful enough, which she accounts a woman's wisdom. She is now greater of the like burden than ever she was before . . . but I doubt and fear it that she will again come before her time, especially if she shall apprehend the loss of my place. . . . I am grown in years, and cannot expect many children. It is come upon me beyond my expectation that she has conceived again since her last so dangerous miscarrying. . . . Sir Edward Conway is my noble friend, and a gentleman. If I know him so right as I think I do, he will not find it in . . . his . . . heart to affect succeeding me so hastily, to the extirpation of my posterity which must be far dearer to me than this fag end of my life.

This touching and subtle plea was honored; late in 1622 Naunton's wife gave birth to the child, Naunton resigned, and early in 1623 Conway became secretary.[10] Conway, at Buckingham's direction, immediately set about to provide some compensation for Naunton. In April of 1623 he wrote a report of the situation to the favorite in Madrid:[11]

Your excellency having imparted to me your resolution to do nobly for Sir Robert Naunton . . . wherein the Lord Treasurer [Cranfield] has shown himself full of faithful care of his Majesty's profit, and yet with willingness and affection to employ himself to your excellency's satisfaction. The three first propositions being £1,000 pension for life, £500 a year improved land inheritance, £500 a year fee farm old rents. The old rents was no way allowed; land improved there is none presently; a thousand pound a year pension is offered, and accepted by Sir Robert Naunton, with two provisions: that it may be for 21 years, and settled upon sure payment. I have moved the Lord Treasurer, but cannot re-move him; yet the work to be done now is to move the King to overrule him, or to procure Sir Robert Naunton to accept it as it will be granted him, which I shall endeavor by the first opportunity.

Here one can see the complexities of patronage and transfer of office. Cranfield was unwilling to allow fee farm old rents because this tied up Crown lands at an unremunerative rate (that is, at the

10   Gardiner, *History*, IV, 409–410.
11   Conway to Buckingham, April 12, 1623, BM, *Harleian* MSS, 1580, fol. 294.

"old," undervalued rental, rather than at rentals which reflected the inflationary trend of the period), he was unwilling to allow land to leave the Crown permanently (improved land inheritance) to the benefit of Naunton's heirs, and he was unwilling to grant the pension for twenty-one years because Naunton probably would not live that long, and thus again Crown income would go to his heirs. Naunton settled for a pension for his lifetime, but he wanted "sure payment" — which is to say, he wanted the pension granted out of one of the reliable, prompt disbursing departments, such as the Court of Wards, rather than out of Exchequer, which had slow and old-fashioned accounting methods, and which furthermore was notoriously in arrears on pensions and other disbursements throughout the Early Stuart period.

During these transactions, Carleton was tending his embassy at The Hague. Conway was too far in Buckingham's favor for Carleton to imagine that an attempt for Naunton's post could succeed. However, in 1623, Carleton made a second attempt to win the provostship of Eton. The incumbent, Thomas Murray, died on April 9, 1623; the office was not formally filled until July of 1624.[12] But even the informal and bargaining phase lasted a full year, from April 1623 to April 1624. Francis Bacon entered the lists first; in late March he approached Conway for the provostship in case Murray should die. Conway went at once to the King and placed Bacon's suit before him, as being favored by Buckingham, but James told him that he had already promised the place at Buckingham's request to Sir William Beecher, a clerk of the Privy Council.[13] Next, Sir John Coke wrote Buckingham that Lord Keeper Williams had suggested that Coke take the provostship and relinquish his office as a master of requests, which could then go to Beecher, thus freeing Beecher's clerkship of the Council for a dependent of Williams.[14] Naunton then took

12   Chamberlain to Carleton, April 19, 1623, July 24, 1624, Chamberlain, *Letters*, II, 489–490, 571.

13   Conway to Buckingham, March 29, 1623, BM, *Harleian* MSS, 1580, fols. 332–333.

14   Coke to Buckingham, April 11, 1623, *ibid.*, 1581, fol. 272.

the field, offering "to quit all pensions, promises, and pretensions whatsoever," in return for the office, but James delayed action on any of these suits until he could confer with Buckingham.[15] One reason for delay was that Buckingham was at this time in Spain (March–October 1623) and all matters of patronage were in suspension.

As it became apparent that the provostship would not be disposed of quickly, Carleton belatedly entered the field. He had sought a reversion to the office unsuccessfully in 1617, and it was a position which had family connections; his wife's stepfather, Sir Henry Savile, had held the office before Thomas Murray.[16] In July 1623, Carleton's friend, Henry Rich, Baron Kensington and soon to be Earl of Holland, wrote that Buckingham was very friendly to Carleton, but that he was already "engaged" for the provostship of Eton, and suggested that Carleton try for some other preferment.[17]

Carleton would not be deterred; early in 1624 he was still trying for the office through Buckingham's good friend, Sir George Goring. He learned, however, that a dark horse was coming up fast on the far side of the track — Sir Henry Wotton:[18]

I have let Sir George Goring know that your lordship has an eye toward Eton College until it be gone; and that Sir William Beecher says that if he must needs compound he had rather do it with your lordship than anybody else. But I find that place must rest yet a while without a provost, and though the speech goes that Sir Henry Wotton has lately presented my lord of Buckingham with a great many curious pictures, which some will have a sign that he is assured to have it, yet Sir Robert Naunton's friends give out that he is certainly the man. . . . But I take the cause of this suspense to be the unwillingness of my lord of Buckingham to interpose in a business that will ask time to be decided among so many competitors.

15   Chamberlain to Carleton, April 19, 1623, Chamberlain, *Letters*, II, 490.
16   Carleton to Chamberlain, September 12, 1617, PRO, *SP* 84/79, fol. 45. See also Chamberlain, *Letters*, I, 14.
17   Kensington to Carleton, July 19, 1623, PRO, *SP* 14/149, fol. 8.
18   Dudley Carleton to Carleton, n.d., *ibid.*, 161, fol. 49. This letter may be dated c. March 28, 1624. Cf. *CSPD*, 1623–1625, 201.

In April of 1624 Wotton clearly had outdistanced the field, and in July he was formally confirmed as provost.[19] Beecher, Wotton, and Naunton had been the major candidates; Bacon, Coke, and Carleton peripheral ones. The latter three were ignored; the former three were all provided for one way or another. Naunton was taken care of by elevation to the mastership of the wards, vacant by the disgrace of Lionel Cranfield.[20] Wotton gave up his reversion to the mastership of the rolls, valued at £5,000, to Buckingham, and his right to fill a vacant clerkship in Chancery, valued at around £2,500, to Beecher; Buckingham then further compensated Beecher by promising him £2,000 out of the sale of the reversion to the mastership of the rolls.[21] Thus, Naunton obtained one of the half-dozen most valuable offices in the realm, and Wotton acquired the provostship, which he apparently thought was worth at least £7,500. Beecher got almost £5,000 in return for surrendering his reversion to the provostship; Buckingham, presumably, kept the remaining £2,500 as a broker's fee.

Buckingham's handling of Naunton, and his subsequent handling of the provostship of Eton in which Naunton was again involved, show how influential proprietary notions of office were. Naunton was leaving office; the favorite clearly felt at least a moral obligation to compensate him for the loss of a possession — first with a pension, later with another office. Both Wotton and the favorite compensated Beecher for relinquishing his reversion. Yet, unlike Naunton and Wotton, who were middle-sized fish in the pond of patronage, Beecher was a small fish. Naunton and Wotton were beneficiaries of notions of patronage as well as notions of proprietorship; although it was Buckingham's patronage which had gotten Beecher his reversion in the first place, in his surrender of the reversion he was primarily a beneficiary of notions of proprietorship. The compensation to him was, in

---

19   Chamberlain to Carleton, July 24, 1624, Chamberlain, *Letters*, II, 571.
20   Chamberlain to Carleton, July 3, October 9, 1624, *ibid.*, II, 568–569, 582.
21   Dudley Carleton to Carleton, April 4, 11, 1624, PRO, *SP* 14/162, fol. 13; *SP* 84/117, fol. 31A. *CSPD*, 1619–1623, 113.

effect, a payment for a quitclaim (his surrender of the reversion) on an estate which was changing hands.

In spite of his failure to gain office amid the complex negotiations surrounding the Eton job, Carleton was still hopeful. A month after he had heard the bad news about Eton (May, 1624), he was negotiating again — this time for a secretaryship.

Sir George Calvert was willing to retire from the office, for his Roman Catholic and Spanish sympathies separated him from the warlike policy toward Spain which Buckingham and Prince Charles were espousing. In May, Carleton's nephew Dudley wrote that Calvert would let Carleton have his office for £6,000, even though one suitor offered £8,000 when Calvert got it, and another had offered £7,000 since. The nephew went on to say that Calvert thought £6,000 was a very reasonable sum, and "he doubted not but by the Queen of Bohemia's [King James's daughter; Carleton's friend and supporter] recommendation and the consideration of your own worth, the Prince and my lord of Buckingham would easily find means to supply such a sum of ready money as that was; it being no more than three years' purchase of a place worth two thousand pounds a year, reckoning the diet, the wages, intelligence money, and other things ordinary and certain . . . besides all extraordinary occasions."[22] A month later Dudley wrote that Buckingham was favorable to the idea of Carleton's taking Calvert's office, but had said "it will be hard to find out the means of satisfaction in so bare a time."[23] Clearly both Calvert and Buckingham assumed that for the transfer to occur, Buckingham — not Carleton — would have to raise £6,000 "ready money" from somewhere.

For a time the negotiations seem to have simmered quietly, but in November of 1624 Carleton was again going on the offensive, sending his nephew Dudley to talk to Conway, and entrusting to Dudley's care a present of statuary for Buckingham if the situation seemed favorable. The nephew reported that Conway

22 Dudley Carleton to Carleton, May 3, 1624, PRO, SP 14/164, fol. 7.
23 Dudley Carleton to Carleton, June 1, 1624, ibid., 167, fol. 1.

insisted Buckingham was favorable to Carleton's replacing Calvert, and that the situation looked promising; he added "as touching the marble, I shall proceed warily, and not engage your lordship in so rich a present without first acquainting your lordship with my reason and receiving your order."[24] In December another friend wrote Carleton to advise patience in his suit, noting that Buckingham "never did anything in his life with post haste but when he went into Spain, and therefore I do not wonder that he uses delay to performance of his promise of a good turn to your lordship; but this is certain, that he has great wants of his own, and everything that he desires does not pass so current but that it depends a season before he brings it about."[25] The friend added that Carleton should not present the statuary yet, but should wait until an opportune moment. The opportune moment came in January of 1625, when Calvert resigned his secretaryship. Carleton's nephew presented the statuary with great indirection. He showed sketches of the items to Buckingham, saying that a merchant of Liège was interested in selling them at a reasonable price. Buckingham sent for his counsellor on art, Balthasar Gerbier, who lauded the worth and beauty of the statuary. The favorite then asked the nephew about purchase and was told that Carleton wished to present them to Buckingham. Buckingham, taken aback, replied that he knew that Carleton could not afford so rich a gift. Sir Dudley's nephew responded that if the favorite did not accept the gift, his uncle would be heartbroken, whereupon Buckingham accepted the gift. Carleton's nephew related the sequel to his uncle:[26]

Being at York House [Buckingham's London residence], Mr. Crow [Sackville Crow, a secretary of the favorite] came to me and told me

24   Dudley Carleton to Carleton, November 23, 1624, PRO, *SP* 84/121, fol. 116.

25   Nethersole to Carleton, December 18, 1624, PRO, *SP* 14/176, fol. 57.

26   Dudley Carleton to Carleton, January 16, 1625, *ibid.*, 182, fol. 4. It is worth noting that Carleton's nephew claimed his uncle sought "any honest revocation." In an unspecialized administration it was possible to make the claim sincerely.

that in the morning my lord had demanded his advice what he should
send your lordship in recompense of some things he had received
from you, saying that you looked for the secretary's place, which was
disposed, and he doubted [i.e., feared] that missing thereof in this sort
it might dazzle your affections to him. Crow answered that sending
you anything back were all one as if he shall bid you . . . 'be there-
with content'; that it would certainly dead your affection to his grace
absolutely, and that he having better ways to do good to his friends
might think of some better to give your lordship contentment. I answered Mr. Crow that I could make it appear to him by your letters
that you never wanted the secretary's place more than any other
honest revocation, that might free you from debts and discredit after
so many years of foreign employment. . . . I gave him thanks for
holding his lordship off from returning present for present, saying
that he had most truly affirmed my lord had many ways of doing for
his friends. . . .

The little tableau described by Carleton's nephew might be
called "Great Moments in Patronage: The Presenting of the
Statuary." The roundabout way of presenting a gift was not uncommon in the early seventeenth century; there was an almost
pathological fear of rebuff. Significantly, when Dudley Carleton
learned from Crow that the secretaryship was already taken, he
immediately did some quick footwork to dissociate the present
from the office. It would have been a disaster to allow Buckingham to think that the statuary was aimed specifically at the
secretaryship, for then the gift would have no further use as a
douceur. One can speculate that Dudley also gave Crow more
than mere thanks for dissuading Buckingham from returning
present for present, since that also would have represented a ter-
mination of the value of the gift as a lever toward an office.

In the short run, the gift brought no fruit, for the secretaryship went to Sir Albertus Morton, who paid Calvert £3,000 himself, thus leaving only £3,000 to be raised "somewhere" for Calvert's compensation.[27] It may well be that the main reason

27   Chamberlain to Carleton, February 12, 1625, Chamberlain, *Letters*, II,
600.

Morton got the office rather than Carleton was that Morton was able to underwrite half of Calvert's compensation, whereas Carleton apparently was not. Nevertheless, Carleton's gift did not go unrewarded. Sackville Crow said that Carleton should write Buckingham freely on anything he desired, for "freedom was the course he loved." Following Crow's advice, Carleton's nephew suggested that he try for the ambassadorship to France, and use that office to sue for the office of vice-chamberlain (soon to be vacant by the resignation of the Earl of Bristol). In any event, Carleton should send his nephew one letter for the ambassadorship and one for the vice-chamberlainship, to be used as the situation warranted.[28]

A week after the gift of the statuary, Carleton was informed that the favorite was going to make him vice-chamberlain, but that it must be kept secret until Buckingham had arranged a settlement with Sir Edward Barrett (also an ambassador), to whom the office had been promised. Buckingham "says plainly and freely that Sir Dudley Carleton must take heed of his rights, knowing and seeming to know much."[29] However, there was another hitch: Bristol refused to resign. In March, 1625, two months after the promise of the office, Carleton still was not in possession. His nephew Dudley wrote encouragingly that "not only the Duke's credit, but part of his fortune, lies at stake until that be made good to you, he having not only declared his Majesty's pleasure therein to his own confidants, but divulged it in a sort, as [one] who would say he gloried in it as one of his good works, and if the present incumbent be not removed shortly, his Grace (in the opinion of some of his own discreet friends) cannot choose but impair."[30]

Fortunately, with the death of King James later that month, Bristol's patent lapsed, and Carleton was installed in the office.

28 Dudley Carleton to Carleton, January 16, 1625, PRO, *SP* 14/182, fol. 4.
29 Dudley Carleton to Carleton, January 24, 1625, *ibid.*, 182, fol. 42.
30 Dudley Carleton to Carleton, March 10, 1625, *ibid.*, 185, fol. 40. See also Chamberlain to Carleton, March 12, 1625. Chamberlain, *Letters*, II, 607.

One ought to note that the letter implied that the financial arrangements for the transfer were underwritten by Buckingham, "part of whose fortune" was at stake until Carleton was installed. Probably Buckingham had bought off Sir Edward Barrett rather than Bristol, who was in deep disgrace with both the new King and the favorite.

Carleton had at last obtained office at home, after eight years' effort. He no sooner had the vice-chamberlainship than he resumed efforts to obtain the secretaryship, which seems to have been his strongest aspiration from the beginning. In September of 1625 Sir Albertus Morton died, having enjoyed his position only seven months, and Carleton was again in the running. Again he was thwarted. Sir John Coke, Buckingham's right arm in the Admiralty, got the office, and his old post as a master of requests went to Sir Thomas Aylesbury, another Admiralty official upon whom the favorite leaned. Sir George Goring wrote Carleton that his friends had not forgotten him, but that there was a "double former engagement" to Coke and Aylesbury; he added that one reason Carleton's preferment had been so slow was that Carleton had depended "on persons averse to the Duke and his undertakers," but that this was now straightened out through the efforts of the Earls of Carlisle and Holland (the favorite's closest cronies) in Carleton's behalf.[31]

Again in 1627 Carleton tried for the secretaryship, which was rumored soon to be vacant by the promotion of Conway, but this was a false trail.[32] Ironically, it was not until December 1628, four months after Buckingham's death, that Carleton finally got the long-coveted secretaryship. Buckingham had promised it to

31   Goring to Carleton, September 8, 1625, PRO, *SP* 16/6, fol. 35. For Aylesbury see Aylmer, *The King's Servants*, 77. There is a very murky reference in a letter from Chamberlain to Carleton about the latter's "mysteries and cabals" with the Earl of Somerset in 1614. Buckingham supplanted Somerset after a fierce rivalry, so it is possible that Goring's reference is to Carleton's dependence upon Somerset. Eleven years had passed, but Buckingham had a long memory. Cf. Chamberlain to Carleton, July 21, 1614, Chamberlain, *Letters*, I, 551.
32   Dumolin to Herbault, April 20, 1627, PRO, *Paris Transcripts*, 31/3, fol. 65.

him before his death, and Charles honored the commitment.[33] Sir Dudley's long diplomatic experience made him influential as an adviser to Charles on foreign policy; however, Carleton did not long enjoy Buckingham's bequest, for he died himself in 1632.

If one wishes to understand the real nature of patronage under Buckingham and the practical difficulties of officeholders and office seekers in the royal administration, here is the case to study. One is immediately struck by the slow, cumbersome, involuted method used to effect transfers of office. In almost none of the posts which Carleton sought was the incumbent summarily dismissed; on the contrary, long three-cornered negotiations occurred among incumbent, favorite, and various aspirants. Even in the case of the vice-chamberlainship, occupied by Bristol, a man whom Buckingham detested (and whom he certainly would have dismissed if he could), appointment of a new man was in fact delayed until Bristol's patent lapsed by the death of James I. It further becomes clear that "sale" of office sometimes was not that at all, but rather another kind of financial transaction, more in the nature of severance pay, or a retirement pension, or unemployment compensation. Students of the period have been too quick to smell money and shout sale.[34] As is shown by the negotiations for the provostship of Eton, the financial arrangements were rather more complicated than the simple term *sale* conveys. This is not to say that sale did not occur; it did. But it did not *always* occur. To think of the monetary arrangements as invariable instances of mere venality obscures an understanding both of Buckingham's patronage and of the "old administrative system." It makes them both purely and simply corrupt, which leaves little more to be said.

33   Gardiner, *History*, VI, 340–341, 372–373.
34   For example, R. H. Tawney, *Business and Politics in the Reign of James I: Lionel Cranfield as Merchant and Minister* (Cambridge: University Press, 1958), 123. H. R. Trevor-Roper, *The Gentry, 1540–1640*, EcHR, Suppl. 1 (Cambridge: University Press, 1953), 28.

In fact, the matter was not that simple. Buckingham's patronage operated in a social context in which dependence and loyalty had to be rewarded (hence, the favorite's efforts for Naunton, and Carleton's efforts to convince Buckingham of his utter dependence), with or without the payment of money, though preferably with. The favorite's patronage existed also in an administrative context in which various proprietary notions of office, coupled with the financial exigencies of Early Stuart officeholders, led to the feeling that to deprive from office without some form of remuneration was arbitrary and unjust. The personal ties of patronage, and the financial ties of office, could combine to create an exceedingly complex web of circumstance which often hindered, or even precluded, "efficient personnel policies." Any system of patronage within an administration is susceptible to corruption (that, after all, is the import of the various national civil service acts), and Buckingham corrupted the English system. But even under Buckingham, corruption was the lesser evil, inefficiency the greater.

ROBERT C. JOHNSON

The Transportation of Vagrant Children from London to Virginia, 1618–1622

During the first quarter of the seventeenth century the City of London contained a large number of vagrant children. Some of them were orphans who literally lived in the streets and managed to survive by begging and pilfering; others came from large families with parents too poor to support them. In either case, the children formed a rowdy element and were responsible for much of the disorder and petty crime that plagued the city. Some of the worst offenders were sent to Bridewell Hospital, which was not a hospital in the modern sense but an institution for the detention of "idle wastrels, petty thieves, and dissolute women."[1] There the children were presumably "kept in arts and occupations, and other . . . works and labors" designed to rehabilitate them,[2] but more often than not the children merely became more confirmed in their delinquency. The records of Bridewell indicate a relatively large number of "old" or "common guests" — that is, persons who were released but soon were returned for having

NOTE: Research for this article was made possible by grants from Temple University and the Penrose Fund of the American Philosophical Society.

1   Edward G. O'Donoghue, *Bridewell Hospital: Palace, Prison, Schools, from the Death of Elizabeth to Modern Times* (London: John Lane, 1929), 18.

2   W. K. Jordan, *The Charities of London, 1480–1660* (New York: Russell Sage Foundation, 1960), 194.

committed another offense. Adding to the problem was the fact that Bridewell, as well as other institutions for the care of the poor, was overcrowded. Most of the vagrant children remained in the streets: homeless, hungry, and sometimes diseased.

One solution to the problem of what to do with these vagrants was to send them to Virginia. This course had long been advocated by the Virginia Company, although in its earlier promotional literature, when the colony was in its infancy, the emphasis was more on adults than on children. By 1618 this emphasis had changed. The colony was now reasonably well established, and with the expansion of agriculture there was a growing need for servants to work the land. In certain respects, young vagrants were much better suited for this work than older ones. The young were less confirmed in their delinquent habits, they could be kept under stricter control, and they could be provided with the necessary training and education that would make them responsible adults. Besides, if the transportation of children to Virginia could be pictured as a project that would benefit both the children and the City of London, the Virginia Company could reasonably expect the City to pay the costs.

The plan to send vagrant children to Virginia originated with the Virginia Company while it was still under the administration of Sir Thomas Smythe. In order to give the project a wider base of support, a petition "under the hands of many citizens" was presented to the Common Council of London in July 1618. The petition complained of the great number of "vagrant boys and girls that lie and beg in the streets . . . having no place of abode nor friends to relieve them" and requested that they (or at least one hundred of them) might be transported to Virginia at the City's expense, there "to be employed in some industrious courses." The Common Council discussed the petition on July 31, "well approved" of it, and appointed a committee to "treat . . . with the Virginia Company for transportation and employing of such vagrant children; the charge thereof; and how the same shall be most conveniently levied; as for other matters which in their wisdoms and discretions they shall think behooveful for the ordering, effecting and managing of the same from time to time hereafter."[3]

The negotiations with the Virginia Company were soon completed, and when the Common Council had its next meeting, on September 24, a bill was presented for adoption. The bill provided that one hundred boys and girls between the ages of eight and sixteen, born in London and having "no means of living or maintenance," should be "taken up and transported to Virginia, there to be educated and brought up at the charge of the [Virginia] Company in such trades and professions as the said Company shall think fit." The bill also provided that each child, after having served as an apprentice, would be given fifty acres of land, the boy when he was twenty-four years of age and the girl on her twenty-first birthday or day of marriage, whichever occurred first. The cost of appareling and transporting the children was estimated to be five hundred pounds, or five pounds for each child. This sum was to be paid by the City of London and would be collected by an assessment upon those responsible for the payment of poor relief. Finally, in order to make certain that the children received all that was promised to them, indentured agreements were to be made between the City of London and the Virginia Company.[4]

The problem of apprehending one hundred children to be transported was quite easily solved. Even before the passage of the bill by the Common Council, the Lord Mayor issued a precept to each of the aldermen of the City requiring them to instruct their constables to "walk the streets within their several precincts, and forthwith apprehend all such vagrant children, both boys and girls, as they shall find in the streets and in the markets or wandering in the night to be apprehended by the watch, and them to commit to Bridewell, there to remain until further

3   City of London, Corporation of London Records Office, Journal of the Common Council, XXX, fol. 374ᵛ.
4   *Ibid.*, fol. 396.

order be given by me and my brethren the aldermen for their enlargement."[5] Although the precept did not mention Virginia, it is quite clear that this was to be the destination of the children. In another precept, issued immediately after the passage of the bill, the Lord Mayor instructed each alderman "to call before you the deputy and churchwardens of every parish within your ward and give them charge forthwith to resort to all the poor inhabitants within their several precincts and require of them that are overcharged and burdened with poor children, if they will have any of their children of the age of ten years and upwards, and how many, sent to Virginia, thereby to ease them of their charge." The parents were to be assured that in Virginia the children would be "well used and provision made for their good education and maintenance." The deputies and churchwardens were expected to make their poll with great speed, for the Lord Mayor further instructed that certificates containing the names of the children to be sent, as well as the names of the parents and the parishes in which they lived, should be returned to the Guildhall by the following evening.[6]

Through these means, ninety-nine children — seventy-five boys and twenty-four "wenches" — were soon collected at Bridewell[7] and were sent to Virginia in groups: some in the *Jonathan*, others in the *George*, and still others in the *Neptune*, all of which left England in the late winter and early spring of 1619. In the following November the City of London was informed that "by the goodness of God" the children had safely arrived in the colony "save such as died in the way."[8]

This first experiment in transporting vagrant children to Virginia was so beneficial to the colony that in the fall of 1619 the Virginia Company sought another group, again at the City's ex-

5 *Ibid.*, fol. 382.
6 *Ibid.*, fol. 397ᵛ.
7 Virginia State Library, Transcripts of Bridewell Hospital Court Book, February 27, 1619.
8 *The Records of the Virginia Company of London*, ed. Susan M. Kingsbury (4 vols.; Washington D.C.: GPO, 1906–1935), I, 270.

pense. By this time, the Company had fallen under the control of Sir Edwin Sandys and his followers, who were formulating vast plans for the colony, including a great increase in the number of settlers. Negotiations with the City began in the middle of November, when Sandys conferred with the Lord Mayor, Sir William Cockayne, about sending another group of children. Cockayne personally approved of the project and advised the Company to draw up a petition to be submitted to the Court of Aldermen and the Common Council. The petition was ready by November 17, was discussed by the Court of Aldermen on December 7, and was submitted to the Common Council on December 18.[9]

The Company's request, as contained in the petition, differed in certain respects from its request of the previous year. In the first place, the one hundred children to be sent to Virginia should be at least twelve years old instead of eight. Secondly, and much more importantly, the Company decided that the children would not be given a grant of land after they had served their apprenticeships; instead they would be placed as tenants on the public lands, where they would "have houses with stock of corn and cattle to begin with, and afterwards the moiety [one-half] of all increase and profit whatsoever."[10]

If there was any objection to this proposal, there is nothing to indicate that it was voiced when the Common Council considered the matter on December 18.[11] The bill that was introduced and passed stated explicity that the one hundred children would become tenants on the public lands after having served as apprentices until age twenty-one. The bill also provided, as in 1618, that the cost of transporting and appareling the children, again amounting to £500, would be borne by the City of London and

<hr />

9 Ibid., 270–271. Corporation of London Records Office, City of London, Repertories, XXXIV, fol. 276; Journal of the Common Council, XXXI, fols. 125–126.

10 Kingsbury, Records of the Virginia Company, I, 270–271.

11 Present at the meeting of the Common Council was a committee of the Virginia Company including Sandys and nine others. Ibid., 287.

would be collected from those responsible for the payment of poor relief.[12]

To carry out the provisions of the act the Lord Mayor issued three precepts. The first was addressed to the churchwardens and the collectors for the poor in the various parishes and ordered them to make the necessary financial assessments. The second, directed to the aldermen, required them to instruct their constables to apprehend all vagrant children found in the streets and commit them to Bridewell. The third, also addressed to the aldermen, ordered that an inquiry should be made of those parents "overcharged and burdened with poor children" whether they wished to send any of the children to Virginia. This time, as an added pressure, those parents who replied negatively were to be told that they would not receive any further poor relief from the parish.[13]

The work of collecting the children began immediately and continued for the next month. The Court Book of Bridewell Hospital indicates that during the period from December 18, 1619, until January 15, 1620, more than sixty persons, two of them girls, were brought in as vagrants and ordered confined until they could be sent to Virginia. Except for their names and in some cases the parishes in which they lived, practically nothing is known about them. Presumably their only "crime" was that they were poor and happened to be found loitering or sleeping in the streets when the constable passed by. On one day alone, December 31, forty-one of these unfortunates were brought to Bridewell and ordered "kept for Virginia."[14]

In the meantime, a serious controversy had developed between the City of London and the Virginia Company over the benefits the children were to receive. Despite the provisions of

12   Corporation of London Records Office, Journal of the Common Council, XXXI, fols. 125–126.

13   *Ibid.*, fols. 128ᵛ–129.

14   Virginia State Library, Bridewell Hospital Court Book, under dates December 18, 24, 31, 1619; January 7, 15, 1620.

the bill passed by the Common Council, the Lord Mayor and some of the aldermen insisted that since the City was paying the costs of transportation and provisioning, the children should be given a grant of land after they had served their apprenticeships. The controversy began on January 11, when the Lord Mayor asked Sir Edwin Sandys how much land would be given to the children. At first Sandys maintained that the children would merely become tenants on the public lands, but when the Lord Mayor became insistent Sandys relented and agreed that the children would be given twenty-five acres each.[15] The controversy did not end with this concession. In later meetings between Sandys and the Lord Mayor and aldermen, other demands were made, the exact nature of which is not known except that Sandys described them to the Company as "strange" and "not fitting for them [the Lord Mayor and aldermen] to ask, nor can no ways by the orders of this Company be granted."[16] By early February the negotiations between the City and the Company had reached an impasse, with the Company stating that it would assume the charge of transportation but that the most the children would receive would be twenty-five acres of land after they had finished their apprenticeships and had served seven years as tenants on the public lands.[17] Finally, by the middle of February, the City yielded and not only agreed to the Company's terms but also paid the £500 that had been authorized and collected.[18]

During the course of this controversy, matters were further complicated by the refusal of some of the children to be transported. In late January a kind of "revolt" occurred at Bridewell, with some of the "ill disposed" among the children declaring "their unwillingness to go to Virginia," where (in the Company's words) "under severe masters they may be brought to goodness."

15 Kingsbury, *Records of the Virginia Company*, I, 293.
16 *Ibid.*, 300.
17 *Ibid.*, 304–307. Corporation of London Records Office, City of London, Remembrancia, V, fol. 67.
18 Kingsbury, *Records of the Virginia Company*, I, 310.

The children probably had outside support, for it was soon discovered that the City of London lacked authority to deliver, and the Virginia Company to transport, the children against their wills. A hasty letter from Sandys to the King's secretary quickly rectified the situation. On January 31 the Privy Council granted the necessary authority and also decreed that if any of the children were "obstinate" and still resisted transportation they should be imprisoned and punished.[19] With this action, the "revolt" ended. By the end of February 1620 the children embarked from London, a number of them on the *Duty*,[20] which arrived in Virginia in May.

Despite these difficulties, the Virginia Company sought another group of children in the fall of 1620. In a meeting of the quarter court of the Company on November 15, Richard Caswell moved that the Lord Mayor should again be solicited for a "like number of children with the like allowance as formerly they had," but he hoped that they might be obtained "upon more easy conditions" than the City had previously tried to impose; in Caswell's opinion, the City's officials had been more interested in obtaining "an over advantageous bargain" for the children than in providing for "the good of the plantation for which they were procured." The Deputy Treasurer of the Company, John Ferrar, added that he had been solicited by the Marshal of London as well as others who had been active in procuring children for Virginia that they should be given some reward "for their care and travail therein, that they might be encouraged hereafter to take the like pains whensoever they should have again the like occasion." The court approved Caswell's proposal and directed that a letter should be written to the Lord Mayor and aldermen requesting another group of children to be sent to Virginia as appren-

19 Sir Edwin Sandys to Sir Robert Naunton, January 28, 1620. *Ibid.*, III, 259; *APC*, 1619–1621, XXXVII, 118.
20 Hence the term "Duty Boys" by which the children came to be known. Alexander Brown, *The First Republic in America* (Boston: Houghton, Mifflin, 1898), 375.

tices. The court also decided that the Marshal of London and some of the other law-enforcing officials deserved rewards and that a sum of money should be distributed among them.[21]

So far as is known, nothing came of the request for another group of children. The Company's letter to the Lord Mayor and aldermen, written by the Earl of Southampton, went unanswered; and when a committee of the Company arranged a conference with the City's officials, the only result was the appointment, by the Court of Aldermen, of a committee to "confer with the Treasurer of the Virginia Company and take an account of the money paid to that Company for transporting of certain persons to Virginia, and to return to this Court an account of money and what persons have been sent."[22] Since nothing was said about sending additional children, it can be presumed that the City was no longer interested.

The Company's last request for children came in June 1622, when a petition was again submitted to the Lord Mayor and aldermen. The City responded by appointing a committee to confer with the Company, but apparently little progress was made in the negotiations until after the news reached England, early in July, that an Indian attack on the colony had resulted in the massacre of almost three hundred and fifty settlers. Then both the City and the Company acted very quickly. On July 3 the Company appointed a committee to make the best possible "bargain" with the City, and on July 9 the Court of Aldermen agreed that one hundred boys should be sent to Virginia at the City's expense and that a bill to this effect should be presented to the next meeting of the Common Council, which was scheduled to take place on July 19.[23]

The bill's preamble expressed some of the shock and indigna-

21   Kingsbury, *Records of the Virginia Company*, I, 424.
22   *Ibid.*, 431. Corporation of London Records Office, City of London, Repertories, XXXV, fol. 58.
23   *Ibid.*, XXXVI, fols. 170, 196ᵛ. Kingsbury, *Records of the Virginia Company*, II, 90.

tion with which the news of the massacre had been received in England:

> *Item* this Court taking into their consideration the plantation in Virginia, by which the Gospel of Christ Jesus hath been by God's blessing and is like to be more and more propagated to the glory of God and the honor of this Kingdom, and being sensible of the great loss which they lately sustained by the barbarous cruelty of the savage people there (who under color of friendship did cruelly murder many of our nation and if their design had not through God's goodness been discovered had endangered the utter ruin and subversion of the whole plantation) have with one heart and voice expressed their readiness to cherish and assist so noble and so pious a work. . . .

Except for the preamble, the bill resembled its predecessors. It provided that one hundred children twelve years and older would be sent to Virginia, that the City of London would pay £500 for their apparel and transportation, and that this sum would be collected by an assessment upon the poor relief.[24] No mention was made of the benefits the children would receive, but no doubt they were to be the same as in 1620: the children would go as apprentices, later would work as tenants, and finally would be given a piece of land.

The task of collecting the children probably began as soon as the bill was passed. By early September, fifty of them were ready for transportation and may have sailed in the *Southampton*, which left England at that time.[25] The remaining fifty left in October.[26] They were the last group of children sent to Virginia at the City's expense.

What happened to these vagrant children sent to Virginia between 1618 and 1622? Did they safely cross the Atlantic and find in the colony a better life than they had in London. No exact

24 Corporation of London Records Office, Journal of the Common Council, XXXI, fols. 66–67.

25 Corporation of London Records Office, City of London, Repertories, XXXVI, fol. 236ᵛ. Kingsbury, *Records of the Virginia Company*, II, 102.

26 Corporation of London Records Office, City of London, Repertories, XXXVI, fol. 275.

answer can be given, primarily because of the scarcity of records and, where records do exist, the commonness of some of the children's names, which prevents accurate identification. The only complete list of children is that of February 1619, which contains the names of seventy-five boys and twenty-four girls "appointed to go to Virginia."[27] As has been mentioned, these children left England in groups during the late winter and early spring of 1619. Some died on the way to Virginia; how many is not known. Those who survived reached the colony before summer and were assigned as apprentices. From that time on, little is known about them except that very few lived to become adults. When a "muster" or census of the colony was taken early in 1625, the names of only seven boys were listed.[28] All of the other boys must have succumbed, either through natural causes or at the hands of the Indians. At least five were killed in the Indian massacre in 1622.[29] The statistics for the children sent in 1620 are equally grim. Of the sixty-six children and young adults admitted to Bridewell Hospital during December 1619 and January 1620 and ordered "kept for Virginia," no more than five were alive in 1625.[30] The children sent in 1622 are not known by name and thus cannot be traced, but there is little reason to believe that they would have fared any better.

One would like to think that some of the few survivors went on to become prominent leaders of the colony or were the founders of great families. This does not appear to be the case. Of the

27   This list is contained in the Bridewell Hospital Court Book under the date February 27, 1619.

28   If any of the girls were still alive, they had probably married and thus had different surnames. The names of the surviving boys were: William Bullock, John Davies, Nicholas Granger, Robert Newman, Stephen Reede (Reade), William Strange, and Nathaniel Tatum. See *Adventurers of Purse and Person, Virginia 1607–1625*, 2nd ed., ed. Annie Lash Jester (n.p., 1964), 5–69 *passim*.

29   The figure was probably higher, since the list of casualties in Kingsbury, *Records of the Virginia Company*, III, 564–571, is very incomplete.

30   They were: Henry Booth, Christopher Browne, Henry Carman, Thomas Cornish, and Robert Whitmore. Jester, *Adventurers of Purse and Person*, 5–69 *passim*.

twelve known survivors, only three can be traced with any degree of certainty beyond 1625. One of these persons was Nicholas Granger, who came with the first group of children in 1619. In 1625, when the muster was taken, he was listed as one of the servants of Captain William Epes on "the Eastern Shore over the Bay." He was then aged fifteen.[31] When he finished his apprenticeship, he presumably received fifty acres of land, and in 1647 he obtained another three hundred and fifty acres for transporting seven persons to the colony.[32]

Another survivor was Henry Carman, who arrived with the second group of children in 1620. (The records of Bridewell Hospital indicate that he was brought in by the Marshal of Middlesex on December 31, 1619.) In 1625 he was twenty-three years old and was a servant of Samuel Sharpe, who lived on Peirsey's Hundred.[33] Carman appears to have been somewhat confirmed in his delinquency, for in October 1626 he was in trouble with the authorities for having "committed fornication with one Alice Chambers, servant to Mr. Abraham Peirsey, and gotten her with child." This offense violated the terms of his indenture, which forbade that any of the children "should commit any great malifice, as whoredom, theft, perjury, drawing of blood and such like," and he was punished by having his period of indentured servitude extended for another seven years.[34] Ultimately he obtained his freedom, and in 1638 he and one Henry Senior were awarded one hundred and fifty acres in James City County for transporting three persons to the colony.[35]

The most successful of the survivors was probably Nathaniel Tatum (or Tatam), who was among the first group of children to be sent. He arrived in the colony in 1619 aboard the *George*, and

31   *Ibid.*, 66.
32   Nell Marion Nugent, *Cavaliers and Pioneers. Abstracts of Virginia Land Patents and Grants, 1623–1666.* (Baltimore: Genealogical Publishing Co., 1963), 170.
33   Jester, *Adventurers of Purse and Person*, 20.
34   *Virginia Magazine of History and Biography*, 3:363 (April 1896).
35   Nugent, *Cavaliers and Pioneers*, 90.

by 1625, according to the muster, he was twenty years old. He had apparently obtained his freedom, and was living in Charles City County, presumably on the land he had acquired as a result of his apprenticeship.[36] In 1638 he began a series of land acquisitions that by 1641 had made him a substantial landowner: one hundred acres along the Appomattox River for the transportation of his wife and daughter, thus indicating that he had returned to England for a time, and fifteen hundred acres in the same area acquired by assignment and purchase.[37] In England, with the same amount of land, he would have been regarded as a landowner of some consequence.

Although the transportation of vagrant children from London to Virginia does not appear to have had any great impact on the colony, its potential effect, if it had been put on a systematic and regular basis, could have been far-reaching. The colony was in desperate need of a cheap labor force, as the commander of the Dutch ship discovered when he brought the first cargo of Negro labor to Virginia in 1619. Sir Edwin Sandys and his colleagues in the Virginia Company were well aware of this need, and searched in all directions to provide a ready supply. Thus, in 1620, Sandys considered soliciting the justices of the peace throughout England to send to the Company "all such young youths of 15 years of age and upward as they shall find burdensome to the parish where they live."[38]

Why the Virginia Company failed to receive the active and continuing cooperation of the City of London, as well as other officials, in furthering its plans is not known. Certainly, the reason was not any lessening of the problem of vagrancy, or of poor relief, for these problems continued for centuries to come. Also the financial "burden" of transportation could not have been an

36   Jester, *Adventurers of Purse and Person*, 14.
37   Nugent, *Cavaliers and Pioneers*, 93, 94, 116, 128.
38   Kingsbury, *Records of the Virginia Company*, I, 411–412. Each child was to be accompanied by the sum of £5 "towards a far greater charge which the Company must be at for [the children's] apparel and transportation into Virginia."

important factor, because the cost of providing poor relief, as well as maintaining such institutions as Bridewell Hospital, was much greater than the cost of sending the children to the colony. Humanitarian considerations may have entered the picture, for there seems to have been a prevailing belief that being sent to Virginia was like being sentenced to death. However, conditions on board ship and in the colony itself could hardly have been worse, or more hazardous to life, than the conditions that existed in the streets and markets of London, or even in Bridewell Hospital. The only possible explanation for the failure of the Virginia Company's plan was the lack of interest in Virginia and its future. The same lack of interest had hampered the activities of the Company on numerous occasions before.[39]

Having lost the support of the City of London, the Virginia Company turned to the Parliament that met in 1621. On April 30, for example, when a bill for the relief of the poor was introduced in the House of Commons, Sir Edwin Sandys made an eloquent plea that "the poor that cannot be set on work may be sent to Virginia." "Never," he added, "was there a fairer gate opened to a nation to disburden itself nor better means by reason of the abundance of people to advance such a plantation."[40] According to Sandys' own report, the House responded to his speech "with a great and grateful applause." Sandys suggested to the Company that a bill should be drawn up, to be presented to the next session of Parliament, that "the poor may hereafter be sent to Virginia at the charge of the parish where they live." In November, a committee was appointed to draft the bill, but before the legislation could be prepared and introduced Parliament was dissolved.[41]

When Parliament met again, in 1624, the colony was about

39   The feuds that had developed in the Virginia Company might also have influenced the attitude of some officials in the government of London.
40   Wallace Notestein, Frances Helen Relf, & Hartley Simpson, eds., *Commons Debates 1621* (7 vols.; New Haven: Yale University Press, 1935), V, 113–114.
41   Kingsbury, *Records of the Virginia Company*, I, 479, 489, 555.

to pass from private to royal control, and the Company, faced with dissolution, was largely inactive. Under royal control the colony struggled on, still faced with the problem of finding an adequate labor force. At the same time the City of London continued to be plagued by the problem of vagrancy and delinquency in its streets. Virginia's loss may also have been London's loss.

ARTHUR P. KAUTZ

The Selection of Jacobean Bishops

One of the pathetic pieces of human flotsam tossed about in the religious tug of war of the early seventeenth century was Marco Antonio de Dominis, Archbishop of Spalato, in Dalmatia. Led to believe that honor and a good living would come from his transfer of allegiance to the English Church, de Dominis, "detesting the Romish tradition, quitted the prelacy,"[1] and late in 1616 fled to England. Burdened with a mixture of motives, by the beginning of 1618 the refugee was becoming discouraged; to one of his remaining friends, Sir Dudley Carleton, the Italian complained that despite glowing promises he was "like the sick man in the porch, who had none to throw him into the waters. Savoy Hospital was promised him, but Jacob supplanted Esau."[2] In 1622 this impotent Esau would pass from the cloudy English scene and return to a coldly suspicious Rome. But the problem the unfortunate man had raised in his letter to Carleton remained germane. In the reign of James I, how could a qualified ecclesiastic gain preferment to a bishopric?

ESAU, THE IMPOTENT

Although proposals to redistrict ecclesiastical England into as many as one hundred fifty sees had been made by reformers

1 PRO, *SP* 14/90/24.
2 *CSPD*, 1611–1618, 510. The Archbishop's allusions are to Genesis 27, 35–36, and John 5, 7.

since the beginning of Elizabeth's reign, at the accession of James I the Church of England, Wales, and the Isle of Man still consisted of twenty-one sees in the Archdiocese of Canterbury, and four sees in York. In the 1590's Archbishop Whitgift and Burghley had tried to refill the depleted episcopal bench, but the bishoprics of Oxford and Bristol, vacant since 1592 and 1593 to slake the financial needs of Queen Elizabeth and her favorite, the Earl of Essex, remained without bishops. In 1604 the Elizabethan Archbishop of Canterbury, John Whitgift, died; Matthew Hutton, the Archbishop of York, died two years later. By 1610 ten of the Elizabethan bishops inherited by James I would be dead, as would Thomas Ravis, a promising Jacobean bishop who died unexpectedly in 1609 at age forty-nine. Thus, the episcopal bench quite soon lost its Elizabethan character and became Jacobean in outlook.

Under the aggressive leadership of the new Archbishop of Canterbury, George Bancroft, Convocation in 1604 codified the canons of the Church. Building on these canons, Bancroft proceeded to reconstruct the English Church. But late in 1610, the year in which Secretary Salisbury's influence began to evaporate, Archbishop Bancroft died. To a far greater extent than heretofore the selection of prelates and the health of the Church lay in the hands of the middle-aged monarch from Scotland, King James I.

In ecclesiastical folklore James I generally is acclaimed for taking his theology seriously, and for being a faithful steward of the Church both in his selection of prelates and in his support of churchmen. Unlike Elizabeth, he did not systematically rob the Church of its patrimony; neither did he leave sees vacant, nor indulge in what had been proved lucrative business, multiple translations. Even when the jackals gathered after the accidental homicide by Archbishop Abbot in 1621, James I did not precipitate scandal by threatening to depose a prelate.

Many of Elizabeth's policies and restraints must be viewed in the context of the wars across the Channel. But with the accession of James I, "the various hand of Time began now to sheath the Sword of War, that had been long disputing the Controversy, which Religion and Policy (that Princes mix together) had for many years so fiercely maintained."[3] During the middle of the reign Europe itself was at relative peace, an unnatural peace before the decades of intensified fury starting in 1618.

Thirty-seven years old in 1603, and experienced in Scottish kingship, the King was eminently pleased with the English Church "as reformed by the Queen." With uncommon frequency he remarked that he would "maintain the Church as I found it." When death seemed at hand in the spring of 1619, the King settled his affairs and then gave instructions in kingship to his heir; "he gave him charge of religion, and of respecting the Bishops, as grave and wise men, and best companions for Princes."[4] There was no Machiavelli, nor Hobbes, found in him.

Like Queen Elizabeth, King James had been trained in theology. But where the wary and pragmatic *politique* Queen always remained the Supreme Governor, King James I identified himself with the prelates and churchmen. When Chaplain John Williams became Lord Keeper, and when Bishop Bilson almost became Lord Privy Seal in 1615, James I seemed to be not only advancing clericalism, but even reverting to pre-Reformation government by prelates. Bishop Williams may have served capably as Lord Keeper, and was much more the courtier-politician than the cleric, but the King stirred fears in the minds of men: "It appears that the King was bent on ruling in his own way, by proclamation, patents, etc., and would abet the clergy against the laity, and thus gradually alter the church."[5]

Despite his background and his vocal devotion to the Church as reformed by the Queen, at the outset the impetuous James I betrayed a lamentable ignorance of the Church. He instructed

3   Arthur Wilson, *History of Great Britain, being the Life and Reign of King James I* (London, 1653), 1.
4   PRO, *SP* 14/108/33.
5   *Ibid.*, 165/61.

the universities to set an example by restoring the impropriate tithes to the Church; the following day Archbishop Whitgift wrote an impassioned projection of the disastrous results of such an action.[6] At the Hampton Court Conference considerable confusion came from the King's complete ignorance of the Lambeth Articles and of the Book of Articles. His prodigal granting of livings repeatedly collided with property rights and legal claims. Shortly after coming from Scotland in 1603 the King promised the deanery of Durham to his Scottish favorite, Adam Newton, if he would remain with the court "so long as till the Archbishop of York were dead." Although Newton had posed as a priest while teaching in France, he was not in holy orders. In 1605, when the Archbishop of York died, Prince Henry reminded his royal father of the promise, and on September 27, 1606, without ever taking holy orders, Adam Newton was installed Dean of Durham. Fortunate were both King and Church in having watch, ward, and tutelage from Archbishop Bancroft and Secretary Salisbury until 1610.

THE SUPPLANTING JACOBS

Only death (there was no deprivation under King James I) created vacancies in the two archiepiscopal and the twenty-five episcopal sees. Hence among those running the race in the Jacobean age, the preoccupation with death seemed to be greater than among the most devout and otherworldly puritans — 1616 and 1621 were vintage years, for five and four episcopal deaths occured; completely frustrating was 1612, a year of death failure. In the North, Tobie Matthew, sixty years old when he became Archbishop of York in 1606, periodically amused himself by planting rumors of his own death; shivers of anticipation regularly spread through London and across the land. Eighty-two years old when he died in 1628, the Archbishop was one of the four Elizabethan prelates who survived into the reign of Charles I. Usually those elevated were not old men; at thirty-nine, John

6   *Ibid.*, 2/37-39.

Williams was the youngest, and only ten, or possibly eleven, of the forty men created prelates during the reign were over fifty-five. Part of the resentment against George Abbot came from the fact that he was only forty-nine when named Archbishop of Canterbury; he lived to a disappointingly ripe seventy-one years. Bishop Giles Thompson caused no such regrets; he was consecrated on June 9, 1611, and died less than a week later.

Vital statistics were at the root of the Archbishop of Spalato's problem of preferment. Since there were only thirty-nine deaths on the episcopal bench during the reign of King James I, and Bishop John Thornborough was translated from the Church in Ireland to one of the two vacant Elizabethan sees, only forty men could be elevated to bishop. All of the forty were either English or Welsh.

If we knew nothing about King James except his prelates, the forty men elevated and the six Elizabethan bishops translated would betray him to us, for they reflected his likes and interests. On the progress to Oxford in 1605, the King visited the Bodleian Library. To his guides he said: "Were I not a King I would be a University-man; and if it were so that I must be a prisoner, if I might have my wish, I would have no other prison than this library, and be chained together with these good authors."[7]

When the puritan representation at the Hampton Court Conference pleaded for an educated clergy, James unhesitatingly agreed with them. No one could fault the Jacobean bishops on their academic credentials. Almost without exception among both the inherited Elizabethan prelates and the Jacobean forty, the list of degrees reads B.A., M.A., B.D., D.D. Bishop Richard Neile had the four degrees from Cambridge University, yet he reportedly said he had never mastered Latin. He left no publications, but was reputed a good preacher. His natural endowment was sufficient cleverness to overcome the academic hurdles.

Neither could one fault either the inherited prelates or the forty on their aptness to teach. Only seven of the twenty-six in-

7   Nichols, *Progresses of James I*, I, 544.

herited prelates and nine (including Richard Neile) of the forty
Jacobeans seemingly were not involved in the academic life, and
Robert Wright resigned as the first Warden of Wadham College,
Oxford, within three months because of the celibacy whim of the
foundress. Otherwise the roster of bishops is a Late Elizabethan
and Early Stuart Who's Who of Lady Margaret and regius pro-
fessors of divinity, chancellors and vice-chancellors, masters and
fellows of Cambridge and Oxford during a period of theological
ferment.

The ferment engulfed much of Western civilization. Calvin-
ism, questioned at a small Netherlands university, moved into
an unpleasant hardening of creedalism. Independently, a similar
movement of thought was raising disturbances at Cambridge and
Oxford. On the Continent, Tridentine Roman Catholicism was
refining its position on church and state in the writings of Cardinal Bellarmine, and catching its Counter-Reformation breath
in the Hapsburg lands.

James I committed his energies to all three conflicts. For a
king who in his first parliament identified himself with peace,
and who prided himself late in his reign for the long peace; for
a king who stressed ecumenism far ahead of his times, this preoccupation with theological controversy was one of the strangest
aspects of a complex character. But it was that aspect which tied
together a number of elevations and translations on the Jacobean
episcopal bench.

The first phase, and as far as personal involvement was concerned, the briefest, was directed against nonconformity. But the
unexpected blandness of the puritan briefs at the Hampton
Court Conference caused the King to dismiss the controversy
from his personal attention and generally to delegate persuasion
and enforcement to the highly uneven administration of the prelates. The fact that Bishop Miles Smith seemed to be indifferent
to the enforcement of conformity was one of the complaints
which gave William Laud the opportunity to climb the first rung
of the episcopal ladder, to a deanery. George Abbot's Scottish mis-

sion, in which he succeeded in persuading the church leaders to conform somewhat to an episcopal system, helped him gain elevation to the bishopric of Coventry and Lichfield. In September, 1606, Bishop Barlow, Bishop Andrewes, Dean John King, and Dr. Buckeridge were the King's preachers at Hampton Court for the reduction of the two Melvilles, and other presbyterians of Scotland. Subsequently all four were rewarded with elevation or translation.

The relative royal quietude did not conceal the explosiveness of the nonconformity controversy. The depth of the King's hostility was made clear a year after his Hampton Court Conference outburst. On February 14, 1605, an unidentified writer reported to Bishop John Jegon of Norwich: [8]

On Saturday last, being the 9th of this present, there was a petition delivered to his Majesty by three or four knights of Northamptonshire, in the favor of the ministers which refuse subscription. Whereat his Majesty took a deep impression, as the next day, being Sunday, he sat eight hours in Council with the Lords. In this meeting he first most bitterly inveighed against the Puritans, saying that the revolt in the Low Countries, which had lasted ever since he was born, and whereof he never expected to see an end, began first a petition for matter of religion, and so did all the troubles in Scotland. That his mother and he, from their cradles, had been haunted by a Puritan devil, which he feared would not leave him to the grave; and that he would hazard his Crown but he would suppress those malicious spirits.

By the end of the reign the long arm of the prelates reaching into the Netherlands caused a shipload of frustrated puritans to sail for North America.

The second phase of Jacobean controversy burst into flame with the Gunpowder Plot and the new oath of allegiance, and was supported with popular apprehension after the assassination of Henry IV of France. When James I, whose training in writing was poor,[9] in this fray stirred the giant of Roman controversial-

8   *Ibid.*, IV, 1064.
9   David Harris Willson, "James I and His Literary Assistants," *Huntington Library Quarterly*, 8 (no. 1):35–37 (1944).

ists, Cardinal Bellarmine, the battle aroused the stubborn pride of the King. He called on his bishops, particularly Andrewes and Barlow, and his guests, the gentle, scholarly Isaac Casaubon or the renegade with inside information, Marco Antonio de Dominis, to help him with research and writing, or he assigned tasks of writing to them. From the beginning of the reign a high road to elevation and translation was participation in this controversy.

An able scholar and divine, Robert Abbot, in 1594 published the *Mirror of Popish Subtleties*, which immediately received favorable notices. In 1603 James made Abbot a royal chaplain in ordinary. The following year Abbot published *Antichristi Demonstratio*, which both Lancelot Andrewes and King James esteemed highly. Other publications brought academic preferments, partly through the good offices of Archbishop Bancroft. In December 1615, Archbishop George Abbot officiated at the consecration of his brother Robert as Bishop of Salisbury. Salisbury had the highest death rate of any see in the Jacobean period. Bishop Robert Abbot died in 1617, leaving a half-completed manuscript against the Arminians.

Even William Laud, of whom the gentlest of his critics would complain, "Today you are in the tents of the Romanists, tomorrow in ours,"[10] was drawn into the outer reaches of the fray. On April 23, 1622, King James I "sent for me, and set me into a course about the Countess of Buckingham, who about that time was wavering in point of religion."[11] William Laud's efforts gained him no translation from James, but the Bishop of impoverished and dilapidated St. David's did gain enormous influence with the Duke of Buckingham, and thus also with "the rising sun."

The anti-Roman Catholic conflict was still blazing when the news arrived in 1611 that Theologian Vorstius was to be named professor of divinity at the University of Leiden. As early as 1602

10   Statement by Joseph Hall quoted in Peter Heylyn, *Cyprianus Anglicus* (London, 1671), 50.

11   *The Autobiography of William Laud* (Oxford: J. H. Parker, 1839), 8.

(which, incidentally, was before the King met George Abbot), King James VI of Scotland had been angered by the liberalizing teachings of Vorstius on general grace. In 1611 the King let the United Provinces know that he would be displeased if Vorstius received the appointment. In January 1612, the King concentrated on a treatise against him which the following month was published in French, Latin, and English. Vorstius lost the position; he lived until 1622, "a troubled soul." In the fullness of time, the King was to interfere not only in the administrative and academic affairs of the foreign university, but to meddle in the domestic affairs of that foreign country, and to give the necessary impetus for the summoning of a synod at Dort to make creedal statements on grace and predestination for the Reformed Church.

It was not until 1617 that this area of controversy directly affected the selection of bishops. For years George Carleton had been seeking preferments in the Church. Although he had followed the usual rituals for an aspiring prelate, elevation eluded him. Then, on October 22, 1617, he reported to Sir Dudley Carleton that he had completed a treatise against Arminius, and had found the elusive key. Less than a month later he was nominated Bishop of Llandaff, although he was not consecrated until July 1618.

When the time came to name the English delegation to the Synod of Dort, the King chose Bishop George Carleton and Drs. John Davenant, professor of divinity at Cambridge, Samuel Ward, archdeacon of Taunton, and Joseph Hall, Dean of Worcester. In October they were busily preparing for the Synod, "though with poor allowance."

Upon their arrival in the Netherlands the delegation gratefully learned that the States were providing a public maintenance for them. Dean Hall fell ill and had to return to England; he was replaced by Thomas Goad, domestic chaplain to Archbishop George Abbot. Both Carleton and Davenant acquitted themselves ably at the Synod, aided perhaps by the fact that "all the religions are anxious about the Synod,"[12] "The Bishop of Winchester [Andrewes] asks tidings from the Synod,"[13] and the Archbishop of Spalato in the Italian Church in London prayed for the success of the Synod.[14] "Over they came into England; and first presented themselves to King James; who seeing them out of a window, when first entering the Court: Here comes, said he, my good mourners, — alluding to their black habit, and late death of Queen Anne."[15] Bishop Carleton that year was translated to Chichester. Two years later, in 1621, Dr. Davenant became Bishop of Salisbury. He broke the see's series of four deaths since 1615. Davenant, a moderate Calvinist, remained Bishop of Salisbury until his death in 1641. Dr. Samuel Ward in 1623 became Lady Margaret professor of divinity at Cambridge. In 1624 Dr. Joseph Hall, who had fallen ill at Dort, "with much humble deprecation, refused the see of Gloucester, earnestly offered to me."[16] Thomas Goad, the chaplain of the Calvinist Archbishop of Canterbury, had been converted to the minority Arminian position at Dort; "the giddy one" received no reward. Happy with the victory of Calvinist orthodoxy, King James in a conversation with Bishop Carleton remarked that "in truth those Remonstrants were Pelagians."[17] Just as happy, Archbishop Abbot wrote to Sir Dudley Carleton, whose chaplain John Hales also had been converted to Arminian moderation at Dort ("at the well pressing S. John iii. 16. by Episcopius — 'There I bid John Calvin good-night' "):[18]

You are not to wonder that your Arminians continue in their pertinacy, notwithstanding the Synod, for so did the Arians after the

12 PRO, SP 14/103/39.
13 Ibid., 103/45.
14 CSPD, 1611–1618, 598.
15 Thomas Fuller, Church History of Britain (12 books, separate pagination for each; London, 1655), Bk. 10, 84.
16 Joseph Hall, "Observations of Some Specialties of Divine Providence" in Works (London, 1788), xi. (Each tract has new pagination.)
17 PRO, SP 14/100/60.
18 John Hales, Golden Remains of the Ever Memorable Mr. John Hales, intro. by Anthony Farindon (London, 1675). No pagination.

greater Council of Nicaea. But a round and severe hand held by the magistrate will first disgrace them, then weary them, and in the end either reform them or remove them. But they must take heed that they do not slack the reins, for . . . it is not to be doubted but if those malignants may get the bit in their teeth, they will do as it now falleth out among the Grisons, so exasperated are they by being broken of their will; if the Prince persist with courage and assiduity.[19]

He wrote prophetically; under "the rising sun" William Laud would negate the victory of Dort in England with "a round and severe hand held by the magistrate."

Bishop Richard Neile did not become involved in any of the controversies, although he became a strict disciplinarian.

What influence did the selection of controversialists for elevation or translation have on the "resurgent clericalism" which Archbishop Whitgift inaugurated?[20] Immediately and directly, very little; indirectly, much indeed. Although to Sir John Harington, "in the Disputations at Hampton Court King James found him [Bancroft] both learned and stout, and took such a liking of him, that passing by the Bishops of Winchester [Bilson] and Durham [Matthew], both men of eminent learning and merits, he made choice of Bishop Bancroft for the filling of the then vacant See of Canterbury, as a man more exercised in affairs of state."[21] To the King "learned and stout" religious disputation became an act of state. Queen Elizabeth had regarded her prelates as "sole executants of the ecclesiastical supremacy."[22] King James's preoccupation with theological controversy tended to make the state clerical.

Sir Thomas Lake, the King's faithful secretary of the Latin tongue, in 1608 and 1609, when the King was engaged in the Bellarmine controversy, wrote letters to Salisbury that came as

19   PRO, *SP* 14/109/15.
20   Patrick Collinson, *The Elizabethan Puritan Movement* (London: Jonathan Cape, 1967), 256.
21   Quoted in John Le Neve, *Lives . . . of the Protestant Bishops of the Church of England* (London, 1720), 81.
22   Collinson, *Elizabethan Puritan Movement*, 284.

close to criticism of the King as a secretary might venture: "The King writes on this business from morning to night. . . . The churchmen will draw the King into writing, contrary to his intention of answering by some mean person, and in scorn only."[23] In the Jacobean age "resurgent clericalism" was not a clerical design; it was a royal abdication, a usurpation by royal invitation in the order of Edward the Confessor. Herein lay the danger of having prelates represented so strongly in the Council. Archbishop Abbot's role in the discussion and formulation of foreign policy would have been unthinkable in the previous reign. On September 23, 1616, Bishop Lancelot Andrewes was sworn to the Privy Council "to put him in heart upon the distaste he had in missing the Bishopric of Winchester."[24] Any report that the seat on the Council was given in lieu of an episcopal promotion constituted a danger to the state.

The reign of Elizabeth already demonstrated one of the strange fruits of controversy. At the request of the Queen, who at the time was debating giving aid to the Dutch rebels in their fight against Spain, Thomas Bilson wrote his *True Difference between Christian Subjection and Christian Religion* (1585). By giving "strange liberty in many cases, especially concerning religion, for subjects to cast off their obedience,"[25] Bilson's volume opened a Pandora's box of troubles, reaped especially by Charles I. Controversial seeds bore strange fruit. By crystallizing areas of difference, James and his bishops were responsible, along with Charles I and Laud, for the exodus to America; worse still, the Jacobean controversialists eliminated possible areas of compromise for the struggle in the next reign.

Blessed were the controversialists who gained the King's approval, for bishoprics came their way. With translators of the Bible it was not so. Among the forty-nine scholars who translated the Authorized Version, there were only seven future members

23   *CSPD*, 1603–1610, 472, 570.
24   PRO, *SP* 14/88/121.
25   Anthony à Wood, *Athenae Oxonienses* (London, 1721), I, col. 404.

of the episcopal bench. The puritans at Hampton Court had requested the translation. King James I, for his own reasons, and
over the objections of Bishop Bancroft, agreed that a new translation should be made. The selection of scholars cut across theological lines. For his sterling performance in translating and in
writing the introduction, Miles Smith in 1612 was rewarded with
a bishopric. A man of puritan sentiments ("there was scarce ever
a Church in England so ill governed"),[26] he is remembered particularly for his refusal to enter his cathedral after changes were
made in an injudicious manner by the newly appointed dean in
1616, William Laud.

Bishops who translated the Bible or the *Book of Common
Prayer* into Welsh or Manx received no royal reward for their
great efforts. William Morgan, Bishop at St. Asaph (1601–1604),
assisted by Bishop Vaughan, first translated the Bible into Welsh.
Richard Parry, Morgan's successor (1604–1623), revised the translation. Welshman John Philips, Bishop of Sodor and Man, in
1610 completed "The Mannish Book of Common Prayer by me
translated," but strong insularity against Welshmen prevented
its printing and acceptance.

"Sermon-tasting was as much the vice of the age as gin-drink-
ing was the vice of the next age."[27] James I, however, raised himself to connoisseur status. He would have agreed with John Chamberlain's criteria of a good sermon by John Donne: "he did
Queen Elizabeth right, and held himself close to the text without
flattering the time."[28] A striking sermon attracted the attention
of the King. Thus, a sermon at Newmarket in 1611 alerted the
King to John Williams. Although Laud had preached before the
King as early as 1609, by 1616 he had learned how to direct his
impact: "Dr. Laud preached, with great applause, from Miriam's
leprosy, as a warning against detractors against government."[29]

26 Heylyn, *Cyprianus Anglicus*, 63.
27 Geoffrey Soden, *Godfrey Goodman, Bishop of Gloucester, 1583–1656*
(London: published for the Church Historical Society by S.P.C.K., 1953), 79.
28 Nichols, *Progresses of James I*, III, 267.
29 *CSPD*, 1611–1618, 392.

It would seem, however, that an excellent preacher would have had a better chance of elevation during Elizabeth's reign. James appreciated and rewarded outstanding preachers, but in general, more than preaching was required for elevation or translation. John King was "the King of preachers," and in 1611 was elevated to the key bishopric of London, but he had also been a member of the episcopal delegation at Hampton Court in 1606. He was one of the King's chaplains. His sermons may have been a factor in his elevation, but it is unlikely that they were the sole or impelling reason.

The strange Robert Wright somehow became a bishop despite the fact that, according to Carleton, of a group of preachers in 1609, "Wright had the honor to do the worst."[30] Lancelot Andrewes, the King's favorite preacher, was almost an institution for Christmas and other festival sermons. He was also an outstanding scholar, controversialist, administrator, and the King's Almoner. The King greatly admired William Barlow as a preacher: in June, 1606, Barlow preached the funeral sermon for the royal infant Sophia. He was also a controversialist and courtier. Excellent sermons helped gain preferment, but were not a guarantee of elevation to a bishopric.

King James felt a very close attachment to the poet-preacher John Donne; the King took great pride in his campaign to get Donne to take holy orders. Although James promised advancement, it was not until 1621 that he named him Dean of St. Paul's (because Donne loved London).

Dr. Richard Field — rector of Burghclere, Hampshire, scholar, member of the episcopal party at the Hampton Court Conference, Dean of Gloucester — also earned the high esteem of the King as a preacher ("this is a Field for God to dwell in"). The renowned Field became chaplain in ordinary to the King, but the dearth of vacancies and prior importunities deprived the outstanding preacher of elevation. In 1616 he died. Saddened, the

---

30   Birch, *Court and Times of James I*, I, 91.

King murmured the timeless human lament: "I should have done more for that man."[31]

Many of the outstanding preachers became royal chaplains. In that and other court posts the courtier-cleric could remain before the King, the royal family, the Court, and the Council, waiting for the moment when the waters of the pool became troubled and preferment became available. But again, there was no certainty that a royal chaplain would be elevated.

Less than three-fifths of the forty men elevated and the six Elizabethans translated during the Jacobean period served as deans of cathedrals. Richard Neile recognized the importance of a deanery as a stepping-stone to elevation. Upon the death in 1608 of the Elizabethan Bishop John Still of Bath and Wells, Neile, Dean of Westminster, suggested a redeployment of deans worthy of a modern general staff.[32]

A deanery provided perhaps the finest training for a prospective prelate. Especially in the North of England the political experience provided an internship for prelates whose nonecclesiastical duties remained largely unchanged from medieval times. It was an organizational weakness of the Jacobean Church not to employ the deaneries more fully for episcopal interns. Pluralist Lord Keeper Williams exacerbated the weakness by clinging cunningly to the deanery of Westminster after his elevation to Bishop of Lincoln. In 1621 Laud was being considered for Westminster. So that he should retain his ideally located deanery, Lord Keeper–Bishop–Dean Williams joined forces with Buckingham to batter down the resistance of the King to the elevation of Laud as Bishop of St. David's. With profound misgivings for the peace of the Church, the King again surrendered to importunists.

Making a mockery of the office of dean was layman (and almost entirely absentee) Dean Adam Newton. He retained the

31 Wood, *Athenae Oxonienses*, II, col. 186.
32 *CSPD*, 1603–1610, 410.

deanery of Durham until 1620, when he sold the office to help pay for his new title of baronet.

Twenty-seven of the bishops had been deans. There should have been more, but the preferment machinery broke down, and the scramble for deaneries was fully as intense as that for bishoprics. To relieve the pressure, the Church needed more sees, an elimination of pluralism, or an ecclesiastical equivalent of the King's new rank of nobility, the baronetcy.

NO MAN TO PUT ME INTO THE POOL

"But Jacob supplanted Esau." The Jacobs who won the blessing of elevation and translation to bishoprics appeared, in general, to have qualification of sufficient maturity, education, teaching experience, scholarship, as well as interests and abilities which the King considered important. Whether they could fulfil the office of bishop was another question, and none could give the answer beforehand.

With his experience in Dalmatia, however, the Archbishop of Spalato would have realized that church preferment had, from about the time of the martyrdoms of Saints Peter and Paul, been an organizational problem. How can a large, widespread organization efficiently choose its officials and provide for an orderly succession? Far from resolving the problem, the Reformation had aggravated it. In Erastian England, Queen Elizabeth had quashed attempts to rationalize the procedure. Even with his proto-totalitarian orderliness, Archbishop Laud would find the problem too spongy for his imposed solutions.

What made the Jacobean age after 1610 distinctive was the deepening official disinterest in the problem. Attempts to find a solution increasingly fell into the instant oblivion of royal disinterest. It was the unpredictability of the Jacobean selection of bishops that made many feel like Spalato's sick man on the porch, waiting for someone to throw him into the troubled waters of the pool.

The king's assent made a bishop. How could a king know who the best candidates were? Here the Church had to bear the burden of the past. Salisbury's suggestion on January 24, 1605, that bishops ought to manage the appointments to church livings was rational (and resurgent clericalism), but it ignored historical property rights which continually plagued rational reform. Out of the welter of property rights that enveloped the Church, the system of patronage emerged. The greatest patron was the king himself. Salisbury as Secretary controlled great patronage, but the complex claims of office and property restricted the great patrons' room for maneuver. The Rev. Thomas Horne in 1615 wrote from Merton College that "the Bishop of London gave him little hope of advancement, being crowded with letters for livings from the King and Queen, and from noblemen."[33] The plaintive remark attributed to the French King Louis XV a century later could have been made by King James I: "If I were Lieutenant of Police, I would ban cabriolets."

The making of bishops was but one of the many royal functions. Hence, the records of the reigns of Elizabeth and James I have frequent instances of remembrancing time that such and such a person is to be advanced. Bishop Goodman, aware of the rising crescendo of complaints that bribes preceded elevation, was moved to protest that Buckingham's sole function in his elevation in 1625 was to remind King James of the promises made to the chaplain of the late Queen.

If the remembrancer failed to do his duty, a part of the machinery broke down; Jacob supplanted Esau. If the monarch failed to wait for the remembrancer, or ignored the message, another part of the machinery stopped functioning; "while I am coming, another steppeth before me." With the passage of years, the Jacobean machinery increasingly became erratic in operation. The King seemed indifferent to proved procedures of selecting bishops, and courtiers knew and exploited his weakness of listening to the last importunists.

33   *Ibid.*, 1611–1618, 301.

In dealing with the Jacobean Church, it is convenient to divide the reign into three periods, with 1610–1612 and 1619–1621 the critical years. In 1610 Archbishop Bancroft died, and Salisbury lost much of the King's confidence. In 1612 Prince Henry died, changing the present hopes for the future. Bancroft and Salisbury, enjoying the confidence of the King, had exercised somewhat selfless power and had kept the Tudor bureaucracy functioning as best they could. After 1610 the Tudor bureaucracy went into a swift decline, which also affected the Church. No Bancroft or Salisbury emerged in the confidence of the King to exercise selfless power. The pattern of selecting prelates was changed.

In the first period, 1603–1610, the letters of importunity went overwhelmingly into Salisbury's hands. Meanwhile, Archbishop Bancroft, not having forgotten his investigating craft, placed an agent in the royal court. The agent, the Cecils' protégé from boyhood, chaplain to Burghley and to Cecil, was Richard Neile.

In the beginning of the reign of King James (by the power and mediation of Archbishop Bancroft) he was made Clerk of the Closet to that King, that standing continually at his elbow, he might be ready to perform good offices to the Church and Churchmen. And he discharged his trust so well, that though he lost the love of some of the courtiers, who [were] too visibly inclined to the Puritan faction, yet he gained the favor of his master, by whom he was preferred to the Deanery of Westminster, and afterwards successively to the Bishoprics of Rochester, Lichfield, Lincoln, and Durham, one of the richest in the kingdom; which shows that there was in him something more than ordinary, which made that King so bountiful and gracious to him.[34]

The information which this clerical Villiers supplied to Archbishop Bancroft made it possible for the Bancroft-Salisbury team of royal servants to instruct their master and thus erase some of the King's original ignorance of Church and State, and, at times, to control the King's impetuosity. They could try to give direction to the elevation and translation of prelates. Early in this

34   Heylyn, *Cyprianus Anglicus*, 55.

period both Bancroft and Matthew, able, hard-working prelates, became archbishops.

From 1603 to the death of Archbishop Bancroft late in 1610, twenty-one other vacancies occurred. Besides Bancroft and Matthew, three Elizabethan bishops (Lloyd, Thornborough, and Vaughan) were translated. Five of the Jacobeans elevated (George Abbot, Andrewes, Barlow, Henry Parry, and Ravis) were translated once before Bancroft's death. Henry Parry had an excellent reputation in his sees; King James considered him one of the best preachers he had ever heard. The five bishops who were translated included a wide range of theological thought; they were notable men of their generation.

Three of the Jacobeans elevated (Harsnett, Montagu, and the court prelate, Neile) would be translated at least once before the end of the reign. Of the four men remaining, John Bridges, Bishop of Oxford, was a noted Anglican controversialist, writing against both the Romanists and the puritans. He had been on the episcopal delegation at the Hampton Court Conference. William James, Bishop of Durham, had a good reputation in his diocese and fulfiled the host of political duties of the bishopric to the satisfaction of the Council. Both Richard Parry, Bishop of St. Asaph, and John Philips, Bishop of Sodor and Man, were resident in their far-off sees, where they earned good reputations. The team of Archbishop Bancroft and Secretary Salisbury ought to receive high marks for their part in the selection of men for elevation.

After the death of Prince Henry in 1612, the King no longer had a number of favorites whose influence was diffused. The aging King was becoming inflexible, and was settling on a single favorite whose influence was not diffused, and, therefore, could play havoc with State and Church.

But in the remainder of the reign a perceptible change of degree or pace took place. Early in 1619 the Calvinist delegation returned from Dort with news of doctrinal victory. Two years earlier, on October 31, Chamberlain had written to Sir Dudley

Carleton that Bishop Andrewes had denied having written in favor of the Arminians. Andrewes, a scholar, had worked with Archbishop Whitgift in the revision of the Lambeth Articles.[35] He was a moderate, one who could regard a difference of opinion in academic terms, not in terms of orthodoxy and heresy. But with the Synod of Dort the lines of demarcation were to be drawn also in England: either one was a Calvinist or one was an Arminian. Perhaps the tensions of the widening European wars and the Protestant defeats hardened men's hearts. The Andrewes (1626) and Overall (1619) generation was passing away.

If one examines the health record of the King and the history of Buckingham, 1619–1621 emerges as a critical period. The years 1610–1612 to 1619–1621 might be called the high Jacobean age, those after 1619–1621, actually extending beyond the death of James to the assassination of Buckingham, might be called the twilight or decline of the Jacobean age.

A powerful ingredient of degeneration in the second of the Jacobean periods was the Essex divorce case. Archbishop Abbot's opposition to the divorce naturally modified his relations with the King for a time. More important was the effect of the Archbishop's opposition had on the reputation of the Church. The Archbishop may have saved the Church from great harm; the vilification heaped upon Bishop Bilson and his son, Sir "Nullity" Bilson, showed how strong and enduring the public disgust was. Most disastrous, but impossible to measure, was the pathological hostility the Archbishop aroused in Bishop Richard Neile. In 1614 Neile had the opportunity to strike back at the Archbishop through his brother Robert. The King intended conferring the Bishopric of Lincoln on his valued controversialist. To frustrate the elevation, Neile obtained Lincoln for himself. When Robert Abbot finally received Sarum in 1615, the King told him: "Abbot, I have had very much to do to make thee a bishop; but I know no reason for it, unless it were because thou writest against one [i.e.,

<hr />

35   H. C. Porter, *Reformation and Reaction at Tudor Cambridge* (Cambridge: University Press, 1958), 363–371.

Dr. Bishop, a Jesuit controversialist]."[36] Since the sycophant courtier Neile remained close to the King, one can only guess what he hissed into the royal ears about persons blackballed by the Durham House cabal.[37]

Arthur Wilson observed one of the tactics of the coarse Bishop Neile. King James I, perhaps about 1621, was smiling at an outrageously satirical sermon preached at Greenwich. "It seems Neile, Bishop of Lincoln was not by him then; for when any man preached that had the renown of piety (unwilling the King should hear him) he would in the sermontime entertain the King with a merry tale (that I may give it no worse title) which the King would after laugh at, and tell those near him he could not hear the preacher for the old B. Bishop."[38]

Although the Queen warned Archbishop Abbot that it was waging a Pyrrhic battle, he tried in 1614 to blunt or eliminate the overweening power of Somerset by bringing Villiers into the King's range of vision. The following year Somerset fell, and the rise of Villiers became spectacular. Since Somerset had been the pioneer mono-favorite, Villiers could profit from the mistakes and successes of his fallen predecessor. Sir Anthony Weldon, an unfriendly witness, but in this case supported by others, made this comparison of the two favorites:[39]

[Prince Henry] being dead, Somerset and that faction bear all down before them, disposing all offices, (yet Somerset never turned any out as did the succeeding favorite), but places being void, he disposed of them, and who would give most was the word; yet not by Somerset himself, but by his lady and her family, [the Howards], for he was naturally of a noble disposition and it may justly be said of any before, or ever will be said of any after him; — he never got suit for himself or friends that was burdensome to the commonwealth.

36   Fuller, *Church History*, Bk. 10, 72.

37   Heylyn, *Cyprianus Anglicus*, 55, 69. Gardiner, *History*, VII, 9.

38   Wilson, *History of Great Britain*, 152. Wilson writes of Neile as Bishop of Lincoln and Cranborne as Lord Treasurer, a confusion of titles and dates.

39   Sir Anthony Weldon, "The Court and Character of King James," Osborne, "Traditional Memoirs," in Scott, *Secret History*, I, 394.

The youthful Villiers had much homework to do before he could expect to exercise power efficiently and with confidence. But in 1616 he jumped into the area of making bishops. Having quickly dropped his "Father," Archbishop Abbot, the youth could have known very little about the problems of the Church. The presumptuous Villiers jumped, stumbled, and retreated in embarrassment.

The episode involved Dr. George Carleton, chaplain to Prince Charles. The Prince assisted Carleton in making a strong suit for the vacant bishopric of Carlisle. They appeared to be successful. "But his Majesty was so importuned by others that now it is gone another way."[40] John Chamberlain related what had gone wrong with Carleton's suit:[41]

. . . but I hear one Snowden, an obscure fellow, is come in at the window and shut him out. Dr. Bayly had better luck, who being both opposed and articled against by the Archbishop of Canterbury and others, yet hath carried the bishopric of Bangor and both by the same means of them that be now in favor; as likewise Sir Robert Naunton (who besides his mastership of requests and waiting in ordinary) hath gotten the Surveyorship of the Court of Wards from Sir Sidney Montague, who had the grant and handgiven earnest. But Sir Robert is of kindred to the new favorite, and so inward with his mother that he is termed her chancellor.

On January 4, 1617, Chamberlain reported how Buckingham tripped: "One Beaumont, an obscure prebend of Windsor, kinsman to my Lord Villiers, was in a fair way to be Bishop of Worcester, but the conferring of Carlisle and Bangor upon Snowden and Bayly, so unworthy men, was so generally distasted that he could not prevail."[42]

The older, experienced Buckingham would not be so clumsy. He learned how to exercise power with finesse. Again Sir Anthony Weldon[43] describes the disposal of offices:

40   PRO, *SP* 14/88/136.
41   *Ibid.*, 88/140.
42   *Ibid.*, 90/8.
43   Osborne, "Traditional Memoirs," in Scott, *Secret History*, I, 437.

Yet did not Buckingham do thing gratis, but what their purses could not stretch unto they paid in pensions out of their places, all which went to maintain his numerous beggarly kindred . . . so Fotherby made bishop of Sarum, paid £3,500, and some also, worthy men, were preferred gratis, to blow up their fames, and trumpet forth their nobleness, (as Townson, a worthy man, paid nothing in fine or pension; after him, Davenant, in the same bishopric;) but these were but music before every scene; nor were fines or pensions certain, but where men were rich, there fines without reservation of rent; where poor, and such as would serve turns, there pension, no fines; so Weston, and many others. There were books or rates on all the offices, bishoprics, deaneries in England, that could tell you what fines, what pensions; otherwise it had been impossible such a numerous kindred could have been maintained with the three kingdoms' revenue.

What made it possible for Buckingham to assume ever more power was the King's bad health and periods of indifference after 1619. On March 2, 1619, Queen Anne died. On April 10 King James was so near death that he gave his final instructions to Prince Charles. The King recovered, but from that time he was an old man. An acceleration of illnesses incapacitated him frequently. In January 1622 he fell from his horse headfirst into the frozen New River. At times he gave the impression that he was surrendering to life's battle. In the words of John Hacket: "It is certain that all grants at the Court went with the current of my Lord Duke's favor. None had the power to oppose it, nor the King the will. For he ruled all his Majesty's designs: I may not say his affections. Yet the Lord Keeper [Williams] declined him sometimes in the dispatches of his office, upon great and just cause. Whereupon the King would say in his pleasant manner: that he was a stout man that durst do more than himself.[44]

Upon Archbishop Bancroft's death, the King decided to select the successor himself. According to Heylyn, the Court bishops conferred, decided that neither Montagu nor Abbot would do, chose Andrewes, and then went to the King. "The motion was no sooner made, but it was embraced, and they departed from the

44   John Hacket, *Scrinia Reserata* (London, 1693), 207.

King with as good assurance as if the business had been done, and Andrewes fully settled in the throne of Canterbury."[45] But while they slept, the Earl of Dunbar approached the King and spoke in favor of George Abbot. When Dunbar died, King James decided on Abbot in memory of his late good friend. Thus the Church of England got an "unwanted Archbishop."

Heylyn's apology does not ring true. How could the Court bishops, particularly Neile, so completely ignore the King's propensity for listening to the last importunist? It is incredible that the Court bishops should have been absent from the Court at a critical time for so long. Bancroft died November 20, 1610. Sir Thomas Lake the following February 25 said that the King had decided on Abbot. The formal nomination was made on March 4, and the installation took place April 9. It was not a selection made in haste.

Was Abbot unwanted? On February 12, 1610, George Abbot was enthroned as Bishop of London. On October 28, 1609, just a few days before his death, Archbishop Bancroft had his last will and testament witnessed. The penultimate clause reads: "And touching my Lord of London, if it should not please God and his Majesty, that he may succeed me in the Archbishopric, then I give and bequeath unto him for his said pains the sum of one hundred marks to bestow in plate at his pleasure in remembrance of me his faithful friend."[46]

No episcopal election of the Jacobean age has raised so many unanswered questions as King James's choice of George Abbot as Archbishop of Canterbury. The King left no diary or memoranda explaining why he chose any prelate; when he made any statements, he clouded them in Delphic obscurity. Since the Interregnum, George Abbot has had a negative press and reputation, for there is a comfortable logic in reading history backward from effect to cause. The life and character of George Abbot made him a natural scapegoat for the sins of many. Abbot lacked a

45 Heylyn, *Cyprianus Anglicus*, 59.
46 Babbage, *Puritanism and Richard Bancroft*, 389.

charming or pleasing personality. Burdened with the memory of an accidental homicide, his painful and forbidding bruskness toward importunists increased. The Calvinist theology which he and his King tried to defend had little emotional or aesthetic appeal to the increasingly secular generations which followed the religious convulsions of mid-seventeenth-century England. Abbot had the thankless lot of a seventeenth-century Wolsey, defending an international theology before a court and people moving toward a national theology. So far, the scapegoat of the Caroline Church, Archbishop Abbot, has defied a definitive biography.

The King chose him to be Archbishop of Canterbury during a period in which old forms were passing and the new forms were still unclear. The King also chose Abbot's successor at London, John King, and most of the men elevated and translated in the period 1611–1619. The bishops represented the full range of theological thought on grace, Calvinist and Arminian. Two Elizabethan bishops were translated, as were three Jacobean bishops. The majority of the King's nominees built good reputations in their sees. But Bishop Miles Smith, who received Gloucester as a reward for his work on the Authorized Version of the Bible, let the cathedral fall into decay and was an outspoken opponent of ceremonies. George Montaigne, a wit and an early Laudian, would be characterized by Charles I as "a man unactive," but James thought him an amusing courtier.

It is the Buckingham nominees who mar the roster. Bayly was in trouble with Church and State when he was nominated. He was a contentious Calvinist, and he remained faithful to his contentions. Snowden, an "obscure fellow," Bishop of Carlisle from 1616 to his death in 1621, remained obscure, not even being listed in the *Dictionary of National Biography*.

From late 1619 to the momentous March 27, 1625, when his "Lords and Servants kneeling on the one side, his Archbishops, Bishops, and other of his Chaplains on the other side of his bed, without any pangs or convulsion at all, 'dormivit Salomon' Solomon slept!"[47] no Elizabethan prelates were translated, but Bishops Carleton and Felton, both moderate Calvinists, and Harsnett, Milbourne, and Montaigne, all anti-Calvinists, were translated to more important sees. James rewarded John Davenant for his work at the Synod of Dort by bestowing Sarum on him. Another factor in that election was the widow and large family of Davenant's predecessor and brother-in-law, Bishop Robert Townson. Godfrey Goodman, friend of the King, of Andrewes, Vaughan, and Williams, but unable to penetrate the coldness of Laud, has been rehabilitated in a sympathetic biography by Geoffrey Soden. John Williams received the bishopric of Lincoln to give him noble status for his position as Lord Keeper. A Richelieu to King James, he was Lord Keeper first, Dean of Westminster second, and Bishop of Lincoln last. He went into partial eclipse after the rise of Laud, who regarded Williams as a rival. Montaigne and Milbourne were Court bishops and, with Neile, pleased the King.

Buckingham and his mother now were supreme. An opportunist and his nouveau riche mother, who for a time used the increasingly fashionable Court Romanism as an attention-getting device, determined the fate, whether as remembrancer or broker, or both, of candidates for high holy offices, "to put me into the pool" or "another steppeth before me." The Spanish Ambassador, Gondomar, duly reported to the Spanish Court: "There was never more hope of England's conversion to Rome than now: for there are more prayers and oblations offered here to the Mother, than to the Son."[48]

Three of the men elevated in the 1620's were definitely Buckingham's candidates. Valentine Carey was "a prudent courtly man" according to Hacket; his high churchmanship in Scotland in 1617 provoked a storm. Theophilus Field ranks lowest among the Jacobean bishops. Impeached by the House of Commons in 1621 for brokage and bribery, he was Buckingham's great dis-

47 Nichols, *Progresses of James I*, IV, 1031.
48 Wilson, *History of Great Britain*, 149.

service to the Church. William Laud, who became Buckingham's agent in the Court during the Spanish adventure, was elevated Bishop of St. David's against the better judgment of King James, who felt that both Laud and the Archbishop of Spalato were radicals who compulsively changed things that were working.

Three of the men elevated during this period left small marks. Robert Townson died within ten months of his consecration. Robert Wright both milked and improved his sees. Rowland Searchfield left an indifferent record in his forty-three months as Bishop of Bristol.

The difference in the quality of men chosen for the office of bishop in the periods before and after 1610 as well as before and after 1619 is actually quite unremarkable. Even when the Buckingham influence was supreme, either fate, or the good sense of King James, made the policy of personal selection of bishops succeed quite well. With Neile, Buckingham, and his mother trying to influence the King, there might have been ten Theophilus Fields instead of one. It was not in the textbook qualifications of the episcopal bench, but in the flaccid government and court that the danger lay. If the episcopal government also became flaccid, and if the theological differences on the episcopal bench became critical, forces other than the selection were at work.

There was variety in the selection process and in the men who were pushed into the pool at the moment the waters were troubled. Among the forty men elevated and the twenty-four bishops translated, there were some who were chosen for the Church's highest positions for reasons not related to the Church; some were chosen in the line of least resistance; too many were chosen without regard to the bitter antagonisms and personality collisions among them; some were chosen with care; some, indeed, because they gave indication that they were worthy risks for the high office of bishop in the apostolic tradition.

It was not in the selection of the bishops that the danger lay. In any age the organized church reflects the society in which it exists. The Jacobean government was lax; so was the episcopal government under Abbot. In a century of revolution the first of the Stuart kings could not have guessed that his was the role of an interim pope. Nor could the Bishop of Lincoln on March 27, 1625, have known that once more after *dormivit Salomon!* the kingdom would become divided.

The Election to the Short Parliament, 1640

The elections for Parliament have been very tumultuary" wrote Sir Francis Windebank in late March 1640. How right he was. Perhaps in no previous seventeenth-century election had such bitterness been displayed, so many "sidings and faction" prevalent.[1] The elections mirrored England's condition. Charles I's government was under extraordinary pressure: the Scots had rebelled, ship money was uncollectible, religion was a burning issue, Charles's personal rule was collapsing. The country was moving toward that bitter division, for or against the court, that was but a few years away.

Historians have said very little about early seventeenth-century parliamentary elections. Unlike those of the Elizabethan era or the eighteenth century, no effort has been made to portray the early Stuart period's election practices. Clientage dominated the Elizabethan political scene; it was the key to parliamentary elections. Personal prestige was the motivation of Elizabethan clientage.[2] In the eighteenth century, clientage had been replaced by connection; furthermore, election patronage had a substantial political purpose. The expense of election had risen enormously.[3]

1   Windebank to Hopton, March 27, 1640, *Calendar of the Clarendon State Papers*, eds. O. Ogle, W. H. Bliss, & C. H. Firth (4 vols.; Oxford: University Press, 1872–1938), I, 196; Holland to Gawdy, November 1640, HMC, *Gawdy* MSS, 176.

2   Neale, *Elizabethan House of Commons*, 24–27, 152.

3   Robert Walcott, *English Politics in the Early Eighteenth Century* (Oxford: University Press, 1956), 36, 45, 68–69. L. B. Namier & John Brooke, *The His-*

Bribery, too, was playing a more significant role in determining the outcome of particular elections.[4] These changes did not occur overnight; their development demands a look at an Early Stuart election. Perhaps the spring election of 1640 can illuminate some of the changing themes of the election story.

Students of the crisis years of the late 1630's and early 1640's have focused their attention on the issues that divided Charles from many of his subjects. Ship money, religion, the grievances that the Long Parliament attempted to rectify, appear as "national" issues. Yet the question still remains, Just how significant were these allegedly dominant grievances in the spring election? Had these issues begun to play an important role or have historians, trapped by their knowledge of the impending political and social crisis, made these questions larger than life? Were the elections still nothing more than the traditional struggle among local interests, patronage, and influence? Was an Englishman's conscience a significant election factor? Or was his concern for political or social prestige in county or borough still the major motive in his struggle for a parliamentary seat? The spring election can suggest some answers, since more information has probably survived about it than for any of the Early Stuart elections preceding it.[5] Of the 233 elections, excluding Wales and Monmouth, evidence has survived for 83, or 35.6 per cent. Not only do the 83 elections provide a basis for some tentative conclusions about the role of "national" issues, but they can also serve to answer other questions as well. The court's election efforts can be analyzed, and the methods of securing election victory can be suggested. The significance of aristocratic patronage can be scru-

tory of Parliament, The House of Commons, 1754–1790 (3 vols.; Oxford: University Press, 1964), I, 4–5.

4   Lawrence Stone, "The Electoral Influence of the Second Earl of Salisbury," EHR, 71:384 (1956).

5   My own research has thus far turned up substantial amounts of material for the spring 1640 election and two of James's elections, those for the Parliaments of 1621 and 1624. The 1626 elections show a fair amount of material but less than the spring Parliament.

tinized. The most vexing problem, that of the "country" or "opposition" group's efforts, may also be tentatively explored.

Thomas Wentworth, Earl of Strafford, was most responsible for Parliament's summons. His influence prevailed first with the Privy Council and then, by December 6, 1639, with the King.[6] The news that Parliament would meet sparked an outburst of election activity. Sir Edward Nicholas, clerk to the Privy Council and a court candidate, wrote "there is very much laboring by divers to be parliament men." Others commented in a similar vein.[7] The reappearance of Parliament after an absence of almost twelve years was to occasion one of the most contentious elections of the Early Stuart period.

Within twenty-four hours of the decision to summon Parliament, the first letters of recommendation for the election had been sent by the court.[8] This was not a new practice. Thomas Cromwell had acted as Henry VIII's selection agent, and Mary Tudor had attempted to secure satisfactory election results. Elizabeth I found it unnecessary to attempt systematically to influence elections.[9] The reigns of James I and Charles I differed sharply from Elizabeth's reign; the Crown was an increasingly active election agent.[10]

The court enjoyed a potentially clear advantage in an election. The Council of the North, the Council of the Marches of

6   *The Works of Archbishop William Laud*, eds. W. Scott & J. Bliss (7 vols.; Oxford: Library of Anglo-Catholic Theology, 1847–1860), III, 233, 282–283. Wentworth to Radcliffe, T. D. Whitaker, *The Life and Original Correspondence of Sir George Radcliffe* (London, 1810). Windebank to Hopton, December 13, 1639, *Clarendon State Papers*, ed. R. Scrope & T. Monkhouse (3 vols.; Oxford, 1761–1786), II, 81–82. King to the Lords of the Council, December 6, 1639, PRO, *SP* 16/435/37. Vane to Rose, February 21, 1640, *ibid.*, 446/3.

7   Nicholas to Pennington, December 12, 1639, *ibid.*, 435/64. Poley to D'Ewes, 1640, BM, *Harleian* MSS, 383, fol. 144, BM, *Add.* MSS, 35, 331, fol. 74ᵛ.

8   Suffolk to the Mayor and Jurats of Sandwich, December 7, 1639, Kent Record Office [hereafter KRO], *Sandwich Letter Book*, Sa/C 1, fol. 8. Suffolk to the Mayor and Jurats of Rye, December 7, 1639, East Sussex Record Office [hereafter ESRO], *Rye Corp.* MSS, 47/131, 39:2.

9   Neale, *Elizabethan House of Commons*, 283–293, 298, 300.

10   Willson, *Privy Councillors in House of Commons*, 104–107, 134, 142–143, 200–204.

Wales, the Duchies of Lancaster and Cornwall, were all capable of exercising significant election patronage. Queen Henrietta Maria's property holdings gave her election influence. The Prince of Wales's Council, and various royal officials such as the Lord Warden of the Cinque Ports could also exert considerable election patronage. The Lord Warden usually returned at least one candidate from each of the Cinque Ports. Churchmen like William Laud, Archbishop of Canterbury, and Richard Neile, Archbishop of York, or courtier noblemen like Edward Sackville, Earl of Dorset, or Jerome Weston, Earl of Portland, could employ their election credit in behalf of the Crown. The universities, too, provided parliamentary seats for royal servants.[11]

But court patronage was declining. Unlike the ambitious Duchy of Cornwall, which nominated sixteen candidates in the spring election, an increase of two over its attempt in 1624, other crown agencies or offices found their influence much reduced by the spring of 1640. The Prince's Council, acting outside the Cornish boroughs, tried to place two candidates that can be identified, a sharp contraction from its effort in 1624 when its letters of recommendation had been sent to at least twelve cities and boroughs.[12] The diminution of crown influence was further reflected in the election records of other crown agencies. Aldborough, Beverley, Knaresborough, and York were far more receptive to the Council of the North in the 1620's than in 1640. By the spring, only York was amenable to its influence.[13]

Two other royal agencies, the Duchy of Lancaster and the Council of the Marches of Wales, also showed the alarming decline of the court's election patronage. Professor Neale has al-

11   M. B. Rex, *University Representation in England, 1604–1690* (London: Allen & Unwin, 1954), 130–131.

12   Duchy of Cornwall Record Office, "Burgesses for Parliament, 1623–1624," fols. 33–40.

13   Aldborough returned Council officials in 1604 and 1621, Beverley in 1621 and 1624, and York City in 1624, 1625, 1626, and 1628. Knaresborough is doubtful, for the Slingsby family enjoyed substantial influence in the borough although members of the family served in the Council of the North.

lowed the Duchy of Lancaster considerable influence within the six boroughs of Lancashire and suggested that some twelve other boroughs or cities were also possibly part of its election network, although the consistency of its success in those outlying places varied greatly.[14] By 1640, the number of potential Duchy boroughs had fallen to eight; local influence usually predominated in all the other places where the Duchy had but a tenuous interest in the Elizabethan period. The story for the Council of the Marches of Wales was similar: it had far greater success early in the century at Ludlow, Leominster, and the other four boroughs of its election base than it was to enjoy in 1640.[15]

The Queen's election influence was also potentially substantial. Including Cambridge University, where her chancellor, Sir John Lambe, was a candidate in the spring election, she could

	Potential	Actual
Duchy of Cornwall	16	16
Duchy of Lancaster	19	8
Council of the North	5	1
Council of the Marches of Wales	8	2
Prince's Council	12	2
Queen's Council	11	11
Lord Warden of the Cinque Ports	7	7
Total	78	47

attempt nominations in at least eleven places. In addition, the Crown could also count on the successful influence of the Lord Warden, who could usually return at least seven court nominees. The accompanying tabulation shows the Crown's foundation of election power and its actual spring 1640 effort.

The Duchy of Lancaster's potential is based on its sixteenth-

14   Neale, *Elizabethan House of Commons*, 224–228.
15   The Council of the Marches of Wales enjoyed election success at Ludlow in 1614, 1621, 1625, 1626, and 1628, and Leominster returned Council officials five times in the 1620's. Council members served for Shropshire in 1604, 1614, 1621, and 1626, but this was more the result of their local influence within the county than their service with the Council. It also enjoyed varying degrees of success at Droitwich and Bewdley earlier in the century.

century influence, and the total for the Prince's Council is judged by its efforts in 1624. The decline in the ability of the court agencies is clear; instead of a possible 78 nominations, there were only 47.

The election potential must also be estimated of those who may be loosely called the "country" or "opposition" group, those anxious for reforms in the king's government. Although this group cannot be described in a precise way, its existence seems clear. Its basis was in its parliamentary opposition to Stuart religious, foreign, and financial policies. Between 1621 and 1628, it focused its energies on the great favorite, Buckingham, and won its major victory when the reluctant Charles I adopted the Petition of Right in 1628. Although it was hardly an organized opposition movement by 1629, it had developed a community of interest and outlook which gave a foundation for future activity.

In the increasingly tense months of 1639 and 1640, the sympathies of this faction became more obvious, as Bulstrode Whitelock noted when he wrote "there was a strange spirit of disunion in the opinions and wishes of most men in these affairs, too many not only favoring but joining with and assisting the proceedings of the Scots Covenanters." [16] Although this comment was made in the late spring of 1640, the development of a "reform" group had been noted earlier. Unfortunately for the historian, the evidence remains elusive (perhaps it was destroyed) but, in late 1636 the group's activities were reported by the Venetian ambassador, who claimed that "many of the leading men of the realm" were urging the summons of a Parliament to correct the alleged abuses of royal government. Two noblemen, Henry Danvers, Earl of Danby, and Robert Rich, Earl of Warwick, openly expressed this view to the King. Secret meetings were supposedly taking place, possibly at Sir William Lytton's home in Hertfordshire, at

16   Whitelock's Annals, BM, *Add.* MSS, 37, 343, fols. 199, 206. Temple to the Earl of Leicester, December 4, 1638, February 7, 1639, Earl of Northumberland to the Earl of Leicester, October 10, 1639, December 12, 1639, Collins, *Letters and Memorials*, II, 579, 592, 612–613.

Broughton Castle, the residence of Viscount Saye and Sele, or at the Knightley home at Fawsley, Northamptonshire. After the Scots revolt broke out, there were numerous rumors of collusion between them and those Englishmen who sympathized with their cause; certainly their goals were very similar.[17]

The Providence Island and Massachusetts companies became the organizational centers of the reform group; the Artillery Garden served as headquarters of their activity in London. The centers were but outward manifestations of the group's most powerful weapon: its network of blood and marriage ties augmented by common religious views.[18] These relationships were as significant in their potential election influences as anything the Crown could muster through the various court agencies.

These reformers also employed another effective election weapon — the powerful propaganda capability of puritan ministers. London was a veritable hotbed of their activity. In the spring campaign the puritan pulpit rang with pious exhortations urging the faithful to vote for appropriate candidates. The ties between the puritan clergy and the leaders of the reform group — Viscount Saye and Sele, the Earl of Warwick, or Robert Lord Brooke — were clear. Both Warwick and Brooke provided refuge for any puritan lecturer who might win Laud's attention because of his zealous religious views.[19]

Before assessing the election influence of the "reform" peers, the electoral patronage of the peerage itself should be deter-

17 *CSPV*, 1636–1639, XXIV, 99, 110–111, 119, 121, 124–125, 136, 387, 418, 457, 506, 535–536, 558–559, 563; 1640–1642, XXV, 35. *Persecuto Undecima* (London, 1648), 28–29. Alfred Kingston, *Hertfordshire during the Great Civil War* (London: E. Stock, 1894), 28. Anthony à Wood, *Athenae Oxonienses*, ed. Philip Bliss (4 vols.; London, 1813–1820), III, 546–547.

18 A. P. Newton, *The Colonizing Activities of the English Puritans* (New Haven: Yale University Press, 1914), 60–61, 65–67, 69–70, 127–128, 240–247. Hexter, *Reign of King Pym*, 77–88. Valerie Pearl, *London and the Outbreak of the Puritan Revolution* (London: Oxford University Press, 1961), 160–168, 170–173. *Persecuto Undecima*, 28–29. Samuel Butler, "A Letter from Mercurius Civicus to Mercurius Rusticus" (1643), Somers, *Tracts*, IV, 580–598.

19 Pearl, *London and the Puritan Revolution*, 160–164, 165, 168.

mined. The list which follows suggests their possible election influence. The political loyalty of the peerage is also indicated, although such loyalties are most vexatious to define. Lord Montagu of Boughton was considered by Parliament's supporters to be a royalist; he died while imprisoned in the Tower for his alleged sympathies. Yet his candidates in Northamptonshire and Huntingdonshire can all be considered either moderate reformers or men of a fully puritan persuasion. Court or reform allegiances are noted; the absence of identification indicates that the loyalty of a particular peer is unclear.

	Actual Nomination	*Possible Influence*
Lord Barrett of Newburgh, court		Andover
Bertie, Earl of Lindsey, court .	Berwick	Lincoln and Lincolnshire
Calvert, Lord Baltimore, court	Christchurch	
Cavendish, Earl of Devonshire, court	Leicester	
Cecil, Earl of Exeter, court . .		Stamford and Peterborough
Cecil, Earl of Salisbury		Hertfordshire, Hertford, and Old Sarum
Clifford, Baron, court	Carlisle	Appleby and Westmorland
Compton, Earl of Northampton, court		Warwickshire and Warwick
Cottington, Baron, court . . .	Berkshire and Hindon	Woodstock
Coventry, Baron, court	Coventry	Tewkesbury and Gloucester
Cranfield, Earl of Middlesex .	Tewkesbury	
Devereux, Earl of Essex, reform		Lichfield, Tamworth, and Newcastle-under-Lyme

	Actual Nomination	Possible Influence
Fiennes, Baron Saye and Sele, reform		Oxfordshire and Banbury
Finch, Baron Finch of Fordwich, court	Sandwich, Cambridge City, and Winchelsea	
Goring, Baron, court	Lewes	
Greville, Baron Brooke, reform		Warwickshire and Warwick
Hastings, Earl of Huntingdon, court	Leicestershire and Leicester	
Herbert, Earl of Pembroke and Montgomery	Gloucestershire, Kent, and Canterbury	Old Sarum, Shaftesbury, Wilton, Salisbury, Wiltshire, and Downton
Howard, Earl of Arundel, court	Christchurch and King's Lynn	Canterbury, Aldeburgh, Castle Rising, Norfolk, and Arundel
Howard, Earl of Berkshire, court		Oxford
Howard, Earl of Suffolk, court	Dorchester	Reigate
Montagu, Baron, of Boughton		Huntingdonshire, Huntingdon, Northamptonshire, and Northampton
Blount, Earl of Newport, court		Shrewsbury
Percy, Earl of Northumberland, court	Christchurch,	Berwick,

	Actual Nomination	Possible Influence
Percy, Earl of Northumberland, court, *continued*	Dover, Rye, Sandwich, Hull, Great Yarmouth, and Scarborough	Northumberland, Portsmouth, Yarmouth (Isle of Wight), and Chichester
Pierrepont, Earl of Kingston-upon-Hull		Shropshire
Rich, Earl of Holland, court .	Windsor and Reading	Cambridge University
Rich, Earl of Warwick, reform	Essex	Colchester, Harwich, Maldon, and Beeralston
Russell, Earl of Bedford, reform		Tavistock and Totnes
Sackville, Earl of Dorset, court	Rye, Lewes, East Grinstead, Bramber, Kent, and Great Yarmouth	
Savile, Viscount	Southwark	Yorkshire
Seymour, Earl of Hertford, reform		Milborne Port, Great Bedwyn, and Marlborough
Stanley, Earl of Derby, court		Lancashire
Stuart, Duke of Lennox, court	Southampton	
Wentworth, Earl of Cleveland		Bedfordshire
Wentworth, Earl of Strafford, court	Boroughbridge, Carlisle, and Scarborough	Pontefract, York, Morpeth, Richmond, Berwick, and Yorkshire
Weston, Earl of Portland, court	Southampton	Newport, Isle of

	Actual Nomination	*Possible Influence*
Weston, Earl of Portland, court, *continued*	and Newton, Isle of Wight	Wight
Laud, Archbishop of Canterbury, court	Canterbury, and Reading	Oxford University
Neile, Archbishop of York, court		Ripon
Piers, Bishop of Bath and Wells, court	Wells	

The peerage and its counterparts of the church made, on surviving direct evidence, 46 nominations. In 68 additional elections, it is probable that they were active participants either because of the candidates involved or their local influence. It appears that they nominated some 128 men in 114 elections. This figure includes Lord Baltimore's 5 nominees at Christchurch as well as other nominations made in behalf of the same men at different boroughs. The total nominated does not include those of Spencer Compton, Earl of Northampton, in the Warwickshire contests since the number of men he nominated is unknown.

The influence of the peerage was still a significant factor in the spring election. Of 233 elections held, excluding Monmouth and Wales, the nobility played a role in 114, almost half — a surprising total in view of the argument that their influence was steadily declining in the early seventeenth century.[20] These figures include duplication where two or more noblemen intervened in the same election. Even with those omitted, the amount of noble patronage attempted was substantial, for 94 of the 233 elections attracted the attention of a member of the peerage (40 per cent). Noblemen made 128 nominations and, of those, 123 were active candidates. Of the 123 nominees, 90 secured election or approximately three-fourths, an impressive record. If noble influence was declining, their efforts in the spring election were

20   Stone, *Crisis of the Aristocracy*, 258–263.

very significant: their activity and success were a major factor in the spring election campaign.

Although assessing political loyalties is difficult, if not impossible, an evaluation of the election influence of the courtier nobles (25 peers and churchmen) and of the reform group (7 peers) has been attempted in the accompanying tabulation.

	Reform Group	Court Group
Actual nomination	1	35
Possible nomination	19	40
Total	20	75

The reform peers successfully nominated all of their 24 candidates; the courtier nobility nominated 82, and returned 49 of 78 active candidates. The court enjoyed an obvious advantage through aristocratic patronage. The reform aristocracy was outnumbered by a little better than three to one, both in its membership and its nominations.

This should have given the court a very decided advantage. The following tabulation tentatively indicates the political loyalties of those nominated by the two groups who won or lost an election. Those designated royalists were men who remained

	Reform Group	Court Group
Total nominations	24	78
Royalists		
Won	1	30
Lost	0	21
Moderates		
Won	3	10
Lost	0	1
Reformers		
Won	19	3
Lost	0	2
Unknown		
Won	1	6
Lost	0	5

loyal to the Crown throughout the Civil War. A moderate was one who, though he managed to remain in Parliament following the Grand Remonstrance of 1642, found himself increasingly out of sympathy with the parliamentary cause and by 1644 had either joined the King or retired from politics. The reform group includes those who steadfastly supported Parliament. The last category, unknown, includes the men who cannot be placed within the three categories.

The cohesion and unity of purpose of the reform group was very evident; all 24 of their nominees won, and 19 of these were of strong reform sympathies. The courtier nobility, lacking the unity and purposefulness of the reformers, returned 49 of their nominees, only 30 of whom were clearly royalists, and lost 29 seats. The stronger ties of family and marital connections, of similar religious views, joint economic interests, and, most important, the strong and distinct sense of purpose and principle that bound the reformers into a tightly disciplined group showed its mettle in their election efforts. Even though such a group may be difficult to define, the work of its noble wing was both visible and successful in the spring election.

THE COURT AND THE ELECTION

The Court's election efforts were both prompt and intense. The Lord Warden of the Cinque Ports, Theophilus Howard, Earl of Suffolk, dispatched letters to the Ports on December 7, reserving his right to nominate one candidate at each port.[21] Algernon Percy, Earl of Northumberland and Lord High Admiral, was not far behind. By December 10, his letters, stressing his election patronage as Lord Admiral, reached Great Yarmouth, Scarborough, Dover, Hull, and Christchurch.[22]

21   Suffolk to the Mayor and Jurats of Sandwich, December 7, 1639, KRO, *Sandwich Letter Book*, Sa/C 1, fol. 8. Suffolk to the Mayor and Jurats of Rye, December 7, 1639, ESRO, *Rye Corp.* MSS, 47/131, 39:2.

22   Northumberland to the Mayor and Corporation of Great Yarmouth, December 10, 1639, C. J. Palmer, *History of Great Yarmouth* (Great Yarmouth, 1856), 205. Sir John Melton to the Bailiffs of Scarborough, December 1639, *Borough*

Other courtier noblemen, too, rushed into action. Edward Sackville, Earl of Dorset, joined Northumberland in recommending a candidate at Great Yarmouth. Windsor was informed by Henry Rich, Earl of Holland, of his choice for its election while Sir Francis Cottington, Chancellor of the Exchequer, was negotiating with his agents in Berkshire, where Sir Francis Windebank, a Principal Secretary of State, desired a knightship of the shire.[23] Cottington (and the court) also received an unexpected bonus; the corporation of Hindon, Wiltshire, urged him "to nominate two such persons as you shall think fit" and they would "most willingly choose them." Cottington promptly replied and the court gathered in two burgess-ships.[24]

Similar stories of noble patronage in the court interest can be repeated many times over. Strafford nominated Robert Read, Windebank's secretary at Boroughbridge; the Lord Keeper, Coventry, just before his death, nominated his son-in-law at Coventry.[25] Reading received letters of nomination from its former citizen and benefactor, Archbishop Laud, and from its High Steward, the Earl of Holland. The Duke of Lennox and the Earl of Portland, employing their credit as joint Deputy-Lieutenants of Hampshire, recommended candidates at Southampton, and Robert Bertie, Earl of Lindsey, used his position as military gov-

of Scarborough MSS, General Letters BL, 1597–1642. Northumberland to the Mayor and Burgesses of Christchurch, December 10, 1639, Christchurch Borough MSS. Northumberland to the Mayor and Jurats of Dover, December 10, 1639, BM, Add. MSS, 18,016, fol. 1. Smith to Pennington, January 30, 1640, PRO, SP 16/443/30. Northumberland to the Mayor and Burgesses of Kingston-upon-Hull, December 10, 1639, Calendar of Manuscripts of Kingston-upon-Hull, ed. L. M. Stanewell (Kingston-upon-Hull: published by the corporation, 1951), 195.

23   Earl of Dorset to the Mayor and Corporation of Great Yarmouth, December 10, 1639, Palmer, Great Yarmouth, 204. Earl of Holland to the Mayor and Aldermen of Windsor, December 9, 1639, HMC, Various Collections, VIII, 53. Harrison to Windebank, December 9, 1639, Sawyer to Read, December 13, 1639, PRO, SP 16/435/52 and 72.

24   John Swift and . . . inhabitants of . . . Hindon, Wiltshire, to [Cottington], December 10, 1639, PRO, SP 16/435/57. VCH, Wiltshire, V, 135.

25   Earl of Strafford to the Boroughmaster and Boroughmen of Boroughbridge, January 17, 1640, PRO, SP 16/442/31. T. W. Whitley, Parliamentary Representation of the City of Coventry (Coventry, 1894), 78–79.

ernor of Berwick to nominate a candidate there.[26] Henry Clifford, heir to the earldom of Cumberland, informed Carlisle of his choice for its election.[27] These efforts are but a sample of the urgency shown by the court's noble supporters.

The clearest examples of the court's determination to influence election contests are to be found in the work of its official appendages. Duchy of Cornwall officials on December 9 sent a letter "touching the Burgesses in Parliament for the towns and boroughs" within the Duchy to its Vice-Warden, William Coryton. He was notified of plans to nominate one candidate for each of its boroughs. The Duchy would brook no failures; Coryton was given strict instructions to prevent any other nominations that would foil the Duchy's plans. No election expense was to be spared, for the Duchy had ordered that Coryton's "charges herein shall be fully allowed unto you." Surprisingly enough, after this early start and clear directive nothing further was done until late February. Candidates were not nominated until February 21, but when the Duchy took that step, it was certainly thorough; a form letter was prepared, differing only in the address and name of the nominee, and directed to each of the sixteen boroughs selected for its election attempt. Coryton was again cautioned against failure and ordered to do his best. Letters survive from that harassed and busy official reflecting his futile attempts to persuade the true election managers of Cornwall, the local gentry, to do the Crown's bidding.[28]

Both the Prince's Council, which worked very closely with the

26   *Reading Records, Diary of the Corporation,* ed. J. M. Guilding (4 vols.; London: James Parker, 1892–1896), III, 472, 475–476. Pescod to Lambert, January 6, 1640, PRO, SP 16/441/48. Sir Peregrine Bertie to the Earl of Lindsey, March 5, 1640, HMC, *Fitzherbert* MSS, 245.

27   Henry Lord Clifford to the Mayor of Carlisle, December 8, 1639, Carlisle City MSS, Ca/2/120, fol. 19.

28   Duchy of Cornwall Record Office, *Letters and Warrants, 1639–1643,* fols. 34, 44v–46, William Coryton to Sir Richard Buller, March 3, 1640, Hicks to Buller, March 3, 1640, Cornwall Record Office, MSS *of Sir John G. Carew Pole, Bart.,* BO 20/63 and 73. Mary Coate, *Cornwall in the Great Civil War and Interregnum, 1642–1660* (Oxford: Clarendon Press, 1933), 5, 23–24.

Duchy of Cornwall — its officials were usually the same men — and Queen Henrietta Maria's Council made intensive efforts to secure parliamentary seats for their nominees. The Prince's Council tried both at Coventry and at Chester to elect its nominees, and the Queen was very active in her campaign.[29] Her Council, both in the spring and fall of 1640, sent letters of recommendation "to the several burgess-towns within her jointure for electing of such persons" as she should nominate. Carlisle enjoyed her full attention. Late in February 1640, she nominated a courtier and complete outsider, Arthur Jones, as her candidate. She was treating Carlisle with the contempt reserved for an eighteenth-century pocket borough, for her previous nominee was a Welshman, probably her servant Henry Wynn — like Jones, a complete stranger to the city. The Queen was lamentably late; a local squire of reputation and influence had nominated his son over two months before.[30] Henry Wynn also turned up in all probability at Higham Ferrers, another borough within the Queen's jointure.[31] The results of the Queen's election labors are the most difficult to assess with any accuracy. Pontefract shows Strafford's influence; his brother, Sir George Wentworth, won one seat there. Henry Benson, victorious at Knaresborough, was the son of an influential property owner there but he also served as a bailiff and steward of the Queen's manor of Knaresborough. Tiverton returned Peter Balle, described as the Queen's Attorney General, which suggests her successful intervention. Sir Frederick Cornwallis, a courtier, was elected at Eye; it is fairly certain that his court connections were responsible. Grantham returned a Chamberlain of the Exchequer, Sir Edward Bashe. Was this

29   List of Government Candidates, April 1, 1640, PRO, *SP* 16/450/15.
30   Tomkyns to Lambe, October 1, 1640, PRO, *SP* 16/469/11. Dalston to the Mayor of Carlisle, December 7, 1639, Mayor and others of Carlisle to Henry Lord Clifford, January 20, 1640, The Queen's Council to the Mayor, Aldermen, and Burgesses . . . of Carlisle, February 21, 1640, Graham to the Mayor of Carlisle, February 28, 1640, *Carlisle City* MSS, Ca/2/120, fols. 14, 18, 21, 22.
31   A. N. Groome, "Higham Ferrers Elections," *Northamptonshire Past and Present* 2:245 (1958).

the work of the Queen's Council? Certainty is impossible but, since a determination should be made, he has been arbitrarily listed among the Queen's election successes.[32]

The Duchy of Lancaster and the Council of the Marches of Wales were also involved in the election venture. The Chancellor of the Duchy, Edward Barrett, Lord Newburgh, successfully secured the return of Simon Avery, one of his officials, at Leicester (with the help of the local patron, the Earl of Huntingdon) and also won a place at Wigan where Orlando Bridgeman, another Duchy official, was elected. The Duchy also possibly nominated a candidate at Higham Ferrers.[33] Ludlow, usually amenable to the influence of the Council of the Marches of Wales, was troublesome in the spring election. It rejected Robert Napier, the son-in-law of the Lord President of the Council, the Earl of Bridgewater, and also refused the Council's solicitor, Timothy Turneur. Turneur, at least, enjoyed some satisfaction; he switched his supporters to another royalist, Charles Baldwin, who managed to win a Ludlow seat.[34] Ludlow was the only borough where direct evidence of the Council's activity can be found, which makes any complete evaluation of its work difficult. Leominster had been under its influence earlier in the century and is therefore included for the spring election. If the Council did nominate candidates, it was notably unsuccessful.[35]

Another listing of eleven court candidates plus the Cornish boroughs, Chester, and the towns of Plymouth and Bewdley has

32   Keeler, *Long Parliament*, 55, 64, 75, 107, 142–143, 383–384. *Members of Parliament; Return of the Names of Every Member Returned to Serve in Each Parliament* . . . (London: House of Commons, Accounts and Papers, 1878), LXII, pt. I, 481.

33   Newburgh to the Mayor and Corporation of Leicester, December 19, 1639, Huntingdon to the Mayor and Corporation of Leicester, February 8, 1640, *City of Leicester* MSS, Hall Papers Bound, 1637–1640, BR II/18/21:548 and 551. James Thompson, *The History of Leicester* (London: W. Pickering, 1849), 359. David Sinclair, *History of Wigan* (2 vols.; London: Kent, 1882), I, 213–215.

34   Martyn to Davies, January 13, 1640, HMC, *Third Report*, 258–259. Brilliana Harley to her son, Edward, March 14, 1640, *Letters of the Lady Brilliana Harley*, ed. T. T. Lewis (London: Camden Society, 1854).

35   Keeler, *Long Parliament*, 61.

also survived, testifying further to the court's election campaign. The list duplicates the Duchy of Cornwall list but adds Bewdley, which returned Sir Edward Herbert, a courtier, and Plymouth, which ignored the court's request and selected two local men. Of more importance is the list of the eleven court nominees of whom only one found a seat, a damaging commentary on the court's lack of election success.[36]

The Council of the North, formerly an election power in Yorkshire, had very little if any success. Sir Edward Osborn, the Council's Vice-President, won at York with the Earl of Strafford's support, possibly the Council of the North's only victory.

The following summary lists the success the Crown's agencies enjoyed in the spring election and indicates where such attempts were made. Both the actual and possible nominations are given and, unless a different indication is made, one nomination is allowed for each borough.

	Actual Nomination	Probable Nomination	Result
Prince's Council .	Coventry		lost
		Chester	lost
Duchy of Cornwall	Bossiney		lost
	Callington		lost
	Camelford		lost
	East Looe		lost
	Fowey		lost
	Grampound		lost
	Helston		lost
	Launceston		lost
	Lostwithiel		lost
	Mitchell		lost
	Newport		lost
	Penryn		lost
	St. Germans		lost
	St. Ives		lost
	St. Mawes		lost
	West Looe		lost

36   List of Court Candidates, April 1, 1640, PRO, SP 16/450/15.

	Actual Nomination	Probable Nomination	Result
Duchy of Lancaster	Leicester		won
		Wigan	won
		Higham Ferrers	lost
		Lancaster	won
		Preston	lost
		Clitheroe	lost
		Liverpool	lost
		Newton in Mackerfield	won (2?)
Council of the Marches of Wales	Ludlow		won and lost
		Leominster	lost
Queens' Council	Carlisle		lost (2)
		Higham Ferrers	lost
		Weymouth (?)	lost
		Leominster	lost
		Grantham	won (?)
		Eye	won
		Knaresborough	won (?)
		Pontefract	?
		Wallingford	lost
		Tiverton	won
Council of the North	York		won
ms. list of court nominees	Plymouth		lost
	Bewdley		won

The tabulation below attempts to reflect the success or failure of the court agencies in terms of the men probably nominated by each agency.

Based on the evidence available and on the past election influence of the Crown's agencies involved, those agencies suffered a staggering defeat in their election endeavors for the spring parliament.

The election history of the Cinque Ports consistently reflected the success of the Lord Warden in securing at least one seat for his nominee at each port. The Earl of Suffolk made every effort to continue that record of court success. By December 18, 1639, he had made his nomination to all of "his" ports.

	Number Probably Nominated	Won	Lost
Prince's Council	2	0	2
Duchy of Cornwall	17	1	16
Duchy of Lancaster	9	5	4
Queen's Council (without Pontefract)	10	4	6
Council of the Marches of Wales	3	1	2
Council of the North	1	1	0
MS list of court nominees	11	1	10
Plymouth and Bewdley	2	1	1
Total	55	14	41

Rye's election testified to the zeal of both Suffolk and the court in pressing its nominees. Before the corporation made its choice, it had received the attention of nine different candidates. The Lord Warden nominated his son, Thomas, but seven weeks later shifted his support to Windebank's secretary, Robert Read. The Earl of Dorset intervened, first for his kinsman Sir John Sackville and then, at the end of February, he replaced Sackville with his secretary, John White. Northumberland, the Lord High Admiral, also pressed his choice upon Rye. Another candidate, one W. Roberts, claimed Suffolk's support in his effort to secure a place. Three local men entered the election contest, Lawrence Ashburnham, John Colepeper, and Thomas Diggis. Diggis offered the most intriguing reason for his candidacy. He claimed that since his father's untimely death had prevented him from showing his "great affection for the town," he would express his father's alleged goodwill by serving Rye in the forthcoming Parliament! Despite all this pressure, including the attention of three noblemen, Rye's corporation rebelled; for the first time in the early seventeenth century it rejected the Lord Warden's candidate and instead chose one local man and Dorset's nominee, John White.[37]

Few boroughs received the attention Rye enjoyed but there was a moral to its election story. The zeal and urgency of the court's campaign was clearly illustrated at Rye. Of its nine candidates, six were nominees of either court officials or of a nobleman, Dorset, who was sympathetic to the King's interest. Four royal officials were involved in the contest as patrons of court nominees. It was quite an experience for a decaying port and something of a letdown for the court since, despite all its efforts, Rye elected but one Crown nominee.

Suffolk nominated at least one candidate at each port. His actual nominations were made at Sandwich (won), Rye (lost), Hastings (won), and Winchelsea (won). His possible nominations included Dover (won), New Romney (lost), and Hythe (won). Suffolk had done rather well to secure five places for his candidates. However, one of the men he probably supported at Dover, Sir Edward Boys of Fedville, Kent, was a court antagonist. John Wandesford at Hythe was his probable nominee, and he supported Read at Hastings, Crispe at Winchelsea, and Sir Edward Nicholas at Sandwich.

Other noblemen acting in the court's interest were not so successful as the Lord Warden. Dorset failed to return a nominee at Great Yarmouth, which preferred local men instead — both strong antagonists of the court.[38] Dorset combined with George

37   W. Roberts to the Mayor and Jurats of Rye, December 14, 1639, Suffolk to the Mayor and Jurats of Rye, December 18, 1639, L. Ashburnham to the Mayor and Jurats of Rye, December 18, 1639, Thomas Diggis to the Mayor and Jurats of Rye, December 24, 1639, Northumberland to the Mayor and Jurats of Rye, December 31, 1639, John Colepeper to the Mayor and Jurats of Rye, January 8, 1640, ESRO, Rye Corp. MSS, 47/131, 39:3–8. John Colepeper to the Mayor and Jurats of Rye, ibid., 47/132, 39:1, Suffolk to the Mayor and Jurats of Rye, February 8, 1640, John Manwood to the Mayor and Jurats of Rye, February 26, 1640, Dorset to the Mayor and Jurats of Rye, February 28, 1640, Windebank to the Mayor and Jurats of Rye, March 18, 1640, ibid., 47/131, 39:10, 11, 13, 14.

38   Dorset to the Bailiffs of Great Yarmouth, December 10, 1639, February 27, 1640, Bailiffs of Great Yarmouth to Dorset, December 14, 1639, printed in Palmer, Yarmouth, 204–207.

Lord Goring, to nominate candidates at Lewes but they were defeated by two men who held violent anti-court views.[39] Suffolk was less successful when he acted without the influence of his office as Lord Warden. He failed to place a notable courtier, Sir Dudley Carleton, at Dorchester. Like Lewes and Great Yarmouth, Dorchester returned local men who were known for their opposition to the Crown.[40]

Henry Hastings, Earl of Huntingdon, the traditional election patron of Leicestershire, suffered a surprising defeat in his bailiwick. He had nominated his son and Sir Henry Skipwith, a Leicestershire royalist, for the knightships of the county and had strongly urged the corporation of Leicester to "send your constables in their several wards to the freeholders to signify my desire unto them" to choose his son in the first place and Skipwith in the second. Alas for the historically proud Huntingdon influence, both were defeated, possibly because of their royalism, by two strong parliamentarians, Sir Arthur Hesilrige and Lord Grey of Ruthin.[41]

It was touch and go as well for the Countess of Devonshire in the Leicester election, where she had nominated Mr. Thomas Coke, son of the venerable principal secretary. He was rejected in favor of one Roger Smith but, when Smith refused to take the "freeman's oath" of Leicester, Coke stepped nimbly into his place. The Countess had her way but it was a close squeak.[42]

39   Burton to Bray, January 27, 1640, PRO, *SP* 16/442/137, *CJ*, II, 3.

40   H. J. Moule, "Notes on a Minute Book (C. 12) belonging to the Mayor and Corporation of Dorchester," *Proceedings of the Dorset Natural History and Antiquarian Field Club*, 15:156–157 (1894). *Catalogue of the Municipal Records of Dorchester*, ed. C. H. Mayo (Exeter, 1908), 435–436. John Hutchins, *History and Antiquities of the County of Dorset*, eds. W. Shipp & J. W. Hodgson (4 vols.; Westminster, printed by J. B. Nichols, 1861–1870), II, 357–358.

41   Huntingdon to the Mayor and Corporation of Leicester, January 20, February 13, 1640, *City of Leicester* MSS, Hall Papers Bound, 1637–1640, BR II/18/21: 550, 552. VCH, *Leicestershire*, II, 110.

42   Countess of Devonshire to the Mayor and Corporation of Leicester, January 20, 1640, Roger Smith to Sir John Coke, March 27, 1640 (two letters of same date), "Common Hall meeting, City of Leicester," n.d., 1640, "Common Hall meeting," March 30, 1640, "Meeting of the 24," April 3, 1640, Countess of Devonshire

Cambridge City was an easier affair for the court. Its High Steward, Lord Keeper Finch, nominated a clerk of the Privy Council, Thomas Meautys, who was duly returned along with Oliver Cromwell.[43] The East Grinstead election was much more contentious, ending with a petition against the election of Robert Goodwin in the House of Commons. Dorset had nominated his secretary, John White, and despite the work of Dorset's bailiff, who made dire threats against all opposing White's candidacy, Goodwin carried the election. He survived the petition as well, thanks to the efforts of the independently minded inhabitants of the town.[44] He, too, was an opponent of royal policies, a factor which curried much favor with East Grinstead's electorate.

Although Kent's election for knights of the shire has been aptly described as a struggle involving the gentry of the county, it was not without its overtones of noble influence.[45] Both the Earl of Dorset and the Lord Chamberlain, the Earl of Pembroke and Montgomery, were involved in the election. Dorset's kinsman, John Sackville, supported Henry Vane's brief candidacy, and his bailiff campaigned in Vane's behalf in the opening stages of the election. The Lord Chamberlain, anxious to avoid faction in the contest, also secured Sir Edward Dering's promise to back

to the Mayor and Corporation of Leicester, April 7, 1640, City of Leicester, April 7, 1640, *City of Leicester* MSS, Hall Papers Bound, 1637–1640, BR II/18/21:549, 578–579, 584–585, 591–592. "Common Hall meeting" of the City of Leicester, March 27, 1640, *ibid.*, Hall Book, 1587–1708, BR/II/1/3:570. Coke the Younger to Sir John Coke, Senior, March 30, 1640, HMC, *Cowper* MSS, II, 252. John Nichols, *History and Antiquities of the County of Leicester* (4 vols. in 9 parts; London, 1795–1815), II, pt. I, 427.

43   Charles Cooper, *The Annals of Cambridge* (5 vols.; Cambridge: printed by Warwick & Co., 1842–1853), III, 296–299. *The Diary and Correspondence of Dr. John Worthington*, ed. James Crossley (2 vols.; Manchester: Chetham Society, 1847), I, 8.

44   Thomas W. Horsfield, *The History, Antiquities, and Topography of the County of Sussex* (2 vols.; London: J. B. Nichols, 1835), II, 40. Wallace H. Hills, *The History of East Grinstead* (East Grinstead: Farncombe & Co., 1906), 33–34. *Sussex Archaeological Collections*, 20:153–154 (1868). *CJ*, II, 10.

45   A. M. Everitt, *The Community of Kent and the Great Rebellion, 1640–1660* (Leicester: University Press, 1966), 69–75.

Vane for a knightship. Vane's withdrawal and Dering's entry, at Vane's urging, ruined Pembroke and Montgomery's hopes of a quiet election and turned the election into a sharp struggle among the leading Kentish families.[46]

The universities as usual returned one court candidate each. Sir Francis Windebank won a place at Oxford University, probably through the "influence of the King and Archbishop Laud"; the Earl of Holland's secretary, Henry Lucas, secured a seat at Cambridge University. Cambridge was not entirely amenable to court pressures because Sir John Lambe, another court candidate (possibly the Queen's nominee), "did lose it" as Dr. John Worthington dryly noted in his diary.[47]

Northumberland, the Lord Admiral, experienced a frustrating election season which testified to the court's difficulties. He cast a wide election net both as a royal official and as a great nobleman. He involved himself in at least twelve different elections in his dual role. As Lord Admiral, he nominated court candidates at Great Yarmouth, Hull, Scarborough, Sandwich, Christchurch, Rye, and Dover. He managed but one success and that was owing more to the influence of Secretary Vane than to his own patronage. In the other contests, where he relied upon his own influence, he was more fortunate. He placed his candidates at Northumberland, Berwick, and Chichester. His nephew, Philip Lord Lisle, was returned at Yarmouth, Isle of Wight, possibly with his assistance, and his brother, Henry, managed a seat at Portsmouth. Northumberland's election record provided a fine example of the court's problems and of local noble success. He managed three victories in his own bailiwicks but suffered six defeats out of nine attempts in his official capacity, a sorry result.[48]

46   George Sondes to Walsingham, December 9, 1639, March 4, 1640, Sedley to Dering, March 7, 1640, Hales to Dering, March 9, 1640, BM, *Stowe* MSS, 743, fols. 136, 138, 140, 142. Sackville to Vane, March 6, 1640, PRO, *SP* 16/447/43.

47   Rex, *University Representation in England*, 120–121. John Windebank to Read, March 9, 1640, PRO, *SP* 16/447/63. Crossley, *Worthington's Diary*, I, 7.

48   Northumberland to the Mayor and Jurats of Great Yarmouth, December 10, 1639, Palmer, *Great Yarmouth*, 205. Northumberland to the Mayor and

The Election to the Short Parliament

The overall results of the court's election efforts are as follows: The efforts of the various court agencies won 14, lost 42; the influence of the Lord Warden won 5, lost 2; and the efforts of the noblemen whose loyalties to the Crown would indicate that their election influence was used in its behalf won 49, lost 29. The totals are thus 68 won and 73 lost. The court, relying on its own efforts and influence, suffered a clear rebuff. When it intervened with the aid of an influential aristocrat, the results were more satisfactory, but still, as Northumberland's record indicated, an official recommendation was often tantamount to election failure.

Two other aspects of the spring campaign deserve attention. One, the question of the role "national" issues played in the election, may offer an answer to the court's predicament. The second, the various methods employed by the candidates and their patrons to secure entry into the House of Commons, may testify to the validity of Professor Neale's suggestion. He wrote that by comparison with elections of the Elizabethan period, 1640 electioneering "had become more intense, more sophisticated, more costly."[49] Elections in Elizabeth's last years also reflected the growing faction and "political jobbery and corruption" at court. Both continued in the Early Stuart period.[50] The spring

Burgesses of Christchurch, December 10, 1639, *Christchurch Borough* MSS. Northumberland to ?, Dover, December 10, 1639, BM, *Add.* MSS, 18,016, fol. 1ᵛ. Kempe to Dering, January 29, 1640, KRO, *Dering* MSS, U 350, C2/73. Smith to Pennington, January 30, 1640, PRO, *SP* 16/443/30. Northumberland to the Mayor and Burgesses of Kingston-upon-Hull, December 10, 1639, Stanewell, *Hull*, 195. Northumberland to the Mayor and Jurats of Rye, December 31, 1639, ESRO, *Rye Corp.* MSS, 47/131, 39:7. Northumberland to the Mayor and Burgesses of Sandwich, December 31, 1639, KRO, *Sandwich Letter Book*, Sa/C 1, fol. 12. Sir John Melton to the Bailiffs of Scarborough, December 1639, *Borough of Scarborough* MSS, General Letters B1, 1597–1642. Popple to Vane, March 21, 1640, PRO, *SP* 16/448/53. *The Household Papers of Henry Percy, Ninth Earl of Northumberland*, ed. G. R. Batho (London: Camden Society, 1962), 43, 150–160. *Members of Parliament*, pt. I, 480–484.

49   Neale, *Elizabethan House of Commons*, 330.
50   *Ibid.*, 244.

contests provide eloquent testimony of the change in election practice.

ELECTION METHODS

The variety of methods employed by the candidates in the spring election demonstrated both their ingenuity and their determination to win a seat in the House of Commons. These methods combined both the traditional practices of their Elizabethan predecessors and innovative procedures which all too often reflected the growing faction, corruption, and moral malaise of the Early Stuart period.

The safest way to Westminster was to enjoy the favor of a nobleman who controlled a parliamentary seat. Christchurch, Hampshire, was just such a place. It might be described as the pocket borough of Lord Arundell of Wardour, who had successfully placed Nathaniel Tomkins, Clerk of the Queen's Council, there five times, 1621–1628. However, Wardour was dead, his inheritance was in dispute, and one of his heirs, Cecil Lord Baltimore, stepped forward to claim his father-in-law's election patronage. For Christchurch, traditionally content to accept the directions of its patron, it was a confusing election. The court was involved, too, for the Earl of Northumberland made a nomination.

Baltimore paraded an apparently inexhaustible number of candidates before the corporation's weary eyes. As soon as Christchurch accepted one of his nominees, it would receive a letter informing it that its previous choice was either too ill to serve or had been chosen elsewhere. With each letter came new nominees. To vex the bewildered corporation even further, Thomas Howard, Earl of Arundel, also trooped out two of his own candidates; Christchurch was paying a heavy price for its past election acquiescence. But even its patience was finally exhausted for, after accepting nominees from both Baltimore and Arundel, it rebelled. It chose one outsider, Baltimore's final candidate, the courtier Sir Henry Herbert, and a local man, Henry Tulse.[51] Even a "pocket" borough's patience could be broken. When the election was finally made, the mayor and corporation could look back on a parade of nominees unique in its history: Northumberland nominated one man, Arundel two, and Baltimore five! The story of Christchurch was one of a nomination borough; its traditional lack of election independence made the tale possible.

Bribery also marked the spring campaign. Hastings returned Robert Read in a hotly contested election that resulted in a charge of bribery. The freemen alleged that Dorset's secretary, John White, promised the corporation that if Read were chosen, Read "would give to the poor . . . of Hastings £20 down, and £10 a year during his life and two barrels of powder yearly for the exercise of youth." Although John Ashburnham, commenting on the affair, thought Read honest, he did admit that were Read "not my friend, I should question his election myself and Mr. White, his impertinences and over busying himself in that place."[52] Read's offer had its effect; he was returned for Hastings. The Earl of Dorset's secretary was involved there; Dorset's friend, Sir John Suckling, was mixed up in the second bribery case, this time at Bramber. An outraged and defeated candidate there, Sir Edward Bishop, petitioned the House for a reversal of the election, claiming that among the "undue means" used by Suckling to carry the election was his practice of scattering his money about the town, offering it "to the meaner sort," thereby "persuading them to vote for himself."[53] Ironically, in the fall 1640 elections Bishop, attempting to emulate the success and perhaps the methods of Suckling, offered a £10 bribe to secure his return![54]

51   VCH, *Hampshire and the Isle of Wight*, V, 86–87, 92–93. Baltimore to the Mayor and Burgesses of Christchurch, December 16, 18, 23, 1639, February 25, 1640, March 3, 1640, Arundel to the Mayor and Burgesses of Christchurch, January 16, 1640, Misham to the Mayor of Christchurch, March 10, 1640, *Christchurch Borough* mss.

52   Cited in John K. Gruenfelder, "The Spring Parliamentary Election at Hastings, 1640," *Sussex Archaeological Society*, 105:49–55 (1967).

53   HMC, *Fourth Report*, 53. *Ibid., House of Lords* mss, 25.

54   Keeler, *Long Parliament*, 67.

Candidates and their patrons could avoid outright bribery but still indulge in expensive and occasionally, if they won election, satisfying corruption. The Earl of Salisbury, in two elections at Hertford and Hertfordshire, spent the munificent sum of £452 10s.4d. to see his candidates returned. His bill for the county contest, £380 2s.6d., "covered the diet and horsemeat for three days at four inns in Hertford of seventy-three of his own company and no less than 899 persons"; it also included his expenditures for about 600 gallons of beverages for the refreshment of the "friends and supporters" of his candidate. Happily for Salisbury, his expenses in the Hertford election were less, only £72 7s.2d., spent in "entertaining the voters." This sum "covered the diet of 217 persons, two hogsheads of sack and claret for the better sort, and four hogsheads of beer for the vulgar," plus several charitable donations including one of £10 for the "poor of the town."[55] The costs of election entertainment were going up as the Earl's accounts proved.

By contrast Sir Thomas Barrington's election costs at Essex were niggardly. Barrington's election, however, thanks to his patron and friend the mighty Earl of Warwick, was practically assured. Even so, Barrington managed to spend £42 2s.6d. in the contest. His largest single expense, £20 2s.6d., was his share "of a bill at the [Lion] for diet and wine & beer." Barrington's custom was not confined to the Lion; he paid part of another bill for a "hogshead of wine and a butt of beer given at the Bell" which totalled £4 8s., and to enliven his victory march employed the Colchester waits for six shillings. A thoughtful husband, he sent a messenger to tell his wife of his victory, which cost him an additional five shillings.[56] When it is remembered that this was a list solely of Barrington's expenditures, then the total costs for Grimston, his election colleague, and for Warwick, his election

<hr/>

55 Stone, "The Electoral Influence of the Second Earl of Salisbury," *EHR*, 71:387, 393–394 (1956).

56 Essex Record Office, "The Expenses of the Election of Sir Thomas Barrington for the Short Parliament," D/DBa, A17.

patron, would probably have made Essex an expensive county on election day as well.

Entertainment was a common, acceptable practice. At Abingdon, Berkshire, the victorious candidate, the royalist Sir George Stonehouse, "persuaded by his beef, bacon, and bag pudding, and by permitting as many of them as would to be drunk at his charge" to cast their voices for him. On election day the "multitude . . . crying in strong drink and zeal" gave Stonehouse victory.[57] The same story with only minor variations was repeated many times over. At Knaresborough the winner, Sir Henry Slingsby, managed to get by for a low £16 "at the least" for his provision of wine for the voters, and at Ludlow one candidate worked diligently "with his friends and purse with the burgesses." Sir Walter Pye, while planning the election campaign with his fellow candidate, Sir Robert Harley, pointed out that "provision must be made at Hereford for the entertain[ing] of the gentlemen and others who will be there" for the election. Pye had already begun the arrangements, assuring Harley that an innkeeper had promised to "provide an ordinary at his old house, of 2s.6d."[58] Such attention to the voter's wants paid off at Knaresborough, Ludlow, and in the Herefordshire contests; those who paid bills often carried the elections.

The puritan clergy also lent their unique talents to election causes in the spring. In Essex the ministers the puritan Earl of Warwick supported, "as Mr. Marshall [the presbyterian divine of Civil War fame] and other, preached often out of their own parishes before the election." They were his campaign orators, exhorting their parishioners and others to support his "opposition" candidates.[59]

57   Whitelock's Memorials, BM, *Add.* mss, 37, 343, fol. 199.

58   W. W. Bean, *The Parliamentary Representation of the Six Northern Counties of England* (Hull: printed for the author by C. H. Barnwell, 1890), 884. *Shropshire Archaeological and Natural History Transactions*, new ser., 7:26–27 (1895). Pye to Harley, February 10, 1640, HMC, *Portland* mss, III, 59.

59   A complete account of the election for Essex can be found in John K. Gruenfelder, "The Election for Knights of the Shire for Essex in the Spring,

The same ministerial election zeal was also repeated in Gloucestershire. John Allibond, holder of two benefices there, was mightily upset by what "men of our own coat" had done in the shire election. He wrote a vivid description of the affair to his close friend, Dr. Peter Heylyn, a chaplain in ordinary to the King. According to Allibond, the puritan candidate, Nathaniel Stephens, was urged to enter the election contest by a "pack of either deprived, silenced or puritanically affected [clergy]men." Fox of Tewkesbury was one. His sons, who were named appropriately enough, "Help-on-High" and "Sion-build," had been reared in Edinburgh. "Marshall of Elmore (who lives under Sir William Guyse [Guise], a great favorer of the side [puritan]"; Baxter, a defender of the Scottish revolt; and Whynnell, "our learned lecturer at Gloucester who that last summer made an expedition into Scotland for Bachelor in divinity," were others involved in Stephens's election bid. All eleven of the clergy mentioned by Allibond either had no livings or acted as lecturers; ten were from outside Gloucester and at least three of them — Whynnell of Gloucester, Fox of Tewkesbury, and Baxter of Forthampton — had either visited Scotland or openly supported the Scottish cause.[60] These ministers, like their preaching brethren in Essex, played a significant role in the election, stirring up the freeholders and lending their oratorical ability to the "reform" candidates. The London election story repeated that of Essex and Gloucestershire. London's four members, Pennington, Vassall, Cradock, and Soames, were all allied with the puritan ministers of the city and enjoyed their full support. Pennington was a close friend of John Goodwin, the famous puritan minister of St. Stephen's parish, Coleman Street. St. Swithin's parish, another puritan hotbed, claimed the allegiance of Cradock. Soames and

1640," *Transactions of the Essex Archaeological Society*, 3rd ser., 2, pt. 2:143–146 (1968).
    60   "Examination of Help-on-High Fox," 1639?, PRO, *SP* 16/440/65. Allibond to Heylyn, March 24, 1640, *ibid.*, 448/79. *Gloucestershire Notes and Queries*, 1:410–413 (1881).

Vassall, too, presumably enjoyed ministerial connections and election support.[61]

More venerable methods were also part of the spring election picture. The usual canvassing and mustering of freeholders, tenants, neighbors, friends, and relatives was a constant practice in most campaigns. The Kent story has already been told, and it could be repeated for other shires throughout the kingdom.[62] A candidate for a knightship in Derbyshire proposed "to try my friends" in his election effort, and another election hopeful, Sir Thomas Hutchinson in Nottinghamshire, wrote to a friend to secure "for the first place all those voices which you intended for Sir John Byron" (who had withdrawn from the race).[63] Pye and Harley's strategy in Herefordshire included the gathering of the relatives of their friends — indeed, of anyone they could lay their hands on — "to give their voices at Hereford upon Saturday come se'nnight" for Harley and Pye in the shire election. One Richard Skinner, who acted as their election agent, even outlined in his letter the eligibility requirements for the voters. They were certainly not narrow.[64] The same procedures or variations thereof were followed in many other elections, although not always with success.[65]

Corruption and chicanery were not absent from musterings and canvassings. Election day at Chelmsford, where the knights for Essex were to be chosen, found many supporters of Barrington

61   Pearl, *London and the Puritan Revolution*, 169, 175–193.
62   Everitt, *Kent and the Great Rebellion*, 69–75.
63   Harpur to Coke, December 31, 1639, HMC, *Cowper* MSS, II, 246. Hutchinson to Clifton, February 27, 1640, HMC, *Various Collections*, VII, 295.
64   Richard Skinner to Edmund Skinner et al., March 6, 1640, HMC, *Portland* MSS, III, 61.
65   Stone, "Electoral Influence of the Second Earl of Salisbury," *EHR*, 121:386 (1956). Sawyer to Read, December 13, 1639, PRO, *SP* 16/435/72, printed in John K. Hedges, *The History of Wallingford* (2 vols.; London: Clowes, 1881), II, 167–168. Huntingdon to the Mayor and Corporation of Leicester, February 13, 1640, *City of Leicester* MSS, Hall Papers Bound, 1637–1640, BR II/18/21:552. *The Diary of Sir Henry Slingsby of Scriven, Bart.*, ed. Daniel Parsons (London, 1836), 50–51. Brerewood to [Sir Thomas Smith], March 10, 1640, PRO, *SP* 16/447/82. Cholmondeley to Sir Thomas Smith, January 19, 1640, *ibid.*, 442/46.

and Grimston present who had already cast their voices in various borough elections.[66] These ambulatory voters probably included Sir Henry Mildmay's supporters at Maldon for, following that election, "the men of Maldon came and we all went to Chelmsford together, where there was such a multitude of all sorts of people as I never before saw."[67] The mustering of tenants could be a two-edged sword, as the Gloucestershire contest showed. Sir Robert Cooke, determined to block the election of the royalist candidate, Sir Robert Tracy, performed one of the most skillful tricks of the spring elections. Lord Berkeley had already mustered his voices, some five hundred of them in fact, for Tracy. But Cooke before the election wrote Berkeley "that there was likely no opposition [to Tracy] and therefore he [Berkeley] might (if he thought fit) spare both his own pains and prevent the attendance of his company."[68] Cooke's scheme was masterful; Berkeley discharged his followers and then watched, no doubt in chagrin, as Stephens, the other, "reform" candidate and Cooke's ally, won many of Berkeley's tenants over to his candidacy. This stratagem almost carried the day for Stephens, who was only blocked by another venerable election practice, the potential for the High Sheriff to twist an election as he saw fit. Tracy's countermeasures were simplicity itself. His brother, the High Sheriff of Gloucestershire, disallowed some of Stephens's voices and then adjourned the election to Winchcombe, a town convenient for Tracy's supporters and his alone. These tactics saved the day for the royalist Tracy.[69]

The High Sheriff of Warwickshire, an ally of the royalist Earl of Northampton, who was engaged in a bitter election battle with

66   Gruenfelder, "The Election for Knights of the Shire for Essex in the Spring, 1640," 143–146.

67   Philip L. Ralph, *Sir Humphrey Mildmay: Royalist Gentleman* (New Brunswick: Rutgers University Press, 1947), 152–153.

68   William B. Willcox, *Gloucestershire, A Study in Local Government* (New Haven: Yale University Press, 1940), 33–34. Allibond to Heylyn, March 24, 1640, PRO, SP 16/448/79. *Gloucestershire Notes and Queries*, 1:410–413.

69   Willcox, *Gloucestershire*, 33–34. Allibond to Heylyn, March 24, 1640, PRO, SP 16/448/79. *Gloucestershire Notes and Queries*, 1:410–413. CJ, II, 4, 7.

the "reformer," Robert Greville, Lord Brooke, also tried to weight the election scale. He allegedly secured the election writ himself, taking it back to the county with him and presenting it at the first county day which he planned to hold so early that "it will not [be] possible for the 10th part of the freeholders to be present, by which means he may have a notable stroke in the election." For some reason, the Sheriff's efforts failed; Northampton's candidates were not returned.[70]

Other officials, sometimes of humble capacity, also tried their hands at election chicanery. The High Sheriff of Suffolk, the diarist and antiquarian Sir Simon D'Ewes, was almost hoodwinked by his own underlings who undertook "to deprive the county of a free election" by adjourning the county court from Ipswich, its traditional site, to Beccles, which "situated in the furthest part of the shire" was chosen in order to discourage the attendance of voters at the contest.[71] D'Ewes denied any complicity in the plot in his customarily long-winded way and bitterly reproached his aides for their wrongdoing. They had attempted the plot in an effort to sway the contest probably in favor of Sir Roger North, who caused poor D'Ewes more trouble by protesting the county election which he had lost.[72] He must have been delighted when his term as sheriff was over.

Any influential county office could be used to sway the voter. In Essex, Warwick skillfully employed his position as Lord Lieutenant to threaten the reluctant voter with possible military charges, should he not be of Warwick's election views.[73] In East Sussex, so Dr. Edward Burton grumbled, "the puritan faction was grown strong amongst the justices upon our bench for the eastern part of this county"; indeed, they were so strong "that such as are moderately disposed were not able to withstand it."

70   BM, *Add.* MSS, 11,045, fol. 96.
71   BM, *Harleian* MSS, 160, fol. 152.
72   *Ibid.*, 97, fols. 5, 7–9, 11; *ibid.*, 388, fol. 43; *ibid.*, 160, fol. 152.
73   Gruenfelder, "The Election for Knights of the Shire for Essex in the Spring, 1640," 143–146.

One justice, Anthony Stapley, later a regicide, used his position as a platform to spread his puritan views to such good effect that both he and his puritan colleague on the bench, James Rivers, won election at Lewes despite the efforts of Lord Goring and the Earl of Dorset. Stapley, in fact, was so popular that he was elected Knight of the Shire for Sussex as well.[74] The labors of Stapley and Rivers alone justified Lord Keeper Finch's fears about the justices who "affect popularity, diving into the people's hearts with kisses, offerings and fawnings . . . [who] domineer over them [their neighbors], and to carry things with a faction."[75] These offices which had once been a monopoly of the Crown's supporters were in the spring contest a weapon of the opposition, a very unsatisfactory state of affairs for the court.

Threats, violence, libels, public campaigning of an almost modern kind, added even more turmoil to the spring election scene. Court candidates, Read at Hastings and Nicholas at Sandwich, ran headlong into election struggles dominated by these methods. Read, whose election story has been told above, managed to secure his place at Hastings, thanks to the determination of the port's corporation and bribery, but nothing could save Nicholas at Sandwich.[76] He was defeated by, as the Mayor described it, "blackmouthed envy" which had "belched out a most false and scandalous aspersion upon you, namely that you were a rank Papist and had not been to church these sixteen years." Poor Nicholas. His denials were of no avail nor was an additional letter of support from the Earl of Northumberland. The Mayor's fears, "that this false scandal will somewhat prejudice our desires and

74   Burton, to Bray, January 27, 1640, PRO, SP 16/442/137. Charles Thomas-Stanford, Sussex in the Great Civil War and Interregnum, 1642–1660 (London: printed at the Chiswick Press, 1910), 31–32. Keeler, Long Parliament, 66.
75   Rushworth, Historical Collections, III, 986, 988.
76   Keeler, Long Parliament, 76. A full account of the Hastings election can be found in Gruenfelder, "The Spring Parliamentary Election at Hastings, 1640," 49–55. Mayor and Jurats of Sandwich to Suffolk, January 13, 1640, PRO, SP 16/441/121. Mayor and Jurats of Sandwich to the Lord Warden?, April 10, 1640, BM, Add. mss, 33, 152, fols. 40–41. KRO, Sandwich Letter Book, Sa/C 1, fols. 12–12v.

aims" to elect Nicholas were correct. The scandal, authored and spread by a sadler, a turner, a hemp dresser, and a glover had ruined the candidacy of one of the Privy Council's clerks, the libel spread by the "factious nonconformists" succeeded, and Nicholas was defeated.[77]

Threats and intimidation marred the East Grinstead election as well. The Earl of Dorset's bailiff, who obviously would do anything to see White, the Earl's candidate, win the election, threatened White's opponents "that if they gave their voices for him [Goodwin, the other election contestant,] their servants should be pressed, and their carts taken away, and other such words of the like nature." Justice however triumphed; the House summoned the bailiff, one Edward Blundell, as a delinquent for his election activities.[78]

Hastings and Sandwich were not isolated instances of the intense campaigning that challenged candidate and voter alike. In Norfolk, Thomas Wodehouse deplored the "workings and counter workings to purchase vulgar tastes and acclamation" that marred his shire's election. Rhymesters, as at Canterbury and Lincoln, coined campaign slogans in verse to both label and perhaps libel the respective candidates.[79]

Borough corporations often played the decisive role in an election. They could, as at Hindon and Chester, either request nominations for their burgesses or seek out candidates who would be acceptable to the town's leadership. Before the Chester election was held, the corporation had already asked Sir Thomas

77 Mayor and Jurats of Sandwich to Nicholas, March 19, 1640, PRO, *SP* 16/448/33 and enclosure I. John Philpot, Bailiff of Sandwich to Nicholas, March 19, 1640, *ibid.*, 448/34. Northumberland to Pennington, March 21, 1640, *ibid.*, 448/54. Mayor and Jurats of Sandwich to Manwood and Finch, April 10, 1640, BM, *Add.* MSS, 33,152, fol. 42. Mayor and Jurats of Sandwich to the Lord Warden?, April 10, 1640, *ibid.*, 44,846, fol. 2. KRO, *Sandwich Year Book*, C & D, Sa/AC 7, fols. 365v–366v. KRO, *Sandwich Letter Book*, Sa/C 1, fols. 14–15.

78 Horsfield, *History of Sussex*, II, 40. Hills, *History of East Grinstead*, 33–34. *CJ*, II, 10.

79 Wodehouse to Potts, [spring 1640]; Bodleian Library, *Tanner* MSS, 67, fol. 189. BM, *Add.* MSS, 11,045, fol. 99v.

Smith to be one of its candidates. He complied and was duly returned.[80] Another method of control which corporations could employ to thwart potential candidates was to refuse to admit them as freemen, thereby making them ineligible to stand. The corporations of both Sandwich and Hastings used this tactic effectively to block the choice of men who were alleged to have "reform" sympathies; it ensured the return of the Lord Warden's nominee.[81] Tamworth's corporation was more blatant in its election methods. It withheld "notice . . . of the time and place of the election" and proceeded to make its own choices. The bitter inhabitants of the town promptly petitioned the House of Commons against the election, protesting against "the usurped power of the corporate body."[82]

Corporations, too, were not immune to the promises of a candidate or an election patron that he would bear all the legitimate charges of a member of Parliament. Whether or not this was decisive is impossible to tell, but no doubt the corporation at Queenborough was delighted by John Harrison's promise to "free and discharge the said town . . . from all manner of wages or other charges whatsover" which he could have legally demanded from them. Beverley, Bishop's Castle, and Windsor also must have been much contented with similar promises from their members.[83] Lord Baltimore also employed this method in his Christchurch election campaign. He promised in his last nominations "that neither of these men . . . shall be any way charge-

---

80   John Swift et al., of Hindon, to Cottington?, December 10, 1639, PRO, SP 16/435/57. Harvey to Smith, December 18, 1639, ibid., 436/5. Brerewood to Smith, January 16, 1640, ibid., 442/17.

81   Gruenfelder, "The Spring Parliamentary Election at Hastings, 1640," 49–55. KRO, Sandwich Letter Book, C & D, Sa/AC 7, fols. 365ᵛ–366ᵛ.

82   BM, Add. MSS, 28,175, fols. 109–109ᵛ.

83   Harrison to the Mayor, Jurats, and Burgesses of Queenborough, March 16, 1640, KRO, Queenborough Corp. MSS, Qb/C 1/37. Beverley Borough Records, 1575–1821, ed. J. Dennett (Yorkshire Archaeological Society, Record Series, vol. 84, 1933), 102. HMC, Westmorland MSS, 403. R. R. Tighe & J. E. Davis, Annals of Windsor (2 vols.; London: Longmans, Brown, Green, Longmans, & Roberts, 1858), II, 144–145.

able to your borough." In his case, even that was not enough; money could no longer induce Christchurch to accept everyone he recommended.[84]

Other kinds of appeals were occasionally employed by candidates. Sir Christopher Abdy wrote to the corporation of New Romney that he esteemed "a free election at a higher rate than the recommendations (which I might have had) of a great man's letter." Like many other candidates, he stressed his local connections and service.[85] Edward Partridge smugly made the corporation at Sandwich aware that although he knew "it is usual to procure [a] lord's letters and make other such like means to get these places," he had "purposely neglected that so I might leave you to your free choice." His disavowals of noble support and promises of loyal service got him nowhere; the port's corporation preferred the Lord Warden's recommendations and the letters of the "great" in behalf of its other candidates.[86] Neighborly connections or services performed were a common method of election courtship. It was one method employed at Hull, Hastings, Rye, Carlisle, and Christchurch, to name but a few. Indeed, in the Hull, Rye, and Carlisle elections, it was decisive in swaying the corporation's election favor.[87]

The tabulation below, based on the evidence that survives for seventy-six of the spring election contests, summarizes the various methods employed.

84   Baltimore to the Mayor and Burgesses of Christchurch, February 25, March 3, 1640. *Christchurch Borough* MSS.

85   Abdy to Smith, December 7, 1639, KRO, *New Romney Corporation* MSS, NR/AEp 45.

86   Partridge to the Mayor, Jurats, and Commonalty of Sandwich, January 2, 1640, KRO, *Sandwich Letter Book*, Sa/C 1, fol. 14.

87   Dalston to the Mayor of Carlisle, December 7, 1639, *Carlisle City* MSS, Ca/2/120, fol. 18. Button to the Mayor and Burgesses of Christchurch, December 18, 1639, Ashburnham to the Mayor and Jurats of Rye, December 18, 1639, ESRO, *Rye Corp.* MSS, 47/131, 39:5. Diggis to the Mayor and Burgesses of Rye, December 24, 1639, *ibid.*, 47/131, 39:6. Colepeper to the Mayor and Jurats of Rye, *ibid.*, 47/131, 39:8. Same to Same, January 13, 1640, *ibid.*, 47/132, 39:1. Gruenfelder, "The Spring Parliamentary Election at Hastings, 1640," 49–55. Popple to Vane, March 21, 1640, PRO, *SP* 16/448/53.

Noble patronage	46
The mustering of tenants, friends, relatives	20
Elections wherein intimidation or libels were used or where campaigning among the freemen against the corporation occurred	13
Payment of expenses, entertainment costs	11
Local service or connections	10
Employment of an office: sheriff, justice of the peace, lord lieutenancy	6
Corporation selection	5
Members serving without pay	5
Employment of ministers as election orators and agents	4
Bribery	2

The months preceding the Short Parliament witnessed a great variety of election methods. Threats and intimidation raised their ugly heads while the puritan ministers lent a novel aspect to the election season. The cost of election was rising; blatant bribery appeared. The usual stratagems were still employed; friends and relatives, indeed almost anyone who might be able to vote, were mustered in a candidate's behalf. Noble patronage still was the most popular method of securing election favor. These elections and the variety of means and methods used provide eloquent testimony to the ingenuity of the politically minded Englishman of 1640.

THE ISSUES OF THE ELECTION

The lines "Choose no Ship Sheriff, nor Court Atheist, no fen drainer, nor Church Papist," from a verse circulated during the spring election in Lincoln, typify the contests very well. They portray the heady mixture of national and local issues which vexed the elections and contributed to the frequent faction, strife, and bitterness which marked many of the contests.[88]

The seriousness of the situation did not escape politically minded Englishmen anxious to serve in the spring parliament —

88   BM, *Add.* MSS, 11,045, fol. 99v.

nor their wives, for Brilliana Harley wrote, "the Lord fill them with wisdom for that work"[89]; her husband, Sir Robert Harley, and Sir Walter Pye had just been elected for Herefordshire. Her sentiments were echoed over all England. A political moderate, Thomas Wodehouse in Norfolk, rebelling against the growing factionalism developing around him, urged his kinsman, John Potts, to stand for one of Norfolk's knightships since, "In these bad times all good men ought to seek such means as might enable them to enterprise good matters." The Cheshire election was the most bitter and factious struggle the county had witnessed in the Early Stuart period. "For the county the labor is indefatigable, and the contestation grows high," complained Thomas Murden from Chester. "I am sorry in my heart to see the preparations of discord, and I sit down in silence to see what God will do in the ambition of these men, who all joined in their own profit where there was a bare pretense of a public good, and now rend the bowels of it to advance their own interests and popularity."[90] Unhappily for Wodehouse, Murden, and others, factionalism stirred by national issues was rising all round men of goodwill; its appearance was often evident in the surviving election correspondence. It is too much to say that in the spring all of England was dividing into two camps, for and against the Crown, for and against Laud, for and against ship money, but to a surprising extent these issues were a definite part of the election struggle. Based on the surviving primary evidence for 83 elections, 33 of them, or almost 40 per cent, reflected the impact of these "national" issues, a substantial figure indeed. That number included those county or borough petitions which were either presented to the House of Commons or which have survived in full where the complaints were enumerated. Other petitions from Norwich,

89   Brilliana Harley to her son, Edward, March 14, 1640, Lewis, *Letters of Brilliana Harley*, 87.
90   Wodehouse to Potts, March 13, 1640, Bodleian Library, *Tanner* MSS, 67, fol. 176. Murden to Smith, March 20, 1640, PRO, *SP* 16/448/43. Murden to Smith, March 27, 1640, *ibid.*, 449/14.

Northampton, Essex, Suffolk, and Hertfordshire, all delivered to the Commons, are not included since the petitions themselves have apparently not survived. Of the 33 elections wherein national questions played a role, it is possible to assess just which issues were most common; the number of elections in which the chief issues arose is shown in the accompanying tabulation.[91]

Religion	20	Monopolies	3
Ship money	13	Forest grievances	2
Impositions	5	Knighthood fines	1
Annual parliaments		Military charges	1
desired	3	Other	2
		Total	50

Illustrations of the complexity of the election picture abound. The developing factionalism between "court and country," the preference for local candidates, and the exhilarating mixture of local and national issues served to obscure the election scene and make it all the more provocative, all the more challenging. The Abingdon contest, fought unsuccessfully by Bulstrode White-lock, exemplified a court-versus-country confrontation. He claimed no intention of standing for Parliament "because of the danger of the time and of the employment" but allowed himself to be persuaded "by my friends, here upon the argument of doing public good and chiefly by divers of the contrary faction to the court, and who favored the Scots Covenanters."[92] The same story, with an admixture of local issues, was reflected in the Lincoln contest where ship money, religion, and a local issue, the draining of the fens, all played some role.[93] The Southwark contest, too, indicated the impact of "national" issues. Robert Holborne was

91   This does not include the reports of eight sheriffs who alleged that ship money in their counties was uncollectible. Complaints about religion and ship money were the most common grievances which hurt the Court's election efforts and contributed most frequently to election success for candidates who appeared to be opponents of royal policies.

92   BM, *Add.* MSS, 37,343, fol. 198.

93   *Ibid.*, 11,045, fol. 99v. J. W. F. Hill, *Tudor and Stuart Lincoln* (Cambridge: University Press, 1956), 145.

aided no end in his victory because "he did always oppose the King, the ship money, and all monopolies whatsoever." He had won some fame by defending in the Court of King's Bench, "a merchant's widow, who was committed to prison for refusing to pay 40s. imposition upon every tun of wine."[94]

Laud, who had every reason to expect continuing favor at Reading thanks to his generosity to his birthplace, should have seen the handwriting on the wall in the first election. To the surprise of many, six of the corporation voted against his candidate and Sir John Berkeley, Holland's nominee, on the grounds that "a stranger . . . can be no friend to the town." The explanation goes deeper than that. Opposition, thanks to the views of Sir Francis Knollys and his son, was growing and displayed itself most vigorously in the second election, held when neither Berkeley nor Herbert accepted Reading's burgess-ships. Sir Robert Heath, former Attorney General for the Crown, stood in opposition to Sir Francis Knollys and his son. Heath, possibly nominated by the court, received no votes at all. Reading's corporation had spoken with a loud voice. Ship money, religion, nonparliamentary taxation, had all been the targets of the vocal Sir Francis Knollys, senior; it is hard to believe that his utterances did not assist both him and his son to victory.[95]

Religion was frequently the key issue in a given election; it was a very important issue generally in the spring campaign. When Lionel Cranfield, Earl of Middlesex, sounded out election prospects for his inexperienced son, James, at Tewkesbury, he was informed that he might not be a good candidate. There, as elsewhere, "an extraordinary care in elections [is taken] at this time, when religion is so much concerned, & the good of the commonwealth never more." Middlesex was told that his son-in-law, Lord Sheffield, would have a better chance, for he was "seasoned tim-

94   BM, *Add.* MSS, 11,045, fols. 73ᵛ, 97, 101ᵛ.

95   A. Aspinall et al., *Parliament through Seven Centuries, Reading and Its M.P.s.* (London: published for the Hansard Society by Cassell, 1962), 50–52, 108. Guilding, *Reading Records*, III, 488–489, 492–493. HMC, *Duke of Leeds* MSS, 186.

ber." Cheshire's tense campaign was also marked by the religious issue. The candidates, Murden wrote, were diligently laboring amongst the freeholders; "Sir William Brereton wins daily amongst the religious," thereby converting potential voters to his side.[96] Religion mixed with desire for local prestige proved almost too exciting a combination for Cheshire's concerned inhabitants.

Antagonism against outsiders was frequently expressed in the elections, often mixed with other grievances: religion, ship money, or the candidate's past court services. Nicholas, whose defeat at Sandwich has already been related, also suffered from this spirit of local animosity to an outsider. Richard Bourne the turner, who had spread the scandal against Nicholas, aptly expressed this view disdaining the strong recommendations he had received since, after all, he "lived at London and it would be no benefit to him [Bourne]." Moreover, Nicholas's past service, "to the Lord Duke [Buckingham]," was also held against him.[97] It was a fine marriage between antagonism to the court, localism, and religion that defeated Nicholas.

His quest was not helped by the fact that his antagonists in the Sandwich contest were both Kentish gentry. Edward Partridge and Sir Thomas Peyton, the freemen's candidates, profited from their local connections and reform views. Partridge kept the puritan Sabbath in his own home because his household was strongly of that persuasion although he was not. Peyton appeared to be another foe of the court. He was on friendly terms with two Kentishmen, Sir Edward Boys and Henry Heyman, both with long records of opposition to royal policy. This mixture of local reputation and alleged opposition to the Crown won for Partridge and Peyton the support of the freemen, those "facetious

96   William Hill, to Lionel, Earl of Middlesex, December 15, 1639, *Sackville* MSS, cited with the kind permission of Lord Sackville, of Sevenoaks, Kent. Murden to [Smith], March 20, 1640, PRO, *SP* 16/448/43.

97   Mayor and Jurats of Sandwich to Edward Nicholas, March 19, 1640, PRO, *SP* 16/448/33, enclosure I.

nonconformists" the Mayor complained about, who were tired of readily accepting "outsiders" as their burgesses and who gave their support instead to men they knew something about.[98] Partridge and Peyton, however, were prevented from standing in the election by the port's corporation; but they enjoyed their revenge in the fall 1640 elections, when the alliance of localism, issues, and the freemen triumphed.[99]

The Hastings election battle featured a similar blend of issues. Thomas Eversfield was a local man laboring, with the freemen's vocal aid, against a candidate with no connection to Hastings. Not only did he have local appeal, he also had an "opposition" air about him. His father had strongly opposed the forced loan of 1621 and had faced the Star Chamber after a dispute with the local vicar. Son Thomas was believed by many to have similar views; his local background and supposed opposition to the court were the foundations of his candidacy.[100]

Local strength and reputation on the one hand and court support or nomination on the other made the Carlisle election one of conflict. The Queen's ownership of the manor and castle of Carlisle had made it a reliable seat for one of her nominees. In five of the parliaments before 1640 a court nominee, usually Sir Henry Vane the elder, had been dutifully returned by the corporation. The story was reversed in the spring election. The local influence of the gentry prevailed despite the Queen's efforts and those of Lord Clifford, a previous election patron at Carlisle. Two local men with strong reputations in the city and county, William Dalston and Richard Barwis, were returned. Sir Richard Graham, Carlisle's recorder and a man of some local influence, also was rejected, possibly because he had relied heavily on his court connections.[101] Localism had triumphed, as it would again in the fall elections despite the Queen's best efforts.[102]

98 Keeler, *Long Parliament*, 298–299, 304–305.   99 *Ibid.*, 77–78.
100 Gruenfelder, "The Spring Parliamentary Election at Hastings, 1640," 49–55.
101 Samuel Jefferson, *The History and Antiquities of Carlisle* (Carlisle, 1838), 445. Henry Lord Clifford to the Mayor of Carlisle, December 8, 1639, Janu-

Even the shire election in Kent was not without its overtones of the issues that appeared elsewhere. Local interests and connections played a great role in the contest, but the grievances expressed in the Parliaments of 1640 cannot be ignored. An early candidate, George Sondes, was apprehensive about the effect of the more national complaints on his own candidacy. He believed he had to stand since "we which have been sheriff and had jury employments in our offices of deputy lieutenant, had need be present to justify ourselves the best we can when our actions are questioned, as undoubtedly they will."[103] Sir Edward Dering, another candidate, also faced the same type of question. His antagonist, Sir Roger Twysden, "has endeavored as far as may be to poison the good opinion the county has of you by possessing them how diligent and eager a servant you were for the court in the knighting monies." Twysden used the religious issue against Dering, pointing out that he "is none of our church," a frequent theme of his letters during the election. Dering, too, made religion part of his election solicitation, noting in one of his campaign letters that "next to the duty of religion, [he would] be careful of your town in particular."[104] Kent was an election battleground fought over by opponents who not only used their local influence, reputation, and connections, but also employed the

ary 12, 31, 1640, *Carlisle City* MSS, Ca/2/120, fols. 11, 18, 19. Dalston to the Mayor of Carlisle, December 7, 1639, *ibid.*, Ca/2/120, fol. 18. Sir Richard Graham to the Mayor of Carlisle, January 30, February 28, 1640, *ibid.*, Ca/2/120, fols. 10, 12. John Wintour to the Mayor of Carlisle, February 20?, 1640, *ibid.*, Ca/2/120, fol. 17. The Queen's Council to the Mayor of Carlisle, February 21, 1640, *ibid.*, Ca/2/120, fol. 14. Aglionby and Baynes to Clifford, January 20, 1640, *ibid.*, Ca/2/120, fol. 21.

103   Tomkyns to Lambe, October 1, 1640, PRO, SP 16/469/11. Keeler, *Long Parliament*, 40.

103   Sondes to Walsingham, December 9, 1639, BM, *Stowe* MSS, 743, fol. 136.

104   Sedley to Dering, March 7, 1640, *ibid.*, 743, fol. 140. Twysden to ?, March 9, 1640, *ibid.*, 184, fol. 10. Dering's five letters "to Dover friends," December 31, 1639, KRO, *Dering* MSS, U 350, C2/72. Twysden to Dering, December 24, 1639, Twysden's notes about the election in Kent, *Proceedings, principally in the County of Kent, in connection with the Parliaments called in 1640*, ed. L. B. Larking (London: Camden Society, 1862), 3–8.

more emotional "national" issues — religion, ship money, and knighthood fines — as weapons in the struggle.

Enough evidence has survived to allow some tentative conclusions. First, what historians can call national issues played an important role in the spring election. These issues, particularly ship money and religion, appeared frequently enough to suggest their significance in the election. Candidates stressed their religious views and worried over their neighbor's questions about their past activities in carrying out unpopular royal policies. Common grievances from as far apart as Bristol, Northamptonshire, and Middlesex testified to an increasing awareness and interest in a change or reform of royal practices.

Secondly, these issues added to the growing spirit of localism, a desire to elect men of reputation and connection within the county or borough. The "outsider" or "foreigner" formerly elected suffered for his real or alleged ties to the court, for his nomination at the hands of a known royal official or courtier nobleman; Carlisle, Hastings, and Sandwich were examples of such election controversies. The court candidate was in difficulty; he could easily be blamed for the very policies which had provoked the grievances under discussion. Local men, aware of the attitudes of their neighbors, could profit either because of their lack of a court connection or because they had been or were believed to be antagonistic toward royal policies. At least 48 of the spring elections for which there is evidence were embroiled in this very question: the conflict between local men of repute and a court or "outsider" nominee. This was the most striking feature of the spring election and was closely associated with the growing concern over what can be called national issues. The seriousness, bitterness, and factionalism which so often emerged in the elections were the result of the mounting interest in such grievances.

THE REFORM GROUP IN ACTION

The historian finds himself frustrated when attempting to show through surviving correspondence, diaries, or letter books the activities of a network of "reform" leaders, busily plotting to work their wills in parliamentary elections or in preparing petitions listing the grievances they had against Charles Stuart's government. The reason for such frustration is depressingly simple: no such papers appear to have survived. Were these letters burned in the dark of night by the "reform" group? Or, more likely, did time itself effect their destruction? Whatever the reason, no such papers have yet been found. Then how can the labors of a "reform" group be shown? Although the methods are less satisfactory, there remain two ways of discerning its performance: the evidence of a particular election and the survival of a petition of grievances. A noted historian has written that "the appearance of the petition marked the revival of a weapon . . . which was to become the strongest in the parliamentary puritan armory."[105] The summer and fall of 1640 provided eloquent testimony to the soundness of that appraisal. If the petition was not yet fully developed in the spring of 1640, it was certainly being experimented with; nine have either survived or were mentioned in the journals of the House.[106] Three petitions have survived in detail, and the others were mentioned either in the journals or are known, like the city of Bristol, to have sent "a deputation . . . to represent the many grievances under which the citizens were suffering." The Bristol deputation must have received a hearing; one of its members, Sergeant Glanville, was elected Speaker and it was to him that the deputation addressed its grievances.[107] Middlesex prepared a petition for the House of Commons designed for the knights elected from the county and read by "divers freeholders then present" who "so well approved thereof that they grew ear-

105 Pearl, *London and the Puritan Revolution*, 173–174.
106 Petitions have survived for Middlesex, Newcastle-upon-Tyne, and Northamptonshire, PRO, *SP* 16/453/52 (Middlesex), *ibid.*, 449/36, enclosure I (Newcastle-upon-Tyne), *ibid.*, 450/25 (Northamptonshire). The Middlesex petition does not survive in detail, but its main points are contained in the examination of Henry Arundel cited in n. 108 below. Petitions from Suffolk, Essex, Hertfordshire, Norwich, and Northampton are mentioned in *CJ*, II, 5–6.
107 John Latimer, *The Annals of Bristol in the Seventeenth Century* (Bristol: W. & F. Morgan, 1887), 147.

nest to have it delivered" to the Commons. It asked for "ease and redress against ship-money, against innovation in the Church, and a request to have a yearly Parliament."[108] It was similar to the other petitions received by the Commons, for in its debates the lower house sharply focused its attention on those three issues expressed in the Middlesex petition.[109]

None of these examples has illustrated a reform group at work, one which attempted to organize either an election or a petition or both. Northamptonshire's election and petition affords a glimpse of such labors. The county had long been a source of trouble for the Crown; its reform and puritan sympathies were clear and unmistakable. In 1639, the High Sheriff, Sir Christopher Yelverton, reported an audacious insult to the Crown when he sent to the Privy Council "a copy . . . of a presentment made by the grand jury at a Quarter Sessions concerning the ship-money" which declared the county's unalterable opposition to the tax.[110] A similar instance of discontent was reported that year when the villagers of Kilsby uttered "disloyal and seditious words" against ship money and about the Scottish revolt.[111]

It is little wonder that the shire election was an occasion of concern for the deputy lieutenants. They complained that "at the election of knights . . . some turbulent spirits by undue practices did cause great clamors amongst the multitude to be raised against the authority of the lieutenancy." The harassed deputies hoped that the Privy Council might take some appropriate action to preserve their maligned reputations and ignored authority. A parliamentary petition also resulted from the spring election which mightily complained that the county had been "of late . . . unusually and insupportably charged, troubled and grieved in our consciences, persons and estates by innovations in religion, exactions in spiritual courts, molestations of our most godly and learned ministers, ship money, monopolies, undue im-

108 "Examination of Henry Arundel," May 14, 1640, PRO, *SP* 16/453/52.
109 *CJ*, II, 4–5, 11–12.
110 Rushworth, *Historical Collections*, III, 991.
111 *CSPD*, 1639–1640, 246.

positions, army money, wagon money, horse money, conduct money, and enlarging the forest beyond the ancient bounds and other such; for not yielding to which things, or some of them, divers of us have been molested, distrained, and imprisoned."[112] It ended with a plea "that it may be so ordered that we may have a Parliament once a year . . . for preventing the like inconveniences for the time to come."[113] John Pym could not have done better; a more complete indictment of Charles Stuart's policies and practices could not have been found.

The Essex election was clearly a well-organized opposition effort which employed the varied talents of all — the Lord Lieutenant and his position of power, the puritan ministers, the movement about the county of potential voters. Sir Harbottle Grimston and Sir Thomas Barrington showed the reform network at its best. Barrington was a kinsman of the great puritan Earl Warwick, he was also related to Oliver Cromwell and John Hampden. Through marriage he was allied to the Lytton and Wallop families, both of the first rank among the reform group. Grimston had long opposed royal policies. He had offended the Court of High Commission and, on at least two other occasions, had incurred the wrath of the Privy Council for his opposition to royal demands.[114] Essex, too, prepared its petition and, although it has not survived, its contents can be easily imagined. Ship money, innovations in religion, forest grievances, and an appeal for more frequent parliaments must have been included, at the very least.

Usual election practices in Gloucestershire were almost overturned by the scheming of the "reformers" who, despite a previous and normally binding election agreement among the gentry over the choice of candidates, introduced a third candidate, Nathaniel Stephens of Eastington, Gloucestershire, whose reform credentials were beyond doubt. Stephens had so nettled the court

112 Deputy Lieutenants of Northamptonshire to William, Earl of Exeter, March 26, 1640, PRO, SP 16/449/4. Same to Same, April 13, 1640, ibid., 450/75. "Petition of the County of Northampton," April 4, 1640, ibid., 450/25.
113 Ibid.
114 Keeler, Long Parliament, 97–99, 198–199.

that he had been put off the commission of the peace. The events of election day clearly indicated a plot between Cooke, the agreed puritan candidate, and Stephens, the "surprise" candidate, to undermine the royalist Tracy. But, previously noted, Sir Robert Tracy's brother, the High Sheriff, was not above a substantial bit of chicanery himself. Gloucestershire's election gave evidence of a reform group at work: the puritan ministers busily campaigning, the plot of Cooke and Stephens to overthrow Tracy on election day and, finally, the usual network of family ties and marriage connections. Cooke's mother-in-law was a sister to that notable puritan, Sir Oliver Luke of Bedfordshire, and Cooke's brother-in-law, Thomas Hodges, was another constant opponent of royal policy and a close friend of Stephens.[115]

Ties of family and friendship, the industry of the puritan clergy, and the campaigning among the freeholders in both Essex and Gloucestershire illustrated the reform group at work. It can be no surprise that John Allibond, deeply worried by what he had witnessed in Gloucestershire, believed what he had heard, "that there is a kind of cunning underhand canvas of this nature, the greater part of the kingdom over." [116] The campaign did not cover the entire kingdom, but it was common enough to cause comment. Such a campaign was nothing new — the puritans had made a similar effort in the 1580's.[117]

The impression of an organized election effort by the reformers was certainly heightened, thanks to the role of "national" grievances or issues in the campaign. Ship money by the fall of 1639 was almost totally uncollectible; the Scottish revolt had been the straw that broke its back. Religious grievances were talked of openly, complained about forcefully. The Scottish example had again provided the impetus. Many other complaints were being heard or written down in the first petitions of grievances that

115   Willcox, *Gloucestershire*, 33–34. HMC, *Fifth Report with Appendix*, 345. Allibond to Heylyn, March 24, 1640, PRO, *SP* 16/448/79. *Gloucestershire Notes and Queries*, 1:410–413. *CJ*, II, 4, 7. Keeler, *Long Parliament*, 351.

116   Allibond to Heylyn, March 24, 1640, PRO, *SP* 16/448/79.

117   Neale, *Elizabethan House of Commons*, 241.

appeared in that hectic spring of 1640. These grievances, ignored by the Crown in the spring Parliament, would multiply through the summer and fall of 1640, providing eloquent evidence of the bankruptcy of Charles I's policies and of the growing gulf between the King and his politically important subjects.

Robert Read complained that "we who were made sure at first of burgess-ships are as likely to miss them as others, men being not able to perform what they promise."[118] His view was echoed by that very active electioneer, the Earl of Northumberland, who grumbled: "The elections that are generally made . . . give us cause to fear, that the Parliament will not sit long; for such as have dependence upon the Court, are in divers places refused; and the most refractory persons chosen."[119] The accuracy of these complaints is incontestable. As an election agent, the court had been rudely stopped in its intensive effort to place its candidates. The Cornish elections alone provided grim testimony of its failure. There were many reasons: the strength of the feelings stirred by the King's policies, the Scottish revolt, the unrequited grievances that had been building up year after year without resolution. Charles I had no one to blame but himself for the growth of the reform group and its efforts in the spring.

Corruption and the growth of faction, first witnessed in Elizabeth's last years, attained even more significant heights in the spring elections and with increasingly costly election "entertainments" pointed the way toward the abuses of the eighteenth century. The development of religious differences, the loud complaints against ship money and other financial exactions, the abandonment of Parliament since its dissolution in March 1629, signaled another important change in election patterns. Battles for local prestige and power there were, but at the same time the very prevalence of more national issues lent a decidedly political complexion to the spring elections.

118   Read to [Windebank], February 20, 1640, PRO, SP 16/445/80.
119   Northumberland to Leicester, March 19, 1640, Collins, *Letters and Memorials*, II, 641.

The Election to the Short Parliament

Local influence was often not enough; most candidates were considered on the basis of their religious views or their political records for or against the court. At Hastings, Eversfield's candidacy was encouraged not by his own activities but by the opposition record his father had earned. These men were also local and therefore more trustworthy than agents of the court which had proved itself the cause of the grievances, the "issues" of the election. Candidates not only labored in traditional ways, securing the aid of friends and relatives, but also emphasized their religious views, their concern over ship money, their demand for more frequent parliaments. Dering was accused of being too diligent in the collection of knighthood fines; Nicholas's service with Buckingham was remembered and his ties to the court scorned. The Queen's candidates at Carlisle were unknown and therefore rejected. Even Graham, a Cumberland man, who relied upon his reputation at court and the court's assistance, was refused. Grimston and Barrington won votes because of their religious views; the same was true for Stephens and Cooke, and for those men who were sent to Westminster from Dorchester, Great Yarmouth, Lewes, and many more boroughs and counties. Traditional patrons, like Huntingdon in Leicestershire, suffered humiliating and surprising election defeats and watched in chagrin as reformers were chosen instead.

Many elections serve to portray the growth of a more political atmosphere in the England of 1640; patronage, clientage were still there but more and more a man's religious and constitutional views were important. Charles I's policies, which vexed so many of his countrymen, served to focus their attention on matters of policy. The court's own spring election efforts provoked similar election endeavors in behalf of those men desirous for reform, for an answer to their grievances. The court's own policies and their failure served to emphasize political issues as election issues. It was still a long way from the eighteenth-century election scene, but the path was clear. The spring elections were one step on that path, but they were a very important step indeed.

HOWARD S. REINMUTH, JR.

Border Society in Transition

Nearly fifty years ago a distinguished book concerned with the history of the Council of the North initiated the modern study of that region.[1] Since that time a number of publications have at least partly remedied the previous neglect of the border counties.[2] Most of these works have primarily treated directly or obliquely the subject of Anglo-Scottish relations, though with some reference to the character of the border area itself. A general assumption has been made that the late medieval domination of the area by the Nevilles and Percies was replaced by that of the Tudors, who brought the north into the rest of England politically through the Council of the North. In many other respects, however, it has been assumed that the north remained largely backward in religious allegiance and medieval in social structure and economic development.

Until recently, historians had also agreed that the advent of James I, by removing the Scottish threat to the north, brought

1   R. R. Reid, *The King's Council in the North* (London: Longmans, Green, 1921).

2   D. L. W. Tough, *The Last Years of a Frontier* (Oxford: Clarendon Press, 1928). A. L. Rowse, *The Expansion of Elizabethan England* (London: Macmillan, 1955). T. I. Rae, *The Administration of the Scottish Frontier, 1513–1603* (Edinburgh: University Press, 1966). C. M. L. Bouch & G. P. Jones, *A Short Economic and Social History of the Lake Counties, 1500–1830* (Manchester: University Press, 1961).

peace to that area, an assumption which has been successfully challenged.[3]

This essay is concerned with one general development whose implications have either been neglected or misinterpreted: the changing social composition of the border counties.

Both late medieval and early modern English society were hierachical. In this regard the north conformed to the national pattern. It has generally been assumed that the power of the Nevilles and Percies (to name the two most powerful border families of the late middle ages) was a threat to national order and to the extension in the north of royal authority. The Tudors have often been seen as supplanting the nearly autonomous rule of these great families with conciliar government imposed from Westminster. It might be more accurate, however, to suggest that members of the border aristocracy were persuaded to share power and to accept an influential place, though at times a subordinate role, both in the Council of the North, and the wardenships of the Marches.[4]

If one may legitimately make this assumption, such cooperation was periodically shattered by events like the Pilgrimage of Grace of 1536 and the Northern Rebellion of 1569. Until that time, however, the northern families had exhibited great endurance: individual members had been disgraced, killed in battle, or executed for treason, yet succeeding members after a time resumed the family's dominance in their "countries," as contemporaries were wont to call them.

This pattern changed in the late sixteenth century partly because the Neville family died out in the direct male line (though a Neville pretender maintained a precarious existence overseas),

3   Penry Williams, "The Northern Borderlands under the Early Stuarts," *Historical Essays, 1600–1750*, ed. H. E. Bell & R. L. Ollard (London: A. & C. Black, 1963), 1–17.

4   The fourth, sixth, seventh, and eighth Earls of Northumberland were members of the Council of the North, for example. The fourth, sixth, and seventh Earls were also Wardens of the East and Middle Marches. See Reid, *King's Council*, Appendix II, 485–493.

partly because the Percies were exiled from the north.[5] Another family of slightly lower rank, the Dacres, also died out in the direct male line. The surviving coheiresses married Howards. Early in James I's reign the border counties were thus largely bereft of resident great nobles.

It is true that the Clifford Earls of Cumberland retained their lands and exercised some political power, but the bulk of their estates were in the West Riding of Yorkshire and in Westmorland. The Whartons also remained in Westmorland, but despite their noble title they were of no political significance in the border area.

In Northumberland Lord Hunsdon, Queen Elizabeth's cousin, had played an important role in the government of the East March. Doubtless through his influence, his youngest son, Sir Robert Carey, had obtained seats in Parliament as a burgess from Morpeth in 1586–1587 and 1588–1589, and as a knight of the shire from Northumberland in 1597–1598 and 1601. Yet, although Sir Robert did not receive his patent of nobility until 1626 (as Earl of Monmouth), he never sat in Parliament for a northern constituency in James's reign. After 1603 he moved south and lived at court.

A Northumberland family temporarily lost its title. Cuthbert Lord Ogle (c. 1540–1597) died without male heirs, and although his younger daughter Catherine was recognized in 1628 as Baroness Ogle in her own right, it remained for her husband's family, the Cavendishes, to rise to power in the later seventeenth century.[6]

According to the traditional interpretation the disappearance of the great families was seen as a blessing. Those who had so often opposed royal authority, especially its extension to their countries, the forces of disorder, the overmighty subjects had

5   Charles, sixth Earl of Westmorland, fled abroad after the failure of the 1569 rising, was attainted in 1571, died in Flanders in 1601. He had no sons, but four daughters.
6   GEC, *Complete Peerage*, X, 36–37.

disappeared. Peace, order, and "good governance" were established.

This interpretation is subject to challenge, however. Whatever the Percies and Nevilles may have meant nationally, they had been the principal governors of the borders, where, indeed, they had been the forces of order. Only locally resident aristocrats who commanded the allegiance of the "meaner sort" could possibly have coped, in Elizabethan England, with the day-to-day problems of the area, and could have suppressed the threat posed by thieves and murderers, Scottish or English, and the ever-present menace of Scottish incursions. Westminster was remote in the sixteenth century (Edinburgh was even more remote!): great lords in residence alone could make their power consistently felt among their tenants and neighbors.

The disappearance of the great border families created an anomaly, a hierarchical border society minus its natural leaders. This removal of the top layer of border society was all the more significant because of the enormous gap in wealth, power, and prestige between the few great magnates with their vast estates and the fairly numerous but infinitely poorer and less prestigious gentry. There was certainly no lack of such families in the border area. Many survived generation after generation, but almost none had ever risen to the rank of noblemen, none had been able to effect great increases in their landholdings over a span of time, none had shared prominently in the exercise of local power, except the Dacres. Viewed over the centuries, border society had been remarkably stable, even static. Each social group had had its place and remained fixed there. The upheavals which convulsed border society did not arise internally from its social composition, but externally from the power of Westminster and of the Scots.

The absence of the traditional great families from the border area created a power vacuum potentially conducive to chaos, not order. No English region so large as the border counties of Cumberland and Northumberland was without resident aristocrats at the beginning of James's reign. To maintain a permanently headless society in contradiction to the pattern provided by the rest of the kingdom was quite impossible. The Stuarts had to rule *through* someone.

Two possibilities existed; neither was novel. One was to introduce noblemen from other areas to replace the local ones who had disappeared. This was certainly risky, especially in the most provincial society in England, one with exceptionally stable and deeply ingrained loyalties. Would an outsider be accepted?

The alternative was to raise members of the gentry to noble rank to replace extinguished or disgraced houses. But whereas gentry had by no means infrequently been ennobled in English history, the process had generally come as the result of a gradual accumulation of lands and local power, though there had been spectacular exceptions. The practice had not usually been to raise modest gentry to become great noblemen.

At the beginning of James I's reign it was the former alternative which seemed the more promising. There were two major candidates: Lord William Howard, by birth a member of a great English noble family, by marriage the resident heir of the Dacres in the north, after 1603; and George Home, Earl of Dunbar, a powerful Scottish favorite of the new monarch, endowed with English lands near the border by a generous king. His handicap as a Scot, however — a complete stranger and, indeed, traditional enemy — was very great.

The more logical candidate from the point of view of land-holding was Lord William Howard. He had his base in Cumberland in the vast Barony of Gisland, his seat at Naworth Castle. He also possessed extensive lands in Northumberland, especially the Barony of Morpeth. Yet from the King's point of view Dunbar possessed the advantage of lands and power in Scotland to combine with his newly acquired English holdings. In that sense he was really the more logical candidate to bring into being the King's concept of the Middle Shires comprising both the Scottish and English border areas.

Dunbar's career, unfortunately, was as brief as it was successful. In early 1607 Sir William Selby, a commissioner for the Middle Shires, wrote to Salisbury, "Northumberland has for months past been much infested with theft, but is now well quieted by the pains of the Earl of Dunbar, who has caused a great number of the principal Riddesdale and Tynedale thieves, and of other parts, to be apprehended and committed."[7]

In 1609 Dunbar himself reported that the course of severity he and the Earl of Cumberland had followed in the Middle Shires had caused a great number of the worst criminals to flee into the heart of Scotland, where, significantly, they had been received by various noblemen and gentlemen.[8]

In the meantime, Dunbar was securing connections with Lord William's family through negotiations for the marriage of his daughter and coheiress Elizabeth to Theophilus, Lord Howard de Walden, eldest son of Lord William's brother, the Earl of Suffolk. The marriage had been arranged although not actually performed before Dunbar's untimely death in 1611. It did, however, subsequently take place. Thereby Lord William's nephew became in right of his wife a considerable landholder in Northumberland. He also strengthened his uncle's position. Lord William Howard in a sense gained more by the Earl of Dunbar's death than merely a share in a royal commission to make secure the Earl's goods![9]

For a few years the Earl of Dunbar had worked diligently though harshly, with complete royal support but with inadequate military means, to effect good order on the border especially in Northumberland. The question was, Who would inherit his position?

It is time to turn now to the central figure in this part of the story, the Lord William Howard. His natural position made him

7 Sir William Selby to Robert Cecil, February 10, 1607. HMC, *Cal. Salisbury* MSS, XIX, 44.

8 Earl of Dunbar to James I, April ?, 1609. PRO, *SP* 14/44/66.

9 Sir William Bowyer to Robert Cecil, February 6, 1611, *CSPD*, 1611–1618, 7.

a logical candidate for the place of the greatest border magnate of the early seventeenth century, but for one handicap: his religion.

That Lord William was a Roman Catholic was common knowledge; that this fact was a handicap in the King's eyes we need not doubt, since we have James's own word for it. At the beginning of 1607 Sir Thomas Lake had written to Salisbury. "His Highness thinks it reasonable that any man of quality resident thereabout [the border] ought to have them [the Berwick garrison] in the like case, [to pursue thieves] and named expressly Lord William Howard; but not with order that any such warrant should be directed for him."[10] It appears that despite this statement there was some misunderstanding and it was assumed that, in fact, Lord William had been given this authority. The King made his position clear to Salisbury in the following letter:[11]

I only spake it by comparison that such a power could not well be refused to Dunbar, when I could have wished that that garrison should be so diligent as not only to ride upon any purpose of Dunbar's making unto them, but even if Lord William Howard or any gentleman of the country could inform them where any of the outlaws were, they should not spare their pains in riding to make a search for them. And in good faith it was a strange fortune that speaking since that time anent the said Lord William in the presence of two or three of the chamber — I chanced to say that the said gentleman's religion did him great harm at my hands, for notwithstanding the infinite trust I had in the faithfulness of his brother [Earl of Suffolk] and uncle [Earl of Northampton], yet I durst never bestow any preferment upon him in my days only because of his religion and devotion to the Jesuits.

This is one aspect of a complex situation. Another is, however, that whereas James would not grant Lord William the offices he might otherwise have held, he would also not permit his prosecution. Attempts were indeed made at various times to have Lord William prosecuted for recusancy, to convict him so that his economic power could be broken. This latter aspect was pointed

10   Sir Thomas Lake to Robert Cecil, January 18, 1607, HMC, *Cal. Salisbury* MSS, XIX, 15.
11   James I to Robert Cecil, February 22, 1607, *ibid.*, 52–53.

out in an anonymous letter. The writer complained bitterly about Lord William's power, and his oppressive rule in the border area, but then continued, "By this means he maketh law which is the refuge from oppression, his sword of oppression, and yet if the law may have course to convict him as a recusant the King shall have two parts [two-thirds] of his land."[12] That the King would not do this, however, was clearly stated in November 1616 when Lord William's legal agent in London, John Dudley, wrote to his brother, "The information that Mr. Salkeld had exhibited against my Lord William Howard for recusancy, is by the King's commandment to be withdrawn."[13] Thus, although Lord William would be denied office because of his religion, he would not be prosecuted for it. This left him in a position which needs careful examination, one which might have both advantages and disadvantages, and in which his economic and social positions were still very powerful. Office in the usual sense was denied him, but was the actual exercise of political power in fact also denied him?

Historians have not generally correlated two characteristics of the Tudor-Stuart period. The first, well known, is that the possession of large estates was a necessary prerequisite to social position and political power. There were men in the Early Stuart period such as the Lord Wharton who though possessed of a noble title were in fact impotent politically and were of little importance in their local society, though of course they could not be denied the courtesies to which their rank entitled them.

Equally, however, men who possessed vast estates, though they were denied office because of their religion, though they were denied, so to speak, the accidents of power, were not necessarily denied the substance, the actual exercise of political influence.[14] Here the failure of the historian is to distinguish between being

12   PRO, *SP* 14/40/11. Undated, possibly 1616 when the attempt was being made to have Lord William convicted of recusancy.

13   Westmorland R.O., D/Ry 97.

14   It is of course both true and important that such a person could not enjoy the *profits* of office.

a recusant and a Roman Catholic.[15] The position of a recusant in Elizabethan and Early Stuart England was indeed difficult. Such a person was at least potentially subject to a broad array of penalties principally fiscal in nature, though also he could be confined to a limited area near his residence. Such families, of which the Treshams furnish a good example among the gentry, had their economic base gradually eroded through the necessity of paying fines. This could ultimately force them to sell their lands and thus to lose their capital in the social as well as the economic sense. Such men were not only denied office, but also any indirect political influence in their localities. Their very social position among their neighbors was precarious. Who, for example, could contemplate with equanimity contracting a marriage for his child with the offspring of such a recusant family?

The position of Roman Catholics who were *not* proceeded against as recusants was, potentially at least, quite different. Although any generalization would be hazardous, one can at least deal with a concrete case. Lord William Howard, a known Roman Catholic, maintained intact his economic base, his vast estates in five northern counties (Cumberland, Northumberland, Westmorland, Durham, and Yorkshire). Such economic power reinforced his social position among his neighbors.

Here, too, an important distinction should be made — at least for Lord William, if not for Roman Catholics in general — the distinction between zealous protestants and establishment Anglicans. The attempts to have Lord William convicted for recusancy, and the evidence that Lord William was the leader of a Catholic party in the north, come from men of deeply protestant convictions for whom religion, reformed religion, was the dominant aspect of their lives. No doubt to such men, especially in the aftermath of the Gunpowder Plot, the culmination of a series of

15   For example W. R. Trimble's book, *The Catholic Laity in Elizabethan England, 1558–1603* (Cambridge, Mass.: Harvard University Press, 1964), is mistitled, for in fact it treats almost exclusively of recusants and largely ignores those noblemen and gentlemen who were Roman Catholic so far as one can determine, but were never proceeded against successfully as recusants.

Catholic plots, Lord William must have appeared the satanic leader of a dastardly papist design to subvert true religion. Certain historians have seemed rather uncritically willing to accept these contentions.[16]

In fact, however, religious differences do not seem to have been so significant to contemporary establishment Anglicans, such as the Bishops of Carlisle, who were Lord William's neighbors. Of the six bishops who held office between 1603 and 1640, four were natives of either Cumberland or Westmorland. There is evidence that the Howards observed some of the usual social courtesies with three of these four men. For example, on August 13, 1609, the following event occurred at the Countess of Arundel's castle of Greystoke: "Sunday the thirteenth day was the Right Reverend father Henry [Robinson], by God's divine providence Bishop of Carlisle at Greystoke Church and did preach I Corinthians tenth chapter and verse third, and this said day was the honorable the Lady Anne, Countess of Arundel at Greystoke Castle, the Lord William Howard and the Lady Elizabeth his wife with many others . . . The Lord Bishop did dine there. . . ."[17] The bishop, Henry Robinson, a native of Carlisle, had an interesting text, "And they all ate of the same spiritual food."

In July 1623 when Richard Milburne, a native of Utterbank, Gilsland, was bishop, Lady Elizabeth Howard visited one of his principal residences, the Rose Castle.[18] Barnaby Potter, a native of Westmorland, sent a gift of tulips to Lord William in 1634.[19] In addition, it appears that Bishop Francis White, whose birthplace is unknown, visited Lord William in September 1629.[20]

16   See Williams, "The Northern Borderlands," 12.

17   Rev. T. Lees, "Extracts from the Registers at Greystoke Church, during the Reigns of Elizabeth and the Stuart Kings," *CW*, I, 338–339 (1866–1873).

18   Prior's Kitchen, Durham, *Howard-Naworth* MSS, 1622 Account Book, fol. 28.

19   Rev. George Ornsby, *Selections from the Household Books of the Lord William Howard of Naworth Castle* [hereafter Ornsby] (Durham, Surtees Society, 68, 1878), 316.

20   *Ibid.*, 263.

All of these instances would seem to indicate that the bishops regarded Lord William as a great landowner, a neighbor, to whom the usual social courtesies were due, despite his religion. Religious differences have perhaps seemed more important to some historians than they were to contemporaries, who had, after all, to function within not only the religious, but also the social, economic, and political frameworks of the age.

Thus, Lord William enjoyed a measure of peaceful coexistence with his Anglican neighbors which made possible the real political power to which his economic position and social rank entitled him, despite the fact that because of his religion he did not enjoy the offices to which he would otherwise normally have been entitled.

Concrete cases can make apparent his political power and Lord William's own awareness of the support he enjoyed at court. In 1606, for example, a notorious felon, William Story, was about to be prosecuted for cattle-stealing. The Bishop of Carlisle wrote to Sir Wilfrid Lawson, one of the border commissioners, that what had moved the commissioners of oyer and terminer to try Story "was that the Lord William Howard in open court gave in evidence that of late the trail was diverse times followed to his [Story's] house and never could be made good after."[21]

In another example, of which many more could be cited, we find the Bishop of Carlisle and Lawson writing to Lord William, "We send your lordship here enclosed a copy of Blackhouse his examination, praying your lordship, after perusal thereof, to signify unto us your opinion, and what your lordship's desire is to have done with him."[22]

Aside from the situation in Cumberland which was itself all-important to a local man like Lawson, there was a further point,

---

21   Henry Robinson, Bishop of Carlisle, to Sir Wilfrid Lawson. October 3, 1606. John Rylands Library, *Earl of Crawford and Balcarres* MSS, Acts of the Commissioners for the Government of the Borders, fol. 164ᵛ [hereafter *Crawford* MS]. I wish to thank the Earl of Crawford and Balcarres for his gracious permission to use this invaluable manuscript.

22   March 5, 1607, *Crawford* MS, fol. 190.

as Lord William made clear. He was about to go to London when he wrote Lawson, but he hoped there would be a gaol delivery in Carlisle before his departure since a man was to be tried whom Lord William suspected of stealing his cattle. He wanted to see Lawson, he said, ask his advice, and speak his own mind, "for though I be silent here, I will not spare to speak where I hope to be heard, but further than you shall direct me I will not proceed, faithfully promising you the small help I am by my friends able to afford you."[23]

A few months later in a similar vein he wrote to Lawson concerning a matter in which the Earl of Northampton, Lord William's uncle was involved. "For the kindness you have pleased to afford me and my friends that I have solicited you for, better than myself shall give thanks and be ready to acknowledge to you upon all occasions that you shall have to make trial of them and me."[24] It is well known that the Howards were close to the King from the beginning of the reign, as James I had said at his first coming to England. In company with the future Earl of Northampton, James met Lord William and the future Earl of Suffolk and said, "here be two of your nephews, both Howards. I love the whole house of them." The writer continued, "the King said they should never repent his coming into this kingdom."[25] The Howard power not only continued but grew, especially after the Earl of Salisbury's death in 1612. Yet that power could also be lost. The elderly Earl of Northampton died in 1614, and much more important, the Earl of Suffolk and his wife were disgraced in 1618.

It is at this point that one may conjecture that the position occupied by Lord William may have involved advantages as well as disadvantages. Had Lord William held office and been closely identified at court with his brother, the Earl of Suffolk, it is in-

---

23   September 19, 1606, *ibid.*, fol. 163ᵛ.
24   January 9, 1607, *ibid.*, fol. 192.
25   John Holland to Sir Bassingbourne Gawdy, May or June 1603, BM, *Egerton* MSS, 2714/1802.

conceivable that he, too, would not have suffered in the family's fall. The position of Lord William may have given him what was most important: the support of a powerful faction at court so long as that power lasted, but protection to some extent from the full consequences of his family's disgrace. A certain detachment, the result partly of geography but also of exclusion from office, meant a lack of attempts at vengeance by the enemies of the Howards.

Moreover, one Howard in addition to Lord William was also relatively untouched and remained to become close to the succeeding sovereign, Charles I. This was Thomas Howard, second Howard Earl of Arundel and Surrey, the only son of Lord William's martyred elder half-brother, Philip Howard. Nor was Lord Howard de Walden's position in the north destroyed by his father's difficulties, since his economic base was his wife's untouched border estates.

But let us return to the border area itself. Not only was Sir Wilfrid Lawson (who was one of the commissioners for the Middle Shires, knight of the shire in James's first Parliament, and twice Sheriff of Cumberland) solicitous of Lord William's wishes, but another of the commissioners, Edward Grey of Morpeth, Esq., was Lord William's receiver for Northumberland. Lord William used Grey more than once as a messenger, as he stated in a letter which also contained the following passage: "if the world were as I thank God it is not nor I trust never shall be, it were too heavy and dangerous a burden to be borne in this place by a southern novice as I confess myself to be."[26] At that very time, however, the English commissioners were writing to Salisbury describing Lord William as "a great furtherer of justice and a persecutor of the wicked cankers of our country."[27]

Perhaps such praise of Lord William's concern for justice prompted the Earl of Dunbar himself to write Lord William ask-

26   Lord William Howard to Sir Wilfrid Lawson, January 9, 1607, *Crawford* MS, fol. 192.
27   January 19, 1607, *ibid.*, fol. 195.

ing his opinion concerning a bill in parliament to take away hostile laws between England and Scotland. The letter reveals that Lord William had already spoken to his brother, the Earl of Suffolk, concerning the matter. Probably Suffolk, in turn, had spoken to Dunbar, who completed the circle by asking Lord William directly.[28]

Later in 1616 the Privy Council addressed a series of questions concerning the state of the borders to the Earl of Cumberland, Lord William Howard, and his nephew, Lord Howard de Walden.[29] In 1618 came a greater recognition: Lord William's inclusion in a commission to survey the state of the borders.[30]

In the next reign, the pattern of protection from prosecution for recusancy was continued, as a 1629 letter from Charles to his attorney general revealed.[31] Similarly, though great office continued to elude the aging Lord William, he found a place from time to time among commissions concerned with affairs in his own "country."[32]

Thus, it may be argued that whereas Lord William's Roman Catholicism prevented him from holding important office at court or on the national scene, and indeed from offices of maximum importance in his own area, it did not prevent him from exercising great political power and influence on the borders — perhaps not so much as his enemies accused him of exercising or with as clear an intent to further his religion (accusations perhaps too readily accepted by at least one historian), but sufficient nevertheless to be the leading aristocrat in the border region in the Early Stuart period.[33] One of the latter accusations was based upon the marital

28   A draft of Lord William's reply to Dunbar, dated June 20, 1607, is in *Castle Howard* MSS, 4/22.

29   Prior's Kitchen, Durham, *Howard-Naworth* MSS, no. 1 in handlist of Lord William Howard's Letters. Lord William sent his own ideas separately, *ibid.*, no. 3. Both are printed in Ornsby, 416–419.

30   May 8, 1618, *CSPD*, 1611–1618, 539.

31   April 11, 1629, BM, *Egerton* MSS, 2553, fol. 73.

32   PRO, *SP* 16/343/75. Printed in Ornsby, 465–469. Included in the commission is Lord William's second son, Sir Francis Howard.

33   Williams, "The Northern Borderlands," 11–12, and references in n. 1, 12.

interconnections of Roman Catholic families such as the Howards and Widdringtons, which zealous protestants saw as evidence
of a northern Catholic conspiracy. These marriages may be ex-
plained much more rationally as attempts to preserve their faith
in troubled times through providing Roman Catholic wives for
their children, thus attempting to ensure that their descendants
would continue to be reared in their faith.

Something else eluded Lord William because of his religion;
a title of nobility. As the younger son of a duke, he was habitually
given the courtesy title "lord." When one considers the honors
heaped upon the Howards by James I, however, one cannot help
concluding that Lord William's religion cost him a peerage. The
family did not have long to wait. Lord William's great-grandson
Charles was born in 1630 and so certainly remembered his great-
grandfather, who died in 1640, as a patriarchal family figure. This
Charles, by steering a careful course through the troubled period
of the English Civil War, managed to satisfy Cromwell and yet
to receive favors from Charles II at the Restoration. The sacri-
fices of Lord William's sons and other family members in the
royalist cause certainly aided this recognition. So, no doubt, did
Charles's decision to change his religion. In 1661 Charles Howard
was created Earl of Carlisle. A new era had dawned for the descendants of Lord William. Certainly Charles had political influence such as Lord William had never exercised: a seat in the
House of Lords, through control of parliamentary elections, for
example, as Lord of Morpeth in that pocket borough. Indeed,
the family moved to a more temperate climate, in the heart of
their Yorkshire estates where the third Earl of Carlisle was to
erect that magnificent Vanbrugh mansion, Castle Howard. But
this takes us far beyond our story.

While in the Early Stuart period Lord William, and much
more briefly the Earl of Dunbar, were acting to fill the void of
nobility in the border counties left by the extinction of the Nevilles and Dacres and the exile of the Percies, another process was

taking place very gradually, the rise of several gentry families to the rank of noblemen.

At the time of James I's accession to the English throne, the border counties abounded in gentry families of remarkable longevity in the direct male line, families who had prestige in their local areas, who had already held and were to continue to occupy positions which gave them limited political prestige and power. These families had lived in social stability, though well beneath the great border families in prestige and power. They almost never ventured as the Nevilles and Percies did so often, and so disastrously at times, into the greater (and more dangerous) arena of national politics.

The principal advances from gentry to noble rank occurred in Northumberland. The Grey family, who had provided a sheriff of the county as early as the reign of Henry IV, is one example. Sir Ralph Grey (died 1623) was knighted by James I at Berwick when the King entered his new realm in 1603. Sir Ralph had already been Sheriff of Northumberland in Elizabeth's reign and served in that capacity in 1611 also. His name appeared in a number of commissions of the peace.[34] His eldest son, William, became Sir William Grey, Bart., in 1619 and was created Baron Grey of Wark, Northumberland, in 1624. He served in the Commons in 1621 and in the 1624 session until his elevation to the peerage.[35] He continued to appear in the commissions of the peace in Charles I's reign.

[34] For purposes of sampling the commissions of the peace, recourse has been had to the following: For Cumberland the commission of 1 James I (PRO, C66/1620), 7 James I (*ibid.*, 1822), 13 James I (*ibid.*, 2076), and 1 Charles I (BM, *Harleian* MSS, 1622). For members of the House of Commons the lists of the knights of the shire, 1603–1629, have been consulted with occasional references to burgesses also. The lists of sheriffs are to be found as follows: For Northumberland, *Archaeologia Aeliana*, 4th ser., 20 (1942), and 21 (1943), two articles by C. H. Hunter Blair, "The Sheriffs of Northumberland," 20, 11–89; 21, 1–92. For Cumberland sheriffs see J. Nicolson & R. Burn, *The History and Antiquities of the Counties of Westmorland and Cumberland*, II, 566–573. For Northumberland justices of the peace, 2 James I (PRO, C66/1662) has been used instead of 1 James I. No additional footnotes will be employed for information to be found in any of the above references.

[35] GEC, *Complete Peerage*, VI, 168–169.

Sir Edward Grey, younger brother of William, had been Sheriff of Northumberland in the reign of Elizabeth also. Certainly by 1612, possibly earlier, he had become Lord William's receiver for Northumberland.[36] He was knighted by James I when that monarch was staying at his father's seat at Chillingham during the progress in 1617. Grey was also, as has been seen, one of the Commissioners for the Middle Shires.

Another important rising gentry family of Northumberland was the Widdrington family, which like the Greys had provided sheriffs in the later middle ages, as early as 1361. The head of the family in the reign of James I was Sir Henry Widdrington, knt. (died 1623). He married into the Cumberland gentry family, the Curwens, who sold Thornthwaite Manor in Westmorland to Lord William Howard in 1610. One of the most important men in Northumberland, Henry had been knighted by James I in 1603. He was Deputy Warden and Keeper of Riddesdale, knight of the shire from Northumberland in the first three of James I's parliaments, Sheriff of Northumberland briefly in February 1606. His name appeared on the commissions of the peace early in James I's reign not only for Northumberland but also for Cumberland. His brother's supposed connection with the Gunpowder Plot may explain the fact that he was on the commissions for Northumberland in 2 and 13 James I, but not in 7 James I, and that his name disappeared from the Cumberland commissions of the peace after 4 James I. The fact that he held office as sheriff so briefly lends credence to this hypothesis. Nonetheless, his family remained one of great importance in the border area. Indeed, his brother, Roger, was not only well known, but actually notorious, being accused more than once as a notable papist by zealous protestants.[37] Since he apparently had no lands (he died heavily in

36 Ornsby, 4. Cf. *Archaeologia Aeliana*, 4th ser., 20 (1942), 89. Hunter Blair makes Edward the younger son of a Sir Thomas Grey, whereas Ornsby, 119n, makes him the third son of Sir Ralph Grey. Ornsby's geneology seems more likely, especially in view of Edward's being knighted at Chillingham, which by Ornsby's calculation was the seat of his father.

37 PRO, SP 14/40/11. *Ibid.*, 86/34. *Ibid.*, 87/15.

debt), it may be assumed that he was dependent upon his brother for whatever power he exercised, though he was not only reputed a dependent of Lord William Howard, but died in debt to his executors.[38]

It is noteworthy that two of Sir Henry's daughters were married to sons of Lord William. Sir Francis, Lord William's second son, took Mary Widdrington as his second wife. Charles, the fourth son, married Dorothy Widdrington.

But it was Sir Henry's son and heir, William (1611–1651) who carried the family from gentry to noble rank. He was knighted in 1631, created a baronet in 1642, and finally Baron Widdrington of Blankney in 1643. He was an ardent royalist who sacrificed his life for the King in a skirmish at Wigan in 1651. Through the fortunes of war and loyalty to the King, the Widdrington family, long a bulwark of the gentry, was elevated to the peerage.

The most notable success story in the county, however, worthy of any Horatio Alger hero and of great importance for eighteenth-century political life, involved the Cavendish family and also the Ogles. On May 5, 1617, King James visited Bothall Castle, Northumberland, the seat of Sir Charles Cavendish, knt. This gentleman was the husband of Catherine, younger daughter of Cuthbert Lord Ogle who had died without male heirs in 1597. Their son William was successively Viscount Mansfield, 1620, Earl of Newcastle, 1628, Baron Ogle, 1629 (succeeding his mother who had been created baroness in her own right in 1628), and, after the Restoration of 1665, Duke of Newcastle. Thus, a man who had been born into a gentry family in 1593 was one of the great peers of the kingdom at his death in 1676, one worthy to pass on to his descendants some semblance of the political power the Percies had once exercised in Northumberland.

No Cumberland gentry family affords a parallel to these developments in Northumberland, since the first creation of a no-

---

38   His will shows goods valued at £1,446 14s.7d., with debts of £6,620 2d. Herbert M. Wood, *Wills and Inventories from the Registry at Durham*, pt. IV (Durham: Surtees Society 142, 1929), 289–290.

bleman resident in that county was to be that of the first Earl of Carlisle in 1661. Only Lord William's sister-in-law, Anne, Dowager Countess of Arundel, sometimes resident at Greystoke Castle within her Barony of Greystoke, gave Cumberland a resident noble in the reign of James I. The leading aristocrat in the county, as we have seen, was Lord William Howard.

In Westmorland the noble houses of Clifford and Wharton remained resident. Francis Clifford, Earl of Cumberland (1559–1641), succeeded his brother in 1605. Thus he became Sheriff of Westmorland, an hereditary office of the Cliffords. He was also lord lieutenant of Cumberland from 1607 to 1641 and lord lieutenant of Northumberland, Westmorland, and Newcastle-upon-Tyne from 1611 to 1641. He certainly exercised some power in the north generally, but his base of power was in the remote interior of Westmorland, where James I visited him in 1617 at his seats of Brougham and Appleby castles. His authority on the borders was no match for that of Lord William Howard.

The Whartons, allied with the Cliffords through the marriage of Philip, third lord, with Frances, granddaughter of Francis, Earl of Cumberland, were also resident in Westmorland but played no significant role in border affairs.

It was not until much later in the seventeenth century that a Westmorland gentry family, the Lowthers, whom Lord William had once characterized as "those lewd Lowthers," and advised his readers to shun as "serpents and viperous beasts whose dealings are odious to God, and their practice hateful to all honest-minded men," attained to noble rank when the grandson of Sir John Lowther (died 1637), one of Lord William's contemporaries, was created Lord Lowther and Viscount Lonsdale in 1696.[39]

When one considers the inflation of honors during the Early Stuart period, the creation of five titles over a period of decades may not seem very impressive. These men however, had a particular role to play in their region, not simply to multiply the num-

39   Ornsby, 390–391.

ber of peers already resident in the area, but to fill a void, small in numbers but great in political importance, created by the exile or extinction of the great border houses: Percy, Neville, Dacre. The old ruling houses were replaced both by the introduction of an outsider by birth, Lord William Howard, though the husband of a Dacre coheiress, and by the advancement of local gentry families to the peerage. Never again, however, would northern noblemen exercise the lordship of those whom they had succeeded. It would not be said of them that the northerners of the late middle ages who had known no lord but a Neville or a Percy would know no lord but a Howard or a Cavendish.

THE HISTORICAL WRITINGS OF
DAVID HARRIS WILLSON

The Historical Writings of David Harris Willson

The following list of the historical writings of David Harris Willson provides a glimpse of his wide-ranging scholarly interests. The list has been divided into books, articles, and reviews; the writings under each classification are arranged chronologically.

BOOKS AND EDITED WORKS

The Parliamentary Diary of Robert Bowyer, 1606–1607 (Minneapolis: University of Minnesota Press, 1931). xxi + 423 pages.

The Privy Councillors in the House of Commons, 1604–1629 (Minneapolis: University of Minnesota Press, 1940). ix + 332 pages.

King James VI and I (London: Jonathan Cape, 1956; Bedford Historical Series, XV, 1959; paperback, 1963. New York: Henry Holt, 1956; Oxford University Press paperback, 1967). 480 pages. Awarded Robert Livingston Schuyler Prize, 1956.

A Royal Request for Trade. A Letter of King James I to the Emperor of Japan (Minneapolis: James Ford Bell Book Trust, 1958). 23 pages.

A History of England (New York: Holt, Rinehart, & Winston, 1967). xiii + 879 pages.

ARTICLES

"The Earl of Salisbury and the 'Court' Party in Parliament, 1604–1610," *AHR*, 36:274–294 (1931).

"Summoning and Dissolving Parliament, 1603–1625: The Council's Advice to James I," *AHR*, 45:279–300 (1940).

"James I and His Literary Assistants," *Huntington Library Quarterly*, 8:35–57 (1944).

Historical Writings

"King James I and Anglo-Scottish Unity," in *Conflict in Stuart England. Essays in Honour of Wallace Notestein*, eds. W. A. Aiken & B. D. Henning (London: Jonathan Cape, 1960), 43–55.

"James I," in *Collier's Encyclopedia* (New York: Crowell Collier, 1964), XIII, 439–440.

REVIEWS

Katherine Anthony, *Queen Elizabeth. SRL*, 6:631–632 (1930).

Acts of the Privy Council of England, 1617–1619, ed. J. V. Lyle. *JMH,* 2:119–121 (1930).

A. F. Pollard, *Wolsey. Yale Review,* 19:620–622 (1930).

E. R. Turner, *The Cabinet Council of England in the Seventeenth and Eighteenth Centuries,* Vol. I. *SRL,* 7:22 (1930).

Memoirs of Sarah, Duchess of Marlborough, ed. William King. *SRL,* 7:208 (1930).

Philip Gibbs, *King's Favorite. SRL,* 7:732–733 (1931).

Acts of the Privy Council of England, 1619–1621, ed. J. V. Lyle. *JMH,* 3:485–486 (1931).

Frederick C. Dietz, *English Public Finance, 1558–1641. AHR,* 38:740–741 (1933).

Hilaire Belloc, *Charles I, King of England. SRL,* 10:334 (1933).

Phillips Russell, *William the Conqueror. SRL,* 10:369 (1933).

Acts of the Privy Council of England, 1623–1625, ed. J. V. Lyle. *JMH,* 6:184–186 (1934).

Calendar of the Manuscripts of the Most Hon. the Marquess of Salisbury, Preserved at Hatfield House, Hertfordshire, pt. 16, ed. M. S. Giuseppi. *AHR,* 39:766–767 (1934).

Acts of the Privy Council of England, 1625–1626. (Issued by the Authority of the Lords Commissioners of His Majesty's Treasury under the Direction of the Master of the Rolls.) *JMH,* 7:327–328 (1935).

Tracts on Liberty in the Puritan Revolution, 1638–1647, ed. William Haller. *AHR,* 41:129–131 (1935).

The Montagu Musters Book, 1602–1623, ed. with introduction by Joan Wake, and biographical notes by Rev. H. Isham. *AHR,* 41:799 (1936).

Harold P. Cooke, *Charles I and His Earlier Parliaments: A Vindication and a Challenge. AHR,* 46:121 (1940); 763–764 (1941).

Willard M. Wallace, *Sir Edwin Sandys and the First Parliament of James I. AHR*, 46:465 (1941).

The Works of Gerrard Winstanley, ed. George H. Sabine. *Yale Review*, 30:853–854 (1941).

The Correspondence of Lady Katherine Paston, 1603–1627, ed. Ruth Hughey. *JMH*, 14:276 (1942).

G. B. Harrison, *A Jacobean Journal: Being a Record of Those Things Most Talked of during the Years 1603–1606. AHR*, 47:839–840 (1942).

R. Coupland, *The Indian Problem: Report on the Constitutional Problem in India. AHR*, 50:337–338 (1945).

Gerrard Winstanley: Selections from his Works, ed. Leonard Hamilton, with an introduction by Christopher Hill. *JMH*, 17:165–166 (1945).

The Basilicon Doron of King James VI, ed. James Craigie, Vol. I. (Publications of the Scottish Text Society, 3rd ser., XVI.) *EHR*, 60:426 (1945).

Zera S. Fink, *The Classical Republicans. SAQ*, 45:119–120 (1946).

Milton Waldman, *Elizabeth and Leicester. AHR*, 51:539 (1946).

J. Max Patrick, *Hugh Peters, a Study in Puritanism. AHR*, 52:366 (1947).

Elkin C. Wilson, *Prince Henry and English Literature. SAQ*, 46:143–144 (1947).

Léon Lemonnier, *Élisabeth d'Angleterre: La Reine Vierge? JMH*, 19:361 (1947).

Wallace Notestein, *The Scot in History: A Study of the Interplay of Character and History. SAQ*, 46:425–426 (1947).

Philip L. Ralph, *Sir Humphrey Mildmay: Royalist Gentleman. Glimpses of the English Scene, 1633–1652. SAQ*, 47:264–265 (1948).

T. Walter Wallbank, *India: A Survey of the Heritage and Growth of Indian Nationalism. AHR*, 54:207 (1948).

J. E. Neale, *The Elizabethan House of Commons. AHR*, 55:885–886 (1950).

H. G. Tibbutt, *The Life and Letters of Sir Lewis Dyve, 1599–1669. AHR*, 56:386 (1951).

A Catalogue of the Library of Sir Edward Coke, ed. W. O. Hassall with a preface by S. E. Thorne. *Yale Law Journal*, 60:755–757 (1951).

The Basilicon Doron of King James VI, ed. James Craigie, Vol. II. (Publications of the Scottish Text Society, 3rd ser., XVIII.) *EHR*, 56:621–622 (1951).

Douglas Nobbs, *England and Scotland, 1560–1707*. *EHR*, 68:640 (1953).

William McElwee, *The Murder of Sir Thomas Overbury*. *AHR*, 59:189–190 (1953).

Sir Percival Griffiths, *The British Impact on India*. *AHR*, 59:381–383. (1954).

G. H. Jones, *The Main Stream of Jacobitism*. *AHR*, 61:171 (1955).

Gordon Donaldson, *The Making of the Scottish Prayer Book of 1637*. *EHR*, 71:155–156 (1956).

A. L. Rowse, *The Expansion of Elizabethan England*. *AHR*, 61:627–628 (1956).

The Poems of James VI of Scotland, ed. James Craigie, Vol. I. (Publications of the Scottish Text Society, 3rd ser., XXII.) *EHR*, 72:172–173 (1957).

Harold Hulme, *The Life of Sir John Eliot, 1592–1632: Struggle for Parliamentary Freedom*. *AHR*, 63:660–661 (1958).

Maurice Ashley, *The Greatness of Oliver Cromwell*. *SAQ*, 57:508–510 (1958).

P. M. Handover, *Arabella Stuart. Royal Lady of Hardwick and Cousin to King James*. *History*, 43:234–235 (1958).

G. B. Harrison, *A Second Jacobean Journal: Being a Record of Those Things Most Talked of during the Years 1607 to 1610*. *William and Mary Quarterly*, 3rd ser., 16:451–452 (1959).

Acts of the Privy Council of England 1628 July–1629 April. (Issued by the Authority of the Lords Commissioners of Her Majesty's Treasury under the Direction of the Master of the Rolls.) *JMH*, 31:272–273 (1959).

William McElwee, *The Wisest Fool in Christendom. The Reign of King James I and VI*. *EHR*, 74:731 (1959).

R. H. Tawney, *Business and Politics under James I. Lionel Cranfield as Merchant and Minister*. *History*, 45:53–55 (1960).

Maurice Lee, Jr., *John Maitland of Thirlestane and the Foundation of the Stewart Despotism in Scotland*. *JMH*, 32:58–59 (1960).

The Campden Wonder, ed. George Clark. *AHR*, 66:198 (1960).

Garrett Mattingly, *The Armada. SAQ,* 59:574–576 (1960).

The Poems of James VI of Scotland, ed. James Craigie, Vol. II. (Publications of the Scottish Text Society, 3rd ser., XXVI.) *EHR,* 76:147 (1961).

G. E. Aylmer, *The King's Servants. The Civil Service of Charles I, 1625–1642. AHR,* 67:108–109 (1961).

Valerie Pearl, *London and the Outbreak of the Puritan Revolution. City Government and National Politics, 1625–1643. AHR,* 67:186–187 (1961).

F. G. Emmison, *Tudor Secretary. Sir William Petre at Court and Home. Renaissance News,* 15:154–155 (1962).

G. P. V. Akrigg, *Jacobean Pageant or the Court of King James I. Canadian Historical Review,* 44:63–64 (1963).

Alan Simpson, *The Wealth of the Gentry, 1540–1660. East Anglian Studies. SAQ,* 62:124–125 (1963).

Proceedings in Parliament 1610. Vol. I, *The House of Lords;* Vol. II, *The House of Commons,* ed. Elizabeth Read Foster. *The Annals,* 372:147–148 (1967).

Gordon Donaldson, *Scotland. James V to James VII.* (The Edinburgh History of Scotland, III.) *JMH,* 40:598–600 (1968).

Lindsay Boynton, *The Elizabethan Militia 1558–1638. AHR,* 73:809–810 (1968).

Lacey Baldwin Smith, *The Elizabethan World. AHR,* 73:1521–1522 (1968).

INDEX

KEY TO ABBREVIATIONS

Add. MSS—*Additional Manuscripts* (BM)

AHR—American Historical Review

APC—Acts of the Privy Council of England

BM—British Museum

C—Chancery

Cal. Salisbury MSS—Calendar of Salisbury manuscripts preserved at Hatfield House, Hertfordshire

CJ—The Journals of the House of Commons

CSPD—Calendar of State Papers, Domestic Series

CSPV—Calendar of State Papers, Venetian . . .

CW—Transactions of the Cumberland and Westmorland Antiquarian and Archaeological Society

DNB—Dictionary of National Biography

EcHR—Economic History Review

EHR—English Historical Review

HMC—Historical Manuscripts Commission

JMH—Journal of Modern History

LJ—The Journals of the House of Lords

PCC—Somerset House, Prerogative Court of Canterbury [Wills]

PRO—Public Record Office

Rep. App.—Report Appendix

SAQ—South Atlantic Quarterly

SP—State Papers

SRL—Saturday Review of Literature

Trans RHS—Transactions of the Royal Historical Society

VCH—Victoria County Histories

Index

Abbot, George: and prohibitions, 26; and *1614* parliament, 44–45; and foreign policy, 50, 163; accidental homicide by, 153; youth at elevation, 156; Scottish mission, 157–158; consecrates brother as bishop, 159; views on Synod of Dort quoted, 161–162; hostility toward Neile, 171; relations with James I, 171; aids in replacing Carr, 172; made Bishop of London and Archbishop of Canterbury, 175; historical reputation of, 175–176; lax administration of, 178–179

Abbot, Robert, 159, 171–172

Abdy, Sir Christopher, 216

Abingdon, Berkshire, 208, 219

Acuña, Diego Sarmiento de, 24–25, 177

Addled Parliament. *See* Parliament, *1614* session

Admiralty, Court of: 24–25; and Spanish shipping, 24–25

Aldborough, Yorkshire, 183, 183*n18*

Aldeburgh, Suffolk, 188

Allibond, John, 209, 228

Ambassadors, 23. *See also* Carew, Sir George; Wotton, Sir Henry

Andover, Hampshire, 187

Andrewes, Lancelot: and preaching, 158, 165; as writer, 159, 171; asks for news of Synod of Dort, 161; sworn to Privy Council, 163; proposed as archbishop, 174–175

Anglican Church: bishops of, 153, 170, 178; and education, 156–157; deans in, 166–167; and Essex divorce case, 171; doctrinal divisions of, 171; allegations of simony in, 174

Anne of Denmark, Queen of England, 67–68, 161, 172, 174

Anti-Spanish faction, 50

Appleby, Westmorland, 187

Arminians, 159, 171

Artillery Garden, London, 186

Arundel, Countess of. *See* Howard, Anne

Arundel, Second Earl of. *See* Howard, Thomas

Arundel, Sussex, 188

Arundell, Thomas, 205–206

Arundell of Wardour, Lord. *See* Arundell, Thomas

Ashburnham, John, 206

Ashburnham, Lawrence, 199

Attorney-General. *See* Bacon, Sir Francis

Avery, Simon, 196

Aylesbury, Sir Thomas, 134

Bacon, Anthony, 72

Bacon, Sir Francis: 40; and Egerton, 35, 59; his quest for office, 54–56, 59, 73; benefits from Coke's disgrace, 57; and Cecil, 64–65, 72, 94; and provostship of Eton, 127

Baldwin, Charles, 196

Balle, Peter, 195

Baltimore, Lord. *See* Calvert, Cecil; Calvert, Sir George

Banbury, Oxfordshire, 188

Bancroft, Richard: 32, 113, 155; and prohibitions, 26; codification of Church canons, 153; and academic preferment, 159; objects to new Bible, 164; and ecclesiastical patronage, 169–170

Bangor, bishops of. *See* Bayly, Lewis

Barlow, William, 158, 159, 165

261